The Road Taken

The Road Taken

A novel

MICHAEL FOSS

MICHAEL O'MARA BOOKS LIMITED

First published in Great Britain in 2009 by
Michael O'Mara Books Limited
9 Lion Yard
Tremadoc Road
London SW4 7NQ

Papers used by Michael O'Mara Books Limited are natural, recyclable products made from wood grown in sustainable forests. The manufacturing processes conform to the environmental regulations of the country of origin.

A CIP catalogue record for this book is available from the British Library

ISBN: 978-1-84317-331-1

1 3 5 7 9 10 8 6 4 2

www.mombooks.com

Designed and typeset by www.glensaville.com

Printed and bound in Great Britain by Clays Ltd, St Ives plc

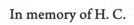

In memory of H. C.

Sunshine Coast
22 April 1999

The gun rested where it had been for the last dozen years, on two rusty nails high on the back wall of the shed. The shed, a ramshackle structure haunted by small mammals and spiders, was part storeroom and part garage, a repository for old junk and also a place to shelter the small Japanese truck when the snows came. Under the low roof, hunched below the downward sweep of the cedar boughs, the light was rubbed out, even on the days of festive sunlight, the interior hung with the gauze of cobwebs speckled with the husks of decayed insects. The gun, too, was filthy, its stock blackened and the metal parts rusted and beginning to pit from the attrition of many cold, wet days. It was not much of a gun – an old bolt-action .22 rifle of unknown provenance – more or less useless against bear or cougar, but against lesser animals it would suffice. Hanging in dun-coloured shadows, it was almost forgotten, since he had no need to blast anything between the size of mice and raccoons.

But some time ago, when its purpose became plain to him, he took the gun off the nails, cleaned and oiled it, buffed the stock, stripped down the action and soaked the metal parts in penetrating oil, then tugged the pull-through down the barrel several times. He reassembled the rifle, loaded it, stuck a can on a hemlock stump and tried a few shots from about thirty yards. He nicked the can once, though he hardly hit it fair and square, but that seemed good enough. The bolt worked and the bullets whistled into the brush with plenty of menace. It would do.

The day was sultry, unseasonably close for late April. He gave it the eye from the big window in his cabin, stirring the last dregs from the pot of breakfast coffee. For several years he had plotted the weather daily, seated in the spring-loaded rocker between the table and the window. Here, in the mornings that were obstinately his own and from which even the most sympathetic of callers were repelled, he took the measure of what he could see while his savage old cat eased herself in and out of the cabin, stiff and mean, until with a baleful look she settled on the patchwork cover of his typewriter. The need for that instrument was long gone; what remained to be said would fit into the creeping sentences of his longhand.

Was there much else to be said? He thought he had covered it. Touching the bitter pain submerged in his jaw and aching along the side of his face, he knew he needed no more confirmation from words. He had set the course of events with studied deliberation, and he would let the levers of motion and the direction of the compass lie as they were.

All that he required now was a kind of adieu. He had to wrestle himself out of the order of life that was peculiar to him, that which he had knocked together out of chance and sloth and temperament and some lucky decisions, yes, and an elemental stubbornness as well. From his chair, picking idly at the place in the arm where the stuffing leaked, he surveyed the forest clearing and the patches of strangled wilderness that he had come to regard as his own, for although he had no formal title to the territory he considered that he had an unwritten lease on it for as long a term as he might wish, granted under the vague but large authority of natural right. Continuously, he had mixed his labour into the property of this world, and that seemed to him to put him at the head of the line to decide the disposition of things.

He emerged from the cabin, into the sticky air. Below the steps, rock outcrops, tree stumps and rank grasses sloped away gently until folded into the edge of the woods. He walked down to the shed, feeling the weight of the restored rifle. In the distance, south on the coast road, he thought he heard a brief wail from a police siren. A few days before he had driven a 6-inch nail into a post of the shed at head height, leaving some 3 inches of the nail proud of the wood. He heard, this time clearly, another cry from the siren. In the cool shade of the shed he contemplated the loaded gun, wryly touching the muzzle to his lips. He tasted the light gun oil and behind that a metallic flavour, sharp and strange. He grimaced slightly and gave himself a half smile. As if the taste mattered, but the habits of being human persist. He fitted the trigger guard over the big nail so that the trigger itself butted against the firm set of the nail. With sudden determination he placed the muzzle in his mouth, grasped the barrel with both hands and pulled strongly towards him.

HOMELAND
THE DEPRESSION YEARS

Long after, when the eternal surprises of youth had given way to greater discretion, he knew he had been born in a bad time. But the malice of that age – the Depression – had been quite impersonal and he wondered if he had any grounds for complaint that went beyond the general misery. It was worse for you, of course, if your folks were poor, or farmers, or small rural businessmen, or just generally down on luck, and his father, at one time or another, had been all of those things. His father, born into a German immigrant family and christened Heinrich Holle but known circumspectly during and after the First World War as Harry, was a man of studious, even philosophical, turn of mind, as became a man of his tradition, one whose family had chivvied hard subsistence from the land for generations, who was also a sometime printer and newspaper stringer. He found he could not put a cap on his curiosity, but still it wandered alarmingly. He saw too much without being able to bring the menacing bloom of this world under the system of a settled view. Reflecting too much, he let everything pass. The poor rural slobs who bilked him of his little bills found forgiveness, in Harry Holle's mind, because they acted under the compulsion of vast economic forces that were as vague as they were potent. It made, for Harry, a rich intellectual life, but it put less and less food on the table.

At the time when his only son was born Harry Holle, dazed by weariness and struggle, quartered the dirty downland of southern Manitoba, delivering flyers and pamphlets and letterheads and invitation cards and public notices to lonesome homesteads sinking under the drift of the prairie, and to little townsites draped like tattered clothes along the line of the railway. Grappling his Model A Ford through gravel-wash and mud and flying dust and the rutted laterite of unmade roads, Harry sometimes pondered, in his bemused way, the achievement of a distant ancestor who, in Pomerania at the start of the seventeenth century, had written, in Latin, a play called *The Dream of Human Life*. This may have been a moribund piece in a dead language but it opened a seam that later talents, such as Calderón and Strindberg, mined to far richer effect. Looking with familiar horror at a prairieland leached out under drought and farming malpractice and lack of capital, Harry Holle saw a particular abandonment that had the quality of a dream and he tipped his hat to his old ancestor, who had surely got it right. How often, in dreams, all steps are wrong, all decisions perverse, all paths circular. The beginning becomes indistinguishable from the end, the road between goes nowhere, and birth is only another kind of death.

In this spirit of indeterminacy Heinrich, later Harry, Holle had named his son Ludwig, which was soon transmuted to Lewis, though the boy so-called grew into a youth and then a man who would always be known as Lew.

*

The first Holle in North America arrived in 1779, quartermaster of a regiment raised by the Margrave of Anspach to fight as mercenaries of King George III in his troubles with the insurgent colonists. Those troubles, at first throwing no more shadow than a man's hand, were swollen by the usual assumptions of arrogant stupidity into an overwhelming darkness that laid the colonial governors under catastrophe.

Holle, a farmer's son, had signed on for the sake of adventure and riches. His fellow soldiers, who were also there to make money, not to be killed, quickly saw the disastrous course of events. They went on their way, with private ends to pursue. Quartermaster Holle, a smart, well-organized young man, as every good quartermaster must be, soon saw the advantages of space and freedom offered by the New World, at least when compared with the feudal cramp and unforgiving hierarchies of his German homeland, that chessboard of tinpot principalities. He detached himself from his role as hired gun and retreated north-east in good order to the Loyalist colony of Nova Scotia, a place where the American revolutionary writ did not run.

Holle, though temporarily a soldier, was still a farmer at heart, and Nova Scotia was well-founded and secure enough to offer productive land and peaceful possession to those with the spirit and money to take up the task. Holle had what was required – a strong back, and ambition, and cash – for if a quartermaster can't make a profit from a campaign who can? He bought a small tract of land in the Annapolis Valley, harnessed the plough team, and set out on the road to becoming a North American.

*

For Harry Holle, descendant of the quartermaster, the time in Brandon, Manitoba, was the beginning of exile. At the start of the Depression, forced from the family holding in Nova Scotia by sinking farm prices which could no longer support all the members of the household, Harry set out to the west. Though newly married, he was young, as yet unburdened by children, and he had a skill. Cannily, he had learnt the trade of printing, for he had seen at an early age the trials of the small farm in the rural economy. Where he went did not matter much. Everywhere underfoot were the shards and wreckage of society. But the West was wider, more empty, not so much encumbered by old familiar landmarks now sinking into decay. His heart could more easily bear a certain amount of wilderness. There was less of man's work to rot, less to grieve over. The prairie horizon, stretching the limit of both eye and imagination, gave some notion also of limitless possibility.

At first, he was heartsick looking at it, that vista of immense grain fields and dirt everywhere. What a landscape needed, Harry thought, was variation of hill and wood and field and settlement. He wanted to read some historical signs of old community. He thought wistfully of cows and horses, wanting to hear the subdued bellow at milking time, and the rattle of harness from the woodlot. He heard instead, from time to time, the gush of grain from the elevators roaring into boxcars hidden under storm clouds of dust and chaff.

In the years before the Second World War, Harry Holle moved many times. Where he went didn't trouble him much, for he was only resting temporarily by a trail that seemed to him inscrutable. His family (he had a boy and a girl now), whose only faith lay in endurance and hope, tagged along. In western Ontario, in Manitoba, in Saskatchewan, there would be a printing shop, a press, a small newspaper, a need for a bit of prose or copy – he had become, among other things, a journalist of a sort. He was intelligent and steady, if perhaps a little too dreamy for a relentless commitment to a nine-to-five routine. But he was adaptable and ready to go at a moment's notice. At Port Arthur, looking out over the huge lake, he considered the United States, the land that his ancestor had helped to let slip. He went instead as far as Regina in Saskatchewan, drawn by the bustle created when Wascana Lake was carved out of the malodorous river, a Keynesian make-work project. 'So this is Regina,' he thought, 'queen of cities . . . '

*

In her childhood, Lew Holle's mother had spoken both German and English.

This was no help to communication in later life, when she found, under stress, the two languages tangled in her mouth. Often, she would cast a clear line in English, then a sudden doubt, the loss of a word, a peculiar construction got her words ravelled up with German. This puzzled and annoyed her son. To him, German was a showy and perhaps sinister embellishment for a good Canadian. Also, his mother sang him German lullabies, and carols at Christmas, in a breathy voice, the kind used to hide an inability to pitch a note. That strange tongue. On the radio the soprano Edith Wiens, who had been raised in a Mennonite community, sang 'Stille Nacht'. Lew could not make out what that *Stille Nacht* business had to do with the Christmas season of Guy Lombardo and The Royal Canadians.

He didn't want to be different. One language was good enough for him. Real Canadian boys at Christmas, if the ice was good, had their skates on, preparing for some hard-muscled hockey.

His education came in pieces, fragments of life on the road, bits shaken in ways that released only disconnected memories. He recalled people more than book learning: Miss Betty, his teacher in first grade, and Miss Gwen, the one in third grade. Miss Betty, a pretty woman with wavy brown hair that bounced as she walked, had patient dark eyes, suggesting a sympathetic perplexity. She favoured tight skirts that showed the little round bulge of her belly, though she was not fat, only plump in a comforting, unassuming way. Miss Gwen was a bottle blonde with thin lips and a challenging eye, a bold one for sure. Both caused in young Lew unaccountable feelings of warmth and alarm.

He was a good student. The three Rs, those tags of learning without which modern life must remain incomprehensible, came to him easily enough. He read anything that came to hand, allowing books to take him into secret places from where the uncertain days of his family wanderings could be viewed with greater safety. Weary of his footloose life, he wanted order and clarity. He tidied his room, hung up his coats, combed his hair, cleaned and sharpened his skates without being told. What was not plain and clear was provisionally suspect.

Away from the sharp light of plain-dealing facts, in the slippery penumbra of doubt, Lew had at first some trouble. When, early in his schooling, Miss Betty had invited each child in turn to sing solo, he had opened his mouth eagerly, but all that had emerged was a low dull tuneless monotone. He saw his own horrified disbelief reflected in his teacher's face. Her lips quivered, she looked at the ceiling, then she burst into laughter. Twenty jeering classmates joined her.

Later, in the early years of the world war, when in the absence of the minister his father acted as lay preacher and took the service, Lew was allowed each Sunday to choose one of the hymns. The congregation soon learnt what was coming – the seamen's hymn: 'Eternal Father, Strong To Save'. When the sounds got deep enough, in the rumbling slough where purity and sense of pitch are drowned, he could enter happily. 'O hear us when we call to Thee,' he bawled, 'for those in peril on the sea.' He felt those vibrations rising from the very roots of humanity. Paul Robeson, he thought, could hardly do better.

Later still, after an affair came to an end, a woman he believed he loved gave him, in lieu of her affection and her body, a guitar. With it came an instruction book. The cover pictured a seated man in a frock coat, with frizzy hair, goatee beard and pince-nez specs. He was strumming a guitar, his left foot resting on a plump tasselled cushion. Before coming to notes on lines, the instructions set out a series of finger and hand exercises that Lew followed with devotion for an hour a day. Calluses bloomed on his fingers but as far as he could tell nothing resembling music emerged. Then one day he plucked a note and to his surprise he recognized it and knew he had got it right. He tried another, and another, and recognized those too. Slowly he picked out the first few bars of 'Yellow Bird', a popular Caribbean song of the day. Over and over he played it, eventually coming up to tempo with a certain swagger. He had the feeling; he had made music.

He stopped there, content that others did it better than he did but knowing now, at least, what it was that they did. He put the guitar in its case and did not touch it again. A few years later he sold it for a hundred dollars, about twice what it was worth. But perhaps not, considering the miracle it had performed.

THE ANNAPOLIS VALLEY

In the war, Lew and his family returned to the farm in Nova Scotia. The younger males, who had been running the farm, had discovered, like many of German ancestry, that in Hitler's war patriotism was for them a psychological necessity, and they enlisted at once to become heroes or dead. But farming too was vital war work, so with others going absent middle-aged Harry Holle was summoned home. He decided he owed more duty to the place where he was born and raised than to the make-work surrounding a stinking lake in Saskatchewan.

On a mild October day Lew, a boy in his teens, stood on an ancient bridge over the highway and surveyed the modest acreage of the farm. He had seen it a couple of times before, on short visits from the prairies, but he saw now that something new was being asked of him. Before him were spread the few good fields in the bottom land, woods and rough pasturage stretching up the hillside, and the steep scree of the mountain above. After the hard Depression years, when farming lay on the margin of mere survival, the land needed work. Lew was young but he could see how it was with the peeled and blistered farmhouse, the outbuildings down on their knees, the patched fences held together with baling wire, ragged fields, and woods full of junkwood and deadwood that should have been cleared.

'Yes sir,' he sighed, wanting the world to know that he would get at it, 'plenty to do here.'

He was a little fellow, small for his age, but lean and wiry and not afraid of hard labour. For some time back he had given his father a hand, spending long hours in the print shop or helping at the press, and he saw now something that would engage him beyond the desire to earn pocket money or to help out his father. There was something to be grasped here, and he was the man – or nearly man – to do it.

The first thing he looked for was a carpenter's toolkit. He felt an affinity with wood, something gained in defiance of the largely treeless prairie. He started with rough work – felling and clearing and splitting and stacking. He was getting to know wood, the look and the lie of the grain, the density, the springiness, the flaws and faults, the cussedness of certain timber. His hand became more sure and he gradually widened his enterprise. Field, farmyard, barn and finally house were slowly gathered in under his eye and hand. He took satisfaction in his work, though his skill often surprised him, so he sometimes looked to see if he had secrets there – the advantage of extra fingers or mysterious double joints.

But there was more to do than to amuse himself with working wood. At first, he pitched in to all the neglected tasks with enthusiasm. Muck on the boots – dung from the byre or heavy loam from the fields – seemed like a mark of honour. Each day, a dozen cows waited to be milked by hand, which was a serious responsibility. It had its enjoyment, even its solemnity – the damp gloom of the milking-shed, misty with bovine breath, his forehead against the warm flank, the rumble of ruminative guts, the silky feel of the teats, the rhythmic gushes of milk pinging into the pail.

After a few years he considered that this might be for ever, and his enthusiasm dropped away.

Still, the life of hard graft and its relentless timetables did him some good, physically and mentally. He became tough and self-reliant. Rural life and the farming seasons allowed no leeway for indulgence, no entry for sloth or self-delusion or sentimentality. His world was what it was, with sharp edges and unequivocal directions. Things grew and bloomed and died, both flora and fauna, and to get in the way led to avoidable wounds. The trick was to sense the flow, waxing or waning, and to keep in step. Respect was better than love, inevitability carried more weight than scruples. When the family favourite, the old collie, was dying miserably of numerous ailments, he took it quietly behind the barn and shot it. The pretty calves went to the abattoir. They were good animals, well and carefully raised, and as far as he could see they came to a good end. All kinds of game, according to season, went into the pot and tasted fine.

He liked animals. They lived in a straightforward, comprehensible way, even when they bit you or savaged you. One of his regular duties was to harness Belle, the draught horse, a stately old Shire with settled ways. Together they went to the woods, to haul out fallen and cut trees, and then to take the wagon of rough-cut logs down to the yard. Belle was big and handsome but faint-hearted, refusing to put out any extra effort. She was hard to shift. When the wagon was loaded she would lean into the collar and see what happened. If the wagon budged immediately she would put some muscle into it, and then she was on her way. But if she felt resistance, or the wheels sticking, she would stop dead and shiver slightly with her head down. Then neither encouragement nor threats nor blows made any difference. At that point, Lew had learnt to offload a few light branches, making sure that old Belle was taking notice. 'Now, you old fool,' he would tell her contemptuously, 'a great lump like you can handle this load.' Then a shake of the reins would get Belle moving, swishing her tail and giving out a number of triumphant farts.

There was some honest humour in this, and Lew felt great affection for the old girl, even as he rode the cart in the slipstream of her noxious gas.

*

He was not exactly lonely – he was far too busy for that – but he lacked something. To help him see what it was, on many an evening, summer and winter, he walked the three miles to the store at the crossroads. This was a general store for country folk, old-fashioned and tumultuous, crammed full of as many essentials and as much frippery as the heart could wish. Here, in daily meetings, the rural folk got under the skin of the land, feeling the bones of their habitual life.

A gallery ran along the front of the building, with a narrow bench beside the door. The rail before the bench bore scuff marks of bootheels and scars from whittling knives. These were the marks of summer deliberation when the loiterers got their coats off, spat into the dust, and put the eye on the traffic of the world. In the winter these same old hats abandoned the outside bench for the fug of the interior, where the speckles of dust and the motes from the stove made the air as hazy as sunset.

Just within the door, smack in the middle of the shop space, was an old pool table, long out of use and now piled high with overalls and denim jackets and heavy blue jeans and long johns and seamen's socks in oiled wool as coarse as burlap and handsome plaid work shirts in wool or cotton. Above the table, hanging from the ceiling like strange ritual offerings, were forks and rakes and axe-handles and rubber boots and gaudy suspenders in powerful elastic and tremendous rain slicks as stiff as statues. Business flowed down aisles either side of the pool table. On the right was the counter where Vida, the red-haired shopkeeper, placidly figured numbers on the thin, crackly pages of her accounts book. To the left, between the pool table and the glass-fronted cabinets for trinkets and candy and cosmetics, was a row of mismatched chairs. Here, on winter evenings or in bad weather, the country philosophers convened.

After a while of standing around and easing his ear into the conversation Lew took an end chair. Since no one moved or even seemed to blink he understood that he was provisionally accepted, on condition that he say nothing. And that was fine by him, for he saw very soon that silence was, with these men (he never saw a woman in the group), part of the language. There was some heavy smoking, almost a part of breathing, working up to some observation, and some old-timers still chewed tobacco, expelling wet globs into the hollowness of the spittoon. Then someone would essay a few words, words as shy as a fawn on the highway, a moment in the harsh light and then gone. The rest gathered in what had been said, without hurry, mauling it about in their minds. A contrary opinion would emerge, even to the most abject platitude. Then a sly grin became the prelude to a story so convoluted and complicated, so packed with cryptic references, so washed with the colour of the place, that only a local could tell its fact from fiction. And perhaps not even that, for behind the straight-faced storytelling lay deliberate playfulness and grotesque wit. They were evenings of obsessions, feuding, score-making, ironic lies, old wounds raked over, twisted intimacies, local mythologies rehearsed and rearranged. Often the tales were cruelly funny, and then the guys might go as far as a chuckle but would not allow themselves a guffaw.

Lew soon learnt to anticipate the good stuff. One lugubrious corpse of a fellow, in full flight, would produce a little bead of white spittle at the corner of his mouth which would grow to the size of a small pea and then burst. A younger man, who knew better than to show too much animation, at ripe moments would whip off his glasses, displaying eyes of naked innocence, while trying to head off his enthusiasm by quietly tapping his glasses on his right knee.

At a late hour, yawning under the night, Lew wondered what he had seen. Life lived under several guises? A reality at home, but artifice when away? Each his own *Homo faber*, constructor of identities according to whim and season? He felt sure he was seeing some avoidance tactic, calculated to make the going home easier, home to milking and ploughing and sowing and harvesting and the accumulation of bills.

But he knew he felt an intoxication, beginning to get high on the power of words.

*

There was school too, and the things you have to do there – study, social rituals, fights, girls, working up a competitive edge on games field or dance floor. He did well enough, though subject, like his father, to dislocating dreams. He had a girl, a high-school sweetheart, no less. He couldn't dance – loathed it – but by God could he skate, he and the girl skimming to music like a pair of migrating swifts.

LAKEHEAD

The long thin man sitting at the dark end of the tavern was so tall that he had to hunch over to get his elbows on the tabletop. His blond hair flopped forward, like a ledge under which his drink sheltered. It looked like a proprietary stance, a man at bay with his beer. The morose face hanging out of the gloom, with pale eyes squinting sideways, did not seem welcoming. So the wave of the hand that directed Lew to an empty chair on the man's right made Lew's heart give a jump. He was shy enough as it was, being a year under age, and he could do without trouble. The two of them, at this early hour, were the only customers.

'I see you come in,' said the stranger flatly, 'itchin' about like you got plague in the feet. Here, sit down.You drink with me.' And then he added, as if the explanation cleared the board of misunderstanding, 'I am a Finn.'

The Finn slumped back in his chair, easing his lips into a grimace that might even have been a smile. His cold eye slowly took Lew apart from top to toe, calculating his age, his vulnerability, his thirst. He nodded, warming a little, knowing that he held the reins firmly on this encounter. He took a pull at his beer and said shrewdly, 'So takin' account of how you look kinda young and nervous and lonely, I guess you're not from here. What you doin' anyway in this pisshole town?'

Lew considered the question, knowing it was a conundrum he himself had yet to solve.

'A damned lousy job,' he mumbled, 'far as I can see.'

'Yeh? Expected the world to be different?' the stranger said with contempt, and the observation seemed to give him pleasure. He looked around, still with the toothy sneer, and crooked a bony finger at the waiter.

'Here,' he ordered, 'get a beer for our dumb friend.'

The waiter was doubtful. 'Hell, Kurt,' he complained, 'he sure don't look old enough.'

The Finn fixed him with a bleak stare. 'You know me,' he said in a harsh whisper, 'and I know this young fella – leastways I will soon. I don't see nobody else in here. Get the damned beer.'

It didn't seem like a good time to argue. 'Okay, just this once,' the waiter grumbled and moved off sullenly, rubbing his hands on his dishcloth as if wiping away some contamination.

Lew sighed and wondered how you got over youth and loneliness and nerves.

*

The problems following the end of the war struck Lew as forcefully as they did any other inexperienced youth who saw himself suddenly unfettered. He was a man now, or at least most of the way there. A scant few months before, farming had appeared to be a safe enough adventure – something he could get his back into, something worth doing. Now it seemed wretchedly narrow and limiting. Somehow he felt on an uneven keel; his ballast had shifted. Farming be damned, he thought. He wanted a bigger palette, brighter colours, a canvas that stretched beyond the Annapolis Valley.

In the war years he had heard his father, rambling on about the wanderings of the Depression, often mention the twin towns of Fort William and Port Arthur. He did so without any pleasure, his account wavering between horror and fascination. Here was a place – a repository, like all human settlements, for hopes and dreams – that looked like the result of some infernal pact, some grim necessary grind to help keep mankind economically buoyant with as little reference to the kindness of civilization as possible. Taking advantage of geography and a fortunate position at the head of Lake Superior, the towns hustled hard labour into ready cash.

The first settlers were drawn to Port Arthur by the discovery near by of a large silver lode. That seemed to be a good enough omen for Lew. He knew himself to be a fortune hunter of a kind, though it was as yet by no means clear to him what form his fortune might take. The construction of the new world fit for heroes (promised by politicians of every colour) required an unknown quantity of brain but certainly a lot of muscle-power. Lew set out for the lakehead. After his apprentice years on the farm he knew the nature of hard work, and he could handle it.

He had to give it time. The topography was so different, not just the abrasive landscape of the cities, but the reformed shape and purpose of his life. To find work was easy. The local economy, whipped into shape by wartime demand, had bounced back from the low of the Depression, from the year 1932 when the Abitibi Power and Paper Company, the largest pulp and paper company in Canada, had gone into receivership. Now, industry and manufacture were going full blast, far too hectic to attend to the blight they left behind. And the immense grain trains from the prairie provinces ghosted heavily down the rails that cut the cities, till the wagons vomited a raw, material plenty into the vast pool elevators on the shoreline, as craggy and overpowering as the buttes and mesas of the American badlands. He took a lowly job in a warehouse that distributed GM auto parts.

When he set the effort of the job (which was slight) against the return in money (which was not bad for a single youth), he could not make sense of the equation. Compared with an industrial worker, a farmer was a free man, though relatively poor and working under the burden of nature. But the blue-collar worker? After a while Lew began to see that he was compensated for boredom and bondage. Each week, after paying for his few wants and necessities, he regarded the money left over as a loan to himself to invest in an undeclared future. He wanted to try to incorporate his Port Arthur present into a beneficial chain leading to something more tangible than mere dreams.

Otherwise, looking around his new town, he saw the point of the old nickname given to the one-time local PD & W railway line, the line that went, despite the boom of the present, no further than Poverty, Distress and Welfare.

*

He found a one-room apartment in a semi-basement off Bay Street. It was a cramped nether space panelled in tongue-and-groove with two slits high on the wall by way of windows. Even on the best of days, natural light in the room never went beyond the dark velvet of shadows. He shared the dingy basement with a heavy-breathing furnace, an accompaniment to the day, and particularly to the night, that he found soporific and friendly.

His apartment was on the edge of the area in Port Arthur known as Little Suomi, a few city blocks given over to Finnish immigrants and their families. Lew knew almost nothing about Finns or their country, though he had learnt very soon to watch out when a Finn was drinking. But he liked the strange sense of being even tangentially connected with an old community. He liked a common history, the warmth of a tightly held tradition. He liked to eat in modest cafés that smelt of baking and root vegetables and home cooking. There, he could peer over shoulders at the headlines of an immigrant paper in an unaccountable language, one that seemed even on the page to have knots in the tongue. From his early years, when he had helped his father with various printing tasks, he had taken a keen interest in the world of newspapers. Even if he could not read the language, he always learnt something from the layout of the page. Now, confronted with the pale, persevering, serious mystery that is the Finn, Lew felt at ease.

He bought a pre-war Dodge of ample proportions, something like an upturned boat. It was a good runner, but had a kick in the steering and the suspension became hysterical on bad roads. He left it parked in the road, for trial and error at the weekends, and got hold of a secondhand English bicycle for weekdays, a choice of transport that marked him immediately as a person heading for eccentricity. If the weather permitted he cycled to work, jolting along, mapping through his bottom the rough terrain of streets eroded by severe winters, pummelled by heavy trucks, and slashed by rail lines.

He discovered that the climate affected him greatly. In the Maritimes on the East Coast he had been used to the full variety of North American weather, from arctic freeze to sunbathing heat. But on the eastern seaboard the days had blown in and out with abandon, sea creatures as unpredictable and exhilarating as the waves. Now he found that the absolutes of continental weather, the rigour of winter and the enervating blast of summer, suffocated the spirit. Day after day, under skies of a terrible sameness, he felt weary and drained before the business of the day had rightly begun.

The big lake, in all its moods, haunted him. Ice shards on the shoreline, fog-bound bulk carriers releasing thin plaints of smoke into air already foully polluted, sullen winter waters that from a certain low angle seemed to swell up above the level of the town; in summer, the metallic glitter hurt the eyes as the little waves shimmied to and fro, playing games with the perspective, and far out in some threatening no man's land the hammerhead clouds of sudden storms rising off the lake like King Kong.

*

For much of the time he found himself at a loose end. The work was nothing, just shifting small material objects from one place to another. From the start, he was on the lookout for something better, though he didn't know what that might be, and wouldn't see if it fitted him until he was in it.

On evenings and weekends he prowled the city centre, in poor spirits, trying to compose fables out of the dull evidence of the life around him. One route was as good as another but often he found his way to the old Canadian National station by the lakefront, on Water Street. Here, at least, he saw signs of aspiration, a loopy construction of mansard roofs and turrets and fol-de-rols and curlicues, so out of place that it assumed an important character. A giant civic belly laugh perhaps, an almost Dadaist joke, richly entertaining and ridiculous. Lew liked it – it was something to chew on – though the end result of reflection might be nothing more than a gut sore from laughing. Opposite the station was a folly of another kind, a pagoda that had been a bandstand. In the rackety old pioneer days – up to the start of the Great War – men of substance alighting from the station, looking for some loophole of advantage in this roughneck territory, were serenaded by a wind band, insinuating into their receptive ears the promise of quick returns and compound interest. Probity and good faith optional.

Frazzled by thoughts that seemed to go nowhere, Lew would dive into eating-places, hungry for something, though not so much for food. He did, and he didn't, want to talk. When tempted or forced to it he preferred old folk, liars, mythologists or storytellers, users of the gift of the gab, wedded to misbegotten pasts. There they were, waving a stick at him as he entered, hoping for handouts with pathetic urgency.

'Hiya again. Here, siddown right there. Okay, son? So I was tellin' you 'bout the blizzard of oh-three – 'bout then anyway, I forget the year now. I was up the Kaministikwia that year, in and outta the woods. Damnedest storm I ever see. Shithole out back as solid as an iceberg. Big firs split like gunshots. Little bitty mice and such-like vermin trying to climb in bed with you, to keep warm. Came across an old bear, kinda shrugged up in a collapsed den, froze to death, four feet in the air like the legs on an upturned table. Hey, you goin' that way, get me a coffee, an' a piece of pie, maybe.'

A piece of pie seemed a small price to pay for many a cock-eyed confidence. After a while, when he had the tale and the old-timer had finished the pie, he could move to a stool at the counter and work on his heartache, sketching suggestive doodles in his mind over the agreeable form of the short-order cook.

After several visits here and there he settled on a favourite place, and a favourite girl behind the counter. She was a tall breezy girl of robust stock, with long legs and a mop of wayward curls. He worked out her roster, then slipped to the lunch counter on the slack afternoons of the weekend, to monopolize her attention and try to size her up. He saw that she was even-tempered and cheerful, impervious to the boorish hints and simple-minded crudities of her worse male customers. From time to time she would let a little sigh escape, or in mute reprimand let her pale eyes rest on a miscreant for a solemn moment. Lew was drawn to her as much by her easy civility and relaxed humour as by the firm flesh of her body, which was nonetheless a matter of anxious speculation to his inexperienced self. She was something of a lanky challenge to one of Lew's bantam build.

She liked to talk, freely and unaffectedly. After circling for a time around the topic of the weather, they advanced to favourite foods and ball games and music. She liked country and western, bluegrass and stride piano. 'Oh my, that Fats Waller,' she would say, rosy with memory. She followed with enthusiasm the fortunes of local sports teams, baseball and ice hockey in particular, and Lew, who had a good head for statistics and team members and dirty tactics, was right on the beam in these matters. He took her skating and cut a dazzle around her own careful swirls and runs. Then she began to look on him with a more comradely, thoughtful eye, sliding her cold hand into his glove on the way home. On the doorstep of her house they kissed tentatively, which was satisfactory, though she had to stoop slightly to meet his lips.

She lived with her parents and saw no immediate reason to leave. She, too, knew herself to be dissatisfied, had plans to be something more than a waitress – not that she was too stuck-up for the job, but she reckoned that anyone with the least brain and personality and two good legs should admit to more ambition that that. Eventually she might go to college, and then have some babies, of course.

She understood that reading would be a good start for future plans but was apprehensive that words all wrapped up in syntax and grammar might make a fool of her, and she didn't know where to begin. Lew had come to words through the presses manned by his father, and words in their peculiar and beautiful order were now something of a drug to him. He offered to take her reading in hand. On the shoddy sofa in his dim little apartment he would set out with her on a ten-mile gallop across some bumpy literary terrain, taking a swing into this pleasant glade or that notorious swamp, till her ears were buzzing and she couldn't remember whether *The Scarlet Letter* was an artist's manual, *Ulysses* a piece of ancient history, or *Go Down, Moses* a collection of spirituals. In the late night hours Lew was still whipping the literary thoroughbreds along with such an alarming passion, the perspiration on his forehead almost matching the beads of condensation on his beer can, that she could only frown at her muddle from which there seemed no way out.

Then Lew ached to give her some comfort beyond words. That ended conversation. In a while he would croak in a voice made hoarse from certain pressures within, 'Do we or don't we?'

'We do not,' she would reply firmly, and that was it for that night.

Still, their friendship prospered. They went to hockey games and movie theatres, and on starry evenings bounced his limping Dodge out to drive-in movies on the edge of town. The night firmament a-glitter with bright eyes gave her a confidence she did not feel in his gloomy room. In the warm car, lapped about in anonymity before the giant screen, she succumbed to the tender smile of a Paulette Goddard or a Douglas Fairbanks and grew wistful. Then one thing seemed likely to lead to another until he whispered once more, 'Do we or don't we?'

'Well, not just yet,' she answered sweetly, which he took to be a hint of a promise for the future.

He persuaded her to take up cycling, and shepherded her early wobbles around potholes and over rail crossings. As she got the hang of it they struck out further, into the countryside, into a tangled world of brush and rock and woods and lakes and streams. In good weather she wore brief cycling shorts, the light golden down on her spectacular legs damp from effort as she pumped the pedals in front of his glad eyes. They took picnics, and sometimes simple fishing gear, something to explain this out-of-the-way enthusiasm. In the high heat of summer afternoons they dozed among the tree roots by waters of a startling blue. Then they sketched plans and dreamed dreams that were different but not necessarily antagonistic. To cool off and to escape a myriad of tiny winged beasties they plunged into lakes, reckless amid the leeches. She swam with strokes of long languid grace then rolled on her back and smiled as he thrashed after her, arms and legs all out of synch.

In the merciless hot days they took to the country more and more. Discovering small private Edens, they were able to become very close to nude, and finally quite naked. One day, humming with soft whirrings and speckled with sharp shadows under birch trees, he was lounging on the bank of the lake with his eyes closed. He heard her commotion as she came to the shore and looked to see her rise from the lake with water sheeting from the taut nipples of her breasts, a dark dell below, and a corona of bright spray shaken from her tousled hair.

Urgently, he pleaded, 'Do we or don't we?'

Then she spread out her wet arms to him, open to a new world, and enclosed him, and they did.

*

What he took to be happiness did not last, for within six months she had moved with her family to a far part of a far province, and in any case he had begun to wonder what particular building block she might be in the uncompleted structure of his life. He feared that she might have become wholly redundant. He never saw her again.

He thought it should be a simple task, to match talents to opportunities. But progress, if it was progress, went slower than he cared to admit. He took a sober look at his abilities and came to modest conclusions. Surely he had not overvalued himself? But he couldn't figure out the obstacles.

Other girls – not many – came and went, attractive and beguiling aides against the curse of a life that was much too ordinary. From time to time he shacked up with one of these young women in a riot of dirty dishes, unkempt clothes and forgotten laundry, in too much intimacy and with overwrought passions, neither of them having the time or the experience to take the heat out of the affair, to lay out parallel and equal lives that might have led to decent ends without unresolved entanglements. He couldn't get hold of the taste for domesticity, even less the taste of marriage.

Eager for better employment, he searched almost daily in the want ads, and at last he slipped into a printing works, where he knew what he was doing. The labour of printing pleased him – the ingenious technology, the dexterity and skill of the printers, the camaraderie, the feeling of get-up-and-go induced by the unrelenting drive of the presses. And then the magical effects of imprints on blank paper. He thought he could be happy with all this. Almost. The foreman, a refugee from an incomprehensible mid-European history, soon had his eye on

Lew and called out to him in a slack moment.

'Hey, you,' he shouted, 'you with your specs on your nose and your head in the air, come and entertain me.'

Lew went to the cubbyhole office and closed the door against the whoosh and rumble of the machines. Then the foreman set out a chessboard and began to teach Lew the moves. From then on, during the odd times of peace, the foreman laughed heartily as he picked off Lew's pawns and then cleaned out his king's-side position. Chastened by these defeats, Lew was quite glad to get back to the boys on the shop floor, to drink after hours in grubby taverns, where he was a friendly observer rather than a convivial buddy, taking stock, polishing his specs, hardly listening to the profanities about girls and the lies about sports, but observing how this man's paunch popped the buttons on his work shirt, how that man added pointless emphasis by slapping a fist into a palm, how another drank luxuriously then sucked the beer foam from his straggly moustache – a second helping. Lew sat there, smiling, smiling.

Fine though the job was in its way, it was not everything that Lew needed. His hands might be busy to good purpose, but his mind was still idling. The imprints on the page were only part of the magic; the greater mystery resided in the meaning of those prints and in the minds that sent the messages forth. He looked for the source of the words and how they were put together. He bought a portable typewriter and began to blot clean white pages with his own compositions. He puzzled himself as to what constituted a story, how its elements should be organized, and most of all how to kick it into life. He made connections through the printing works and badgered them for leads and introductions. The foreman, magnanimous after so many chess victories, was a great help in this respect. Then Lew, with some small offerings, began to sniff around newspaper offices – not so much the dailies with decent circulations but weeklies and community papers and little cyclostyled magazines, any publication that served any general interest whatsoever.

He had more sense than to try to chase the big stories. He let drift by the political shenanigans, administrative corruption, plane crashes, derailments, big storms, floods, droughts, murder in Main Street at high noon. At this stage he could not have handled them. Rather than look for the big punch he went for the sly jab – the humorous, the eccentric, the cock-eyed, the kinky. He sought out peculiar accidents, coincidence, misunderstandings, long-shot bets, tragedy turning to smiles, comedy leading to tears: fish that drown; father dates long-lost daughter; gymnast falls from doorstep; wheelchair user gives chase and catches burglar. In effect, 'Man Bites Dog,' that old newspaper chestnut.

He was surprised when a few of his pieces were picked up here and there. The small fees were welcome (when there was a fee), though better than that was a momentary but profound satisfaction. Very occasionally a publication – a little local rag perhaps – would condescend to give him a byline. Once, he was granted a byline and a headshot photo. He gazed at the picture and fancied he could detect the keen, hawk-like visage of an implacable news-hunter. But from another angle he feared he might be viewing the vulture beak and bare mottled throat of an opportunist scavenger.

WESTERN ONTARIO

A paper in Kenora had an opening for an office boy-cum-cub-reporter. Lew shot off a resumé and followed it to the front desk by eight in the morning. The front desk was only a thin partition away from the newsroom and in no time Lew was sitting before a middle-aged man with craggy brows. He appeared to be harassed.

'Okay, let's get on with it,' said the man, who was news editor and also chief reporter – it was a small outfit, where everyone doubled up. 'Let's see what you have to offer.'

He began to read the resumé, which he hadn't bothered to look at till then.

'Already done some writing, eh? Scattering pearls of wisdom in the benighted lands of western Ontario?'

There was nothing to say to that. The news editor went on reading, puffing out his cheeks in mock amazement.

'Well, I don't know that we were expecting this much talent,' he continued, digging deep in the reporter's tub of irony. 'But I'm glad to see that you know something about the technical side of the business. Printing and production and all that. Always comes in handy, if you care to use it. Most reporters are too damned lazy to think of problems on that side. Don't care to get printer's ink on their lovely white hands.'

'I don't mind work,' Lew offered boldly, 'with head or hands.'

'Is that so? That's good, very good. You look hale enough to put in some long hours. But it's no picnic here. Lots to do; not many people to do it. No time for mistakes. Takes too long to put them right. No one to hold your hand either; you'll have to scrabble about, make your own destiny. Also, the money's lousy. You start on less than nothing and work up to not very much. But there's some fun to be had, and maybe just a little bit of value to be added occasionally to the public good.'

He paused, staring at Lew quizzically, working his great eyebrows like street-cleaners' brooms. Then he went on, 'From what I can see, it looks as if you might have what it takes. What do you say – yes or no?'

Lew said yes and started the same day. He learnt later that, at the time, he was the only applicant.

*

The work could be fun, the news editor had said. Lew had not thought of it like that. The image he had was more or less the conventional stereotype of the reporter: cunning, resilience, bulldog tenacity, bare-faced cheek, mollified somewhat by kinder-sounding virtues such as truth-seeking, public service and social accountability. At this stage he knew nothing of grasping, barely literate proprietors peddling influence and advertising space.

But if hard work and long hours were fun, then he soon had amusement up to the neck. He had a ringside view, sometimes too close for comfort, of events and happenings which, for want of a better word, might be called life – or at least modern life. He saw so much of town halls, police headquarters, law courts, fire stations, building and health departments that he sometimes felt as if he had left his skin on a peg in one of those places overnight and taken it up again the next morning. A part of him, the front that faced the world, resided there. The rest of his existence seemed leached out, too pale to leave an impression.

He was industrious and wrote copy by the yard, and some of his words – his own innocent creations – even staggered into print, after the rewrite man had worked them over with the hatchet.

Like many reporters, he was at first fascinated by crime. He remembered his first murder case. It was a hot summer and the provincial court was stuffy, lawyers and court officials fretful, wanting to get their coats off. The courtroom was too small for its own pretensions, overburdened with symbolism and dark oak. The prisoner in the dock was a junior in a real-estate office, a lacquered young man with oiled hair, a light fuzz on the upper lip, a shirt with button-down collar under a dark suit tightly closed, despite the heat, for the whole proceedings. He was anxious about his appearance and frequently swept a pocket comb through his sticky locks.

The facts of the case were not really in doubt. He had killed his girlfriend at the breakfast table. Some days before she had warned him that she might be pregnant (in fact, the autopsy had shown that she was not). For days they had been batting this development back and forth. She, who wanted the baby, grew frantic and shrill and sour enough to set his teeth on edge; he, who didn't want the baby, became more frightened and conscience-stricken and whey-faced by the hour. Both were young and inexperienced and no worse than the next boy and girl. That morning, as they sat down to try to eat, she was at him again, screeching sadly and banging the table enough to make the cups rattle and his head ring. He grasped his head in his hands and shut his eyes, since he could see the path no clearer than it had been before. After a while, he rose quietly, as if in a dream, went to the kitchen counter, picked up a heavy skillet and suddenly launched a blow at the back of her head. It seemed to call for a full baseball swing. It was a solid blow, but to make sure that the task was complete, he then struck her two or three times in the neck with the bread knife. Neighbours in the downstairs apartment, hearing what was but the latest and most noisy part of a now familiar ruckus, phoned the police. When two uniformed officers arrived, bursting exuberantly through the door, the dead girl was slumped forward on the table, blood oozing from her neck on to a bowl of breakfast food, while he sat frozen, a cup of black coffee locked in his hand.

The prisoner did not – could not – deny the facts but claimed some kind of blackout, some lesion of sanity. 'I can't remember, I just can't,' he repeated ad nauseam to anyone who would listen. The prosecution was not impressed. Nor was it much of a defence for his lawyer to work on, although he did what he could, bringing up the question of *mens rea* and the degree of responsibility.

In the dock the young man seemed pathetically anxious to get things straight. He nodded at the lawyers' good points, both for and against him. 'Yes sir!' he was heard to mutter, and once 'Now hold on there,' for which he was reprimanded by the judge. His head swivelled in jerky spasms, as if at a knotty tennis match in which the points were going by too fast. In moments of extra stress, confronted by painful witness statements, he developed a slight tic in the left eyelid so that he appeared to be winking without discrimination at court, lawyers, public, judge and jury. Perhaps the jury saw some sort of message written there, in the stiff, pleading, ashen, twitching face, which allowed them to accept mitigating circumstances. He was declared to be sufficiently insane and sent down to the hellhole of a psychiatric prison ward.

The trial made good copy but Lew was stumped as to what sense he should try to put behind the description. In a blazing, unforeseen moment death had misappropriated a young life. That was the raw look of the matter; everything else was gloss. Of course, in the interests of order, stability and cohesion, society demanded some accounting – a dignified drama, some money in lawyers' pockets, a penalty. Out of charity, the court and the jury gave the prisoner a sentence that many thought worse than death. As he was led out to the cells the young man was still frowning, turning here and there, looking questions at the warders, the iron-bound door, the steps out of a bearable life. He was whispering, as if for ghosts to hear, 'What, sir? What?'

That night, in the fancy hotel where many of the participants in the trial were staying, a couple of the young lawyers were making a racket over martinis and pungent cigars.

'Hardly seems worthwhile to come all the way out here to the boondocks,' said one of them, 'except for the money of course.'

'Professionally, it *was* disappointing,' the other agreed. 'No fight in that fellow. He just went under and drowned.'

At a nearby table Lew got well and truly drunk, and forgave himself for doing so.

*

So it went on, a long slow road, nothing dramatic, stumbling over stones not boulders, yesterday's hopes revisited as today's emptiness. Years of wandering, learning his trade forwards and backwards until he was damned good at it. No one could take that from him.

Nothing, in the misapplication of brain or will or ability, in the way of small-minded petty mischief as well as larger errors, surprised him any more. Big cases were no more illuminating than little cases. After covering several murder trials he found himself bored, very bored, yawning at the indefatigable misery of lives coming apart.

Timmins, Sault Sainte-Marie, Sudbury, Owen Sound. At first he was just chasing jobs, looking for a variety of experience. But glancing at the map one day he realized that he was edging towards the big city and he decided that was where he wanted to be. Patience and persistence – that should do it. He had no doubt that he possessed whatever professional ability might be needed.

On the way to Toronto, city of hopes, Lew landed in London, Ontario, working for *The Free Press*, a paper that espoused Family Values. After nine months he was sent to cover the story of a ten-year-old boy knocked off his bicycle and killed by a car in a suburban street. The story was sad and unexceptional. A bright fall day with leaves turning colour; a kid, feeling good after school, letting life get to him, swooping his bike about without looking behind; a car, not driven dangerously, but going a little too fast in a quiet road. Then a sudden silence and some shutters drawn for ever in a family home. The story hardly needed writing. It told itself.

Lew turned in his copy to the city editor.

'Yeah, yeah, that seems to hit most of the spots,' said the editor after barely a glance. 'But we need a picture of the kid. Go out there and get me one.'

'I already asked around,' Lew replied. 'The mother didn't have a suitable one, or she wouldn't let it go. The poor kid was new to the district. Nothing at the school; no yearbook or sports photos. Nothing in the neighbourhood. I reckoned the family had enough troubles without pestering them any further.'

The editor looked up in amazement. 'Don't give me that bleeding-heart respect crap,' he snapped. 'You're a reporter, aren't you? Get out there and goddamn report. Listen, I'll even tell you how you do it. We had a guy here – Danny Smithers – a sure-fire ace. I sent him out one time to get a photo for a story very like this. The family wouldn't play ball, though Danny knew there was a photo, having seen one on the piano. So early next morning he waylaid the milk-delivery man, paid him five bucks to borrow his apron and cap for a few minutes. Then Danny rang the doorbell and gave the lady of the house some cock-and-bull story about the last milk bill being wrong, about owing the lady some money. Could she check? As she stumbled off in her dressing gown to find the bit of paper, Danny snuck into the living room and popped the photo under his apron. And *voilà*, we had the picture.'

'Shows what a creepy asshole your reporter was,' Lew replied angrily. 'I'm not going to do anything like that.'

'Suppose I order you to?' The editor was giving him the baleful eye.

'Then you'd better fire me.'

'Maybe it doesn't warrant that yet. But you should watch out.'

He sent Lew away and rewrote the story himself. He got it down to one paragraph, carefully eliminating all expressions of sympathy and regret and small tragedy that Lew had put in.

Within a week Lew handed in his notice.

*

In a pre-war book about the Press, written by a hardened old Fleet Street pro,

Lew had read: 'The reporter's thick skin is required as a protection against his own self-contempt. He may be asked at any moment to behave in a way that every decent instinct in his nature revolts against.'

He knew this, of course, had known it years ago, without admitting it. He had got used to the fix given by the reporter's adrenalin rush. He liked to feel the copy grow and change under his fingers on the typewriter. His profession was a dangerous fix, but a useful skill. So, trying to distance himself a little from the ragged line where people were hurt, he applied to, and was accepted by, Canadian Press in Toronto. It was an editing job, to take material off the wire, then to rewrite it and condense it for transmission to local papers.

'Looks easy, eh?' said the cheerful interviewer, Steve, who later became a pal of Lew. 'I guess you've done plenty of rewrite work in your time. But let me tell you, it's not so simple, with stuff whizzing off the wire and deadlines waiting, to get to the core – the soul – of every story. How it's done – there's an analogy here that I like to use. You know how the first golf balls were made? Seems there in old Scotland they took a top-hatful of feathers, boiled the feathers down, squeezed them into a little core and sewed that into a ball covered with sheepskin. There you have it. An amorphous mass of useless feathers reduced to a neat handy ball that you can play with. So that's what you do here. Boil and boil away until you can squeeze the kernel into a neat-looking coat of sheepskin.'

Lew didn't mind that. Though he had always been infatuated with words, he didn't mind pruning and squeezing them a bit, getting them into a tidy shape. Just so long as he could rub up against them every day.

Toronto

He felt fully awake, perhaps for the first time since his early years in the Annapolis Valley. Toronto was no paradise. In those days it had a reputation for transcendent dullness. But it had what the big city usually has: much coming and going, restlessness, diverse communities, immigrants, students, commerce, roughhouse politics, stubborn old prejudices, ancient relics, new conceits, tills ringing in shops and offices. In the mêlée of peoples and ideas some intellectual ferment might arise, or lives become jarred out of frame by strange rewards and torments. In all, there were good chances for a personal revolution.

Steve Atkinson, the sunny CP interviewer, had a view of life that put things, as it were, in lower case. A recognizable journalist for sure, he was not exactly cynical. The term 'cool' was becoming fashionable north of the US border and it seemed to apply to a disposition that was real and significant. Steve took a step back from the city and found it appalling but amusing. In the hours after work he liked to smoke a little grass, and that made things even more amusing. It was not as if he personally were going to do anything about the grotesque lapses of city government. But he was glad to bring to notice, according to best journalistic practice, any breach of humanity, honesty and decency that came to his attention. So he was not short of material. For the rest, he lived with the looser rules of those who do not quite conform. He gave offence to city fathers, working without too much responsibility, sometimes high and occasionally drunk, and he talked too much. He lived in Yorkville, even then a place that was exchanging inner-city poverty for romantic squalor.

Lew had taken a look at that part of the city and decided that it was not for him. His days of slovenly rapture were long gone. At an earlier stage in a hard-working life he had discovered the value of comfort. He knew that a little effort and organization could get him a heated apartment with proper plumbing, a warm bed, a bathroom without cockroaches, and a kitchen free of salmonella. The carnival lives of Yorkville looked suspect, too much like poor theatre. After a few mistrials he settled in a semi-industrial area to the west of the Gooderham and Worts Distillery, where blue-collar workers kept their lives under wraps and the breeze off the lake sent the distillery fumes to penetrate his top-floor apartment. He liked to imagine that he could detect on the breeze a tincture of spices and spirits, and that was almost as good as a double whisky.

As a newcomer to the city Lew was glad to let Steve Atkinson waltz him around town, to show him the ropes, or at least the ropes that Steve's unfastidious and disrespectful hands could get a grip on. In idle hours they would smoke some grass, have a beer or two, then sally forth renewed in the hope that some sprightliness or daring had managed to creep that week under the portcullis of the city's Presbyterian defences. They found that what passed for shock and vice in town was generally just the tedium of excess that the rich can always purchase at will. That was easy to avoid; it was merely a matter of better taste and leaner pockets. So, still mildly elevated by the dope, and bulging with undelivered talk, Steve most often led them to university territory, to student hang-outs, where he could buttonhole some footloose acquaintance for a good-natured rant. He seemed to know a host of willing listeners, from undergraduates to junior instructors. Under his devil-may-care good fellowship Steve had something of the scholar's sober quest for knowledge. He wanted to know how matters stood on a heap of subjects, and the habits of a reporter made him a powerful inquisitor. He was particularly playful with student philosophers, having again the newspaperman's eye for evasion and bullshit, and he loved to plunge the knife of derision into vulnerable spots. He used to say, laughing, that one day he would study the subject properly – at the University of Toronto, why not? – then he would be able to tell what he was really talking about.

One of Steve's favourite places was the King Cole Room, a bar where students and the university crowd mixed easily with journalists. In the course of many visits Lew had his eyes drawn to a tense young woman with a dark clouded frown on her face who sat usually on the edge of a group of students, severe but attentive, opening her mouth suddenly as if passionate to speak, then saying nothing. It was a very eloquent silence which Lew, for ever a listener, wanted to hear broken. He watched her and gradually worked his way towards her, in the tumble of ever-changing places, bringing himself within range of those haunted eyes.

Her name was Elaine Friedman, a Jewish girl, a graduate student of political economy. We live, of course, then as now, in the best of all political and economic worlds, but Lew considered that, if any people had a right to demand a reckoning from Providence and the so-called beneficial progress it is said to provide, then it had to be the Jewish people. Elaine had a query about Western society, and her looks, her family history, her inability to speak of that, and in general her reticence about the world, let society know of her unease. Lew felt that he could be at one with her on that subject, and he grew interested enough to wonder if he, too, had something Jewish in him. He did a little digging into his background, making enquiries among his family in the Maritimes, and discovered, without great surprise, that his distant forebears in the old Holle clan in Pomerania and East Prussia had had more than a little Jewish blood in them, before chance and circumstance had thrown them boldly into the New World as undeviating Protestants.

Lew was determined to get to know her. After a low-key siege, which both approached uneasily, with caution on his part and timidity on hers, he prevailed on her to smile a bit, to talk, to take a drink with him, to relax with some mild grass. Slowly, they were led into further convergence – the normal consequence of attraction and sympathy.

Elaine was a non-practising Jew. This was a relief for Lew since he had come to regard the institutions of religion – any religion – as the worst ball-breakers of society, the cause of much madness. Still, she couldn't help being a Jew and she certainly didn't want to be anything else. If not religious, she was nun-like in her habitual reserve and solemnity before life, though not at all nun-like in bed where the ferocity of her screwing sometimes left Lew with palpitations and minor abrasions. He was not among those who thought pain a welcome part of sex. But she seemed to need – seemed eager for – these rough animal encounters, though her orgasm, if she had one, was followed too often by a crying jag. At that point, to comfort her might be offensive. How far was he allowed to trespass? And what if life really did warrant such topsy-turvy emotions? For her, pleasure itself appeared to be part of a life under a curse.

They set up house together, in trepidation, fearful for the present and blind to the future. Since he was earning good money, they lived in his apartment, but nervously, afraid to give away too much, scared by too much contact. Large parts of their lives were kept private by unspoken agreement. At times, she passed him silently on the stairs. Her strained little smile might have been for the newel post, for all he could tell. In the course of a week, one or the other of them was likely to be in the King Cole Room bar; they didn't have to be there together.

For both of them, winter was a bad time. When the temperature dived below zero, often for weeks on end, Lew's good spirits went into hibernation. On certain days the light was glaring, as brittle as glass, stabbing the eye. On other days of low cloud and high humidity the air was almost unbreathable, a dank suffocating medium in which small fish might have lived happily, an exhaust compounded of fumes and icy mist. It smelt of sourdough. A winter wind cut through the city canyons, a razor diminishing Lew's body into a clenched huddle beneath too many clothes. His mind became semi-frozen and null, locked into dreams of avoidance and escape. Earmuffs clamped to his head, mizzling snow on a fur cap, spectacle frames giving a chilly pinch to the bridge of his nose, bloated in padded winter coat, feet as clumsy as cinder blocks, he felt woefully reduced, a stricken and hardly animate lump of being.

For weeks on end he and Elaine prowled the small apartment, stepping warily, protecting themselves against slight provocations, guarding their frailties. For days, they barely spoke. They took to adding a dash of rye whiskey to the morning coffee; they were drifting into a blue minor key.

MEXICO

In the winter, as often as they could get away, they fled for Mexico. These flights had the look of a holiday but were more in the nature of a surrender to lack of hope. For brief moments they could find some satisfaction in sunlight and the rewards to rich foreigners that grew out of others' poverty. The feelings were complicated, blurred by warm days and lazy nights.

They followed some of the familiar trails of young gringos out for fun, taking in the west-coast beaches all the way down to Acapulco, and ending usually at Oaxaca or thereabouts, or in the small hilltop towns of Sierra Madre del Sur given over to the blatant sexual morals and unquenchable idle thirst of North American dropouts and wastrels.

For low cost, and to try to make some sense of Mexican life on the gritty edge, they travelled for preference by train or bus. They shared incomprehension and bottomless courtesy on wooden benches in slow, creaking carriages, bathed in blown dust and sticky sunrays. Occasionally, soldiers or armed police intimidated them with malignant stares, insolently strolling the aisles and bumping the foreigners with boot or rifle butt. This told them, if they needed reminding, that not all in this perplexing land was booze and beaches. The residue of long history, filmed over by economic necessity and Yankee power, still left a stain. Bus travel was often easier; glued by sweat to tight-fitting seats, they presented less of themselves as a target for misunderstanding. And some of the long-distance buses were comfortable and swift.

They learnt some rough-and-ready Spanish of the tourist kind. The cheap meals were generally thin tortillas with a pleasant mush of beans, exploding sometimes into fire as if booby-trapped with hidden explosives. The drink was good and cheap, too cheap for sustained sobriety. Marijuana appeared to be dealt around every corner, usually by North American expatriates.

They saw, if they wished, the wounds of the land – wounds of history, of conquest, of colonization, of revolution, of underdevelopment too close to a frightening neighbour. The picture was there, but too often they had not the courage to face it.

*

In San Miguel de Allende they had taken two rush-bottomed chairs outside the cantina to watch a lurid sunset boil down towards the distant Pacific. Leaning chairbacks against the whitewashed wall they held thick glasses of tequila in hand. Clouds massing over the mountains to the south-west hinted at the diversion of rain. In a while, sleeping might be easier. Down the street a fat workman had his shoulder under the haunch of a mule, trying to goad it into motion. The mule, loaded with two large woven panniers of building rubble, swivelled its long ears and cocked its head back for a solemn look, as if to get a proper take on the torrent of abuse afflicting its rear end. Then it backed up a pace and squatted into an even more stubborn resistance. The labourer, seeing the uselessness of language, reached in one of the panniers for a machete and began to whale at the mule's rump with the flat of the blade. Some urchins, who had been appreciating the contest of man versus beast, gave up jeering and started to wham a child's rubber ball against a goal outlined in burnt stick on the blank end wall of a house.

'Those *chicos*,' Elaine said, 'you'd think they are happy.' Her voice was low, as if ruminating with herself.

'So, why not?' Lew replied lazily.

At this stage of a pleasing day he was not disposed to argue. He had a drink, the sunset, prospects of the evening and night to come.

'Well,' she began. Then she stopped and decided to think about it, screwing her face up as she sipped the sour tequila behind the rim of lemon and salt. After a long pause she dropped her chair back on to its four feet and continued firmly.

'What I'm wrestling with is a simple fact. We're scared to be deprived of things these people don't even have theoretically within reach. You know the things as well as I do – wonderful consumer goodies, security for life, steady income, leisure, comfort, good health, easy and frequent fucks, that sort of thing. What I want to know is how come we grow faint and practically have a heart attack if we are denied *anything*, yet these people still show themselves to be human, as much and maybe more so than we do. They even show signs of contentment, with nothing more stable and reassuring then sun and sky overhead?'

'Maybe that's the key,' he replied, 'plenty of sun and blue sky.' He was feeling relaxed and didn't want to be pitched into depressing thoughts. There were enough of those lying in wait back in Toronto. But she was not put off.

'What is this place, then?' She was looking around, searching for clues.

'Perhaps a laboratory to test the validity of our political and economic certitude? I feel I should have a white lab coat on, with some quantifying measuring device in hand. But let's say the measurements taken here falsify our bold predictions, those that we are never tired of laying on other societies. Isn't that just frightening? As good followers of Karl Popper we should then abandon our social and economic hypotheses. Is that possible? Could you, for example, accept the readings of the instruments? How do you stand on our measured scale – let's call it the Holle Scale of Bliss? Are you happy? You don't always look it, and I have some personal reasons to doubt it.'

'I don't know that I'm in a position to make scientific world judgements,' Lew replied.

He was taking her more seriously now, apprehensive about where this might lead them.

'As for me,' he suggested cautiously, 'perhaps there are always holes and pitfalls on every road.'

'Just a bad road surface?' she said with amusement. 'But it looks to me as if you're on a perfectly smooth and lovely stretch of tarmac, only it's leading in entirely the wrong direction.'

'It's true, I'm trying to deal with some issues in work and life.' He held up his tequila glass, twisting it, testing the last of the sunset through the opaque imperfections of the glass, wishing that her suspicions would shimmer as quickly into obscurity. 'I'm embarrassed that I'm not able to clarify them even enough for myself.'

'Oh come on now,' she teased him. 'I know this is Mexico, the land of *mañana*, but you'll win no more time by equivocating.'

'But this bears down on both of us,' he protested. He was not ready to go on until she had shown something of her hand. 'What about you? Could you be happy here?'

'I don't know for sure. Probably not.' She said it sadly, clutching her blouse against her throat, as she might in a sudden chill. 'I'm the representative hero of our time – the Kid of the Capitalist West. City born, city bred, product of a long and useful line of burghers, merchants, dealers in every available commodity; financiers, middlemen, hustlers, swindlers; the core members of modern society. A few scholars and musicians too. Our kind, we take a couple of steps off the city sidewalk and we're lost. You know that old jibe about the Jew? The one who goes in the revolving door last and comes out first? The whole point of the insult requires a building with limited openings, a revolving door, an apparatus for control, a means to apportion people, a reason to get in first. Without all that, the virtue of precedence – if it is a virtue – is useless. Outside the modern city our special qualities desert us. We become at the mercy of hicks who can tell a Hereford from a Holstein, or farmers who know land and nature well enough to sit back and watch the corn grow. We harvest dockets, bills of sale, contracts, memoranda of agreement, financial instruments, dollar notes. There's no season for these, and nature isn't going to help you at all. So for me, I fear that this place can be no more than temporary therapy. Modern life – what we have made of it – takes a tough toll, and I need some repair. But I know I'm going back, even for heartache and disillusion.'

'Buying and selling,' he replied truculently, 'you're going to wind down your stock till you're damn near naked. A shell with no more trappings to dispose of. What are you going to offer the citizens then? Who the hell wants your naked shell?'

'I'll face that,' she said sadly, 'when the world's last commodity has gone under the hammer.'

Gloomily, she licked the rim of her glass, thinking how peculiar this drink was, filtered through salt and lemon, wondering if she should have another.

'So you're not going to fight it, the tentacle that strangles the world?' He sounded upset. 'Just wait until the last option, the one on death, is sold and claimed?'

'I think I *am* fighting it,' she protested. 'It's not commerce I object to – in our present state of being that is very necessary – but to commercial society taken to our extreme. I look at this land and people and weep to see unsophisticated peasants, unable to defend the traditional order of their lives, so ruthlessly exploited for our gain. I would like to look at humans who don't have dollar signs flashing behind their eyelids. But I can only fight with weapons made for my use. There's nothing to hand here that I can wield effectively. The weapons I can use arise out of the technology and society that I hope one day to help curb and civilize. Ironic, isn't it?'

'That doesn't sound like cheerful news for us, or for me.'

He definitely needed another drink and stomped inside to get it. When he returned the spark of her cigarette seemed no more than the weakest of beacons in failing light. She waited until he had squirmed peevishly on to the uncomfortable chair, then went on in her most reasonable voice.

'You know very well that we've been on edge for some time. I'm not talking about fault, and it's not affection that we lack. I feel we have plenty of that. But we seem to be hobbled together in a three-legged race, stumbling about without getting the swing of it. Are you content as you are? Admit it, you're not.' She beamed at him kindly, hoping to soften the message. 'You're a hayseed at heart, a farmer's boy, countryman, husbandman, woodsman, ploughman, as well as carpenter, printer and long-time newspaper man. I can't see you abandoned in this world for lack of abilities. And I can very well see space and satisfaction for you in a place like this.'

'I thought I was a wordsmith,' said Lew ruefully.

She smiled and took his hand and gently kissed his knuckles.

'Perhaps you could be,' she whispered close to his ear, 'but I think you're not really trying.'

*

They departed Mexico City on a morning flight. Already, the city smog – that notorious climatic inversion – was as foul as the lining of a smoker's lungs. Suddenly Mexico was a place to leave and it didn't matter a damn how quickly they got back to Toronto. Lew was not feeling well. Who knew what might have caught him out south of the Rio Grande? Contaminated food? Spiked drinks? Infection from unclean beds? The flux from poverty? It turned out that it was hepatitis, an affliction that made alcohol taste disgusting.

Elaine was staring out of the window, watching Popocatépetl diminish as the plane swung into its northern route. Then, slumped in her seat, she nervously smoothed her dress over her knees until coffee was served. That seemed to shape her up. She laid her hand on Lew's arm, securing his attention, and spoke in a low voice.

'Lew,' she said flatly, 'I've missed my period. I'm quite sure of it.'

TORONTO, 1961

The winter blanket of white was now growing patched and filthy. The apartment, unopened for a couple of weeks, was stuffy with stale air. They opened windows and let arctic currents roust about for a while, cleansing corners and throwing in their faces some ill-timed thoughts.

'Let's talk about it later,' Lew had said on the plane, stiff with shock.

'Not too much later,' she had replied sharply. 'These things don't wait for your convenience.'

Then he was thinking about it most of the time, and whatever premiss he started from he could not make the syllogism click on to any logic that made complete sense to him. The difficulty of being two – he and Elaine – was hard enough; to reduce that to a unity had seemed to be, for some time past, beyond his courage. Now, to smuggle into the unity, as it were, a third being who was some naked, pleading, wanting part of themselves appeared, at first and second judgement, inconceivable. Emotion had little to do with it. Even if his heart desired this child – on the whole he thought that it did – a navigator with a faulty compass approaching reefs of doubt would be a fool to carry such tender and vulnerable cargo.

He had known for some time that his newspaper life – his career – was holed, perhaps fatally, and shipping water fast. Only his proximity to words and the ways to handle them kept him going. But now he needed to separate his words from the professional occasions that gave rise to them.

At home, he saw a pile of blank paper stacked to the side of his typewriter. He took this as an accusation. The pile waited patiently for the moment, but for how much longer? And now there was another accusation, a living speck growing by the day in Elaine's womb. Two confusions. Could not both be simply resolved by straightforward decisions surely within reach of rationally self-interested Cartesian man? But every time he tried to rehearse possibilities in his mind he seemed to generate only white noise. Then a small voice in his head said 'Cut and run.' He would make some strong coffee, stand at the window overlooking a city of lives just as shipwrecked as his, wish that hepatitis allowed him a drink, and know that decisions couldn't be *that* clear.

At the tail end of the winter Lew was invited to a retirement party given out at Kawartha Lakes by a hearty, overweight editor of invincible cynicism who liked to dwell on the theatrical implausibility, the charade, of the world he laid out daily in his pages. He had stipulated for his guests, with typical mischief, fancy dress based on medieval themes. Lew had tried to persuade Elaine to go, but she was in no mood for foolishness; she would leave the pranks to the boys. But Lew decided to let go of his anguish for a while and give himself over to an idle entertainment. He rented from a theatrical costumer an impressive-looking suit of armour, made up in a heavy cloth that had the sheen of steel, with a helmet and visor in stiff plastic.

The weather, at the time, was unreliable, the familiar unreadable composition of a season about to change. Dirty snowbanks, under the day's weak sun, shrivelled at the edges into slush that leaked thin sheets of water across the road. In the deep chill of twilight the water froze again into black ice. At night, a tenacious mist clung in the trees and oozed furtively into the hollows and dips of the land. Driving, in particular night driving, was tricky. But Lew was a confident driver, with a sporty and powerful little Triumph car from England, and he backed his skill against the elements. To him, long resident in the middle lands of Canada, the road conditions were no mystery.

He drove out in late afternoon in his full medieval gear, on a brisk day that promised no more than it delivered. The party was in a large old rambling wooden frame house with its feet almost in lake water. On one side was a neglected orchard with low, rank vegetation in which fallen branches rotted. Behind the house, sparse woods ruffled by the wind were close enough to peer over windowsills into comfortable, dishevelled rooms. As he entered the warm and noisy interior Lew thought he might be going to enjoy himself. He was surprised to find that he could leave his puzzlement and dejection at home.

His plump host had made an early start at the bar. Ever alert to rub a raw spot, he feigned indignation when he heard that Lew's hepatitis stopped him drinking – drinking, in the editor's view, being one of the sacred duties of newspaper hacks. Then he took a firm grip on Lew's arm, growling 'Pretend this isn't happening in my respectable home,' and led him to a little study in the far corner where some crime reporters were preparing and exchanging joints of marijuana. A few tokes left Lew, if not on the primrose path, at least temporarily free from the sensation of wading a swamp in diver's boots.

In a while he found he *was* enjoying himself. Drifting from room to room, glass of fruit juice in hand, he came upon colleagues and friends under the caricature of fancy dress, sometimes so shifted out of the normal that he barely recognized them. He noticed conversations taking tortuous turns, sly and often flirtatious, the speakers surprising themselves into new personas beneath the disguise of the strange clothes. A squeezed-out financial journalist, well known for her rigid virtue, was dressed as Maid Marian and had a jolly hand tucked deep into the rear waistband of a young squire wearing a large codpiece. A notorious gay, in papal robes, was loudly recommending abstinence and orthodoxy. A shy young Chaucer was so drunk he might as well have been speaking Middle English.

All this Lew took as encouragement for change, not just an alteration of clothes but perhaps of skin and guts also. His own figure, as knight-in-armour, argued for a big view, for idealism and errant adventure in foreign lands.

He left the party after midnight in high good spirits, visor pushed up and a cigar jutting out through the open face of the helmet. The night was clear and sharp, stars blinking, the frost biting at his heels as he hurried to the car. He started the engine and sat for a while, smoking, waiting for the heater to flush some tepid air over his feet in their party shoes, listening to the muscular rumble of all that eager horsepower. When he had some feeling in his toes he eased the clutch out and juggled the Triumph slowly over the black holes of the unpaved drive to the country road. The late-night radio was moaning some hillbilly lament, making as much sense as a baby whimpering in a cot. He felt the rear of the car fishtail for an instant as he swung out on to the blacktop. He settled into the bucket seat, flung the remains of the cigar away, and began the stiff canter home.

In the darkened woods there was ice in places, and from time to time swaths of mist wrapped the car up for a few moments. But in the main visibility was good and the road surface not too treacherous. After a few miles he shook the reins out a bit and felt exhilarated by the rush of the night. The car was going fast and steady but just on the nervous edge of letting go. On a long sweeping curve through a patch of forest he drove with no more than delicate fingertips on the steering wheel, anticipating the limit of adhesion that the car seemed keen to go beyond. He was beginning to grin at his competent skill when of a sudden two small brilliant lanterns, like lights shot from a gun, pierced the beams of his headlights. A deer, transfixed in the road, turned uncomprehending eyes on its onrushing executioner. Lew flung the wheel to the right but knew better than to get on to the brakes too fiercely. For an instant he thought he might skid safely by. But the left fender caught the deer with a dull, solid blow. There was a crunch of splintering bone and the car was thrown into an uncontrollable wobble. Before Lew could conjure it back on course, awkwardly burdened as he was by fancy dress, the front wheels hit roadside ice and Lew was heading fast for the woods.

A world exploded in his ears, a squat birch split and tumbled, with the car climbing up the ragged stump. Then the Triumph keeled over on to its right side in a mess of steam and frozen mud, the engine roaring and then dying. Lew was left hanging limp over the handbrake and the gear lever. He knew he was hurt, perhaps badly so, but in the seconds before he lost consciousness he could not quite locate the source or the extent of the pain and he wondered if that was relevant. The last he remembered was the low, mean hiss of the punctured radiator.

*

The louvres of the Venetian blind were closed so only a little strained sunlight relieved the gloom. A machine by the bed made a steady ticking noise and various wires and tubes attached him to a reality out there that he knew nothing about. Someone – not him – stirred and coughed.

He was reluctant to open his eyes, though circumstance seemed to demand that he take just a glimpse, if only to register what part of limbo he occupied. His body felt as if it was on an obscure journey, one that was weirdly pleasant.

He cracked his eyes open a fraction, looking through slitted eyelids, letting in a blurry image of a white room in which loomed a blurry white figure. He wanted to say something clear but his jaw was not working too well. It seemed to be stifled with some lagging or other bulky material. With effort, he managed a small noise.

'Where am I?' he mumbled woozily, as if through a packed mouthful of sand.

'Hospital of course,' replied a severe female voice. 'Where did you think? You've been in a car crash and have some injuries – quite bad I'd say.'

'Man, I wouldn't know it,' he sighed, as indistinct as distant static. 'It's warm and strange down here, feels pretty good.'

'Don't think you're here for fun,' said the unfriendly voice. 'Your jaw was broken and has been reset. You're on morphine now. But don't think we give you that so you can have fun.'

He remembered fragments of time and place. He thought he had been awake before and hadn't liked it. But now he was having an interesting time, almost on the brink of pleasure, with heightened perceptions, convoluted dreams, intimations of other futures. He wanted to think about these things free from the nurse's sad medical moralism. He closed his eyes and settled back into the mystery tour of the drug. Morphine could help.

He had suffered a broken jaw and concussion and busted ribs and a torn ligament in his shoulder, plus lacerations and severe bruising where his body had been thrown forward into the steering wheel and windscreen. The visor of the helmet had buckled into his jaw, breaking it, but the ridiculous party headgear had saved him from even worse head damage when he hit the glass. He would mend, said his doctor, poking about to see where it hurt. But the jaw might give trouble in the future and would certainly need careful dental work. 'You're lucky,' the doctor added.

When he was ready for visitors Elaine came as often as she could. She looked withdrawn and haggard, and since talking was a trial for him for the most part she sat silent, holding his hand. After some days – he was not sure how long – she became more animated, her resolve in place at last. In the midst of long pauses, when he was beginning to drift again, she suddenly gripped his hand tighter than before.

'Lew, I've been waiting to tell you this,' she said in a voice from which all emotion had been washed. 'I've arranged a termination.'

Just climbing out of drugs and sleep, he was astonished. What could she mean? *His* termination? The doctors had given him good hope. He squeezed her hand as hard as he could and looked as perplexed as a whipped puppy.

'The child of course,' she added hastily, understanding his fright. 'Well, what do we call it? Abortion? Murder? Timely disposal? There is no way to put it nicely. I feel that, at heart, you want the baby. But you're a case, battling with yourself, and now you're injured, who knows how badly? And I'm afraid and unready. I can't face a mother's burden. Together, we're so tangled up emotionally that we're likely to strangle each other if we're not careful. Poor little mistake, with us as parents he or she would be launched into quicksands. I can't face the thought of that. Another's pain growing out of our insecurity and selfishness. I've taken advice. I'm in good time, and there should be no problem.'

He closed his eyes and let go of her grip. Perhaps he had wanted it – he was still not sure – but only in the way that he coveted some other supposed good. The abstract idea of fatherhood. For him, perhaps, a form of insanity. Thank goodness one of them had been brave enough to face it.

'Lew?' she said. 'Are you smiling? I wish I could tell under all those injuries. Please look at me. I'm leaving you now – I mean permanently – though of course not until you're fit and well. Yes, I'll be all right, and I hope with all my heart that you will be, too.'

He *was* smiling, and he might have laughed had his jaw permitted it. Could it be the effect of the drugs? Drugs my eye, he thought, it was something new taking hold.

ANDALUCIA
WINTER 1962

He'd heard it said, somewhere in this uncomfortable land, that a word is like the throw of a stone; once released, it could not be recalled.

He intended to throw some stones – loose off a few words – and that was the reason he gave himself for coming to this place. His arm, he felt, was limber and ready to start throwing, but so far he had released nothing. The act of letting go scared him. Who knew where a stone might land? It went beyond expectation, into the blue, able to help or damage, both others and himself.

Writing needed faith. He was still unsure of what kind, or how you acquired it.

THE ATLANTIC

In the late autumn after his crash, after deciding to get up and go, Lew found it strangely easy to leave. In Toronto, he talked matters over in the King Cole Room, canvassing thoughts on what to do and where to go. The philosophers at the university, doodling syllogisms on beermats, always had an opinion.

'Look at it this way,' said a logical positivist, 'While you're pulling yourself together and puzzling yourself with designs, what you want is the most life for the least money. Get the basics right: sun, good air, lots of space, lots of time, all free. Let nature provide in the most handsome way possible. It's yours to take. Then cost the bare necessities – food, drink, accommodation – and balance the equation between availability, quality and price. Give some sort of weight to the imponderables: peace of mind, intellectual stimulation, conviviality, ease of communication, compatibility with local society, the pleasure of the present moment, that sort of thing.' He was ticking the points off on his fingers. Then he stopped and grinned, lolling back in a corner of the bar, glad to be going nowhere.

'What's so hard about all that?' he demanded. 'Give yourself a chance. I can see you're practically on your way.'

And so he was. He had savings in the bank, dependencies all untied, clothes for summer or winter, a portable typewriter with a supply of spare ribbons. His destination swung into view as if preordained. At first, having a little primitive Spanish, he had thought of Latin America or Mexico. But Latin America posed problems he didn't need to solve, alien lands still savage with the beasts spawned by a history made miserable by fraud, greed, violence and cruelty. He was not an anthropologist and felt no desire to investigate the varieties of colonial malaise. Mexico he had already tried, nibbled at it a bit but found it unhealthy, contaminated by the run-off from North American culture that he was anxious, for the moment, to escape.

In the King Cole Room, suggestions flew around as if each one was a speculative move in a new game: the reinvention of a life according to pure principles. Behind each suggestion – conventional or outlandish, funny or cynical – there seemed to be some personal fantasy, some sigh for what might have been if courage or chance had been different. They were cheering Lew on, but they were a little jealous too, wanting to imagine themselves as new men and women in new landscapes.

Finally, they settled it to their own satisfaction and left Steve Atkinson to give the verdict.

'Look, where have you ever been?' he ribbed Lew cheerfully. 'Just bumping around North America in a gloomy way. You need to get out from under this swath of territory. Get offshore both physically and mentally. Discard the whole lousy hand dealt you by the accident of birth. Reshuffle the pack, lay out fresh cards, slip yourself a few off the bottom to ease the way. Considering your peculiar mixture of hopes and talents I'd say that southern Spain would suit you to a tee.'

Of course, Spain was the powerful archetype of all those little Latin pieces of America, the ones that seemed to offer false promises. And now southern Spain, under the sanguine wash spread by Steve's genial nature, took on a rosy hue. Steve had a friend who had made the move and claimed to live on ambrosia and happiness, snug in a whitewashed village about the size of a handkerchief, on the hot bare expanse of shale, rock and sand beginning to be known, in the tourist brochures, as the Costa del Sol. Between the mountains and the beach days slipped by, waiting for you to make what you could out of them.

After a few days and several rounds of beer Lew saw doubts blow away. A sunny exploration shone through. Southern Spain looked like the place for him, and he didn't want to live with the regret that he had never tried it.

*

He bought a one-way ticket on the Yugoslav freighter that plied between New York and Casablanca in Morocco. On the Greyhound out of Toronto he took an inventory of himself, trying to assess his fitness for a new life. He judged that he had the moral and mental stamina for the task ahead, whatever that might be. The material resources were there, in his bank account, in his many years of self-sufficiency. And he thought he was now in adequate physical shape. He had shaken off the hepatitis and could look a drink in the eye once more without retching. Exile in a hot climate, even if self-imposed, seemed inconceivable without a fond attachment to wine and beer at least. And Spain was, historically, a land of wine. Of the injuries sustained in the car crash, the lesser ones had healed nicely. Only his jaw and teeth gave reasons for worry. The break had been reset and mended and then a good, and very expensive, dentist had gone to work on his teeth. Everything was now firmly in place, held by some discreet scaffolding, but the dentist had told him that the whole structure of his mouth was very fragile. The man in the spotless white smock had sucked in his cheeks, looking pensive.

He was a good man, but was he aware how steep his prices were? Lew was content to chance his luck in Spain. No doubt there were talented Spanish dentists – much cheaper too – though perhaps they did not have the very latest technology, and certainly not the preoccupation with the Hollywood smile. Lew could think of nothing in his new life that required the Hollywood smile.

The bus unloaded him on the West Side of an autumnal New York, with a cold wind fingering the skyscrapers and driving filth into the potholes. It was a place he was eager to leave behind. He had visited New York on a few occasions for short periods of curiosity and careless indulgence, but he was well aware how the city tempted you to rush towards danger, to make megalomania and vanity a large part of the day's work. As the taxi took him towards the Hudson Piers, through the stink of fish and raw meat, past the crumbling ironwork and the angry dementia of men whose work tussled constantly with the gargantuan disarray of the city streets, a soft drizzle loafed off the river from the Jersey shore and wrapped what had merely been ugly in a sodden cloak of misery. In haste, he paid off the cabbie, a smartass with a dead cigar in his face, brutal with grammar, as much an ornament of the city as the ragged cat looking ferocious on a window ledge. He pulled the collar of his jerkin around his ears against the rain and hurried into the embarkation shed.

Among the horde of fretful and puzzled youth that flowed at this time out of the North American universities, among those with more complaints than degrees and with aspirations to serve a hundred vexatious causes, among those who had finally said 'to hell with it,' the Yugoslav freighter gave a popular means of escape. Taking only a limited number of passengers, it offered, for a reasonable price, an easygoing but spartan journey, amid an affable equality of crush and democratic intimacy and execrable food, in a leisurely drift to North Africa. From there, a variety of trails lay open to disaffected youth, most of them requiring caution and good sense and a determination not to become lost.

The cabins were small, stuffy and smelt of cleaning-fluid. Lew found himself bunched into a two-berther with a stained basin in the corner and a short run of buckled linoleum on the floor. He chose the lower bunk, laid out a few night things from his suitcase, then sat on the bunk breathing deeply, suddenly agitated by unknown fears and wondering if a quick retreat would get him back on shore in time. Then a rap on the wood was followed by a broad freckled face taking a quizzical look around the edge of the door.

'Cabin number three?' said the newcomer, shoving a suitcase before him with a foot.

He looked the place over, wrinkling his nose. 'Very cosy,' he added amiably. 'I see you got the bottom bunk. I'll try not to step on your face in the night.'

He chuckled, cocking an eyebrow and seemed to be more amused than upset by the tightness of the cabin. Having dumped his case he was intent on a swift exit, but just before backing nimbly into the corridor he remembered his manners and held out his hand.

'Everett,' he said. 'I won't bother you with the last name, which is Polish, tricky, and much too long.'

Lew shook hands, a neutral expression on his face. His cabinmate appeared to have an agreeable looseness but it was wise to await the fall of events. Formerly, with new faces, Lew had trusted his reporter's instinct. Right or wrong, he put his money on the first impression. But now such hastiness might well be a mistake.

At the first meal, the captain, a hefty fellow in a threadbare nautical jacket, made an appearance. Thereafter he rarely attended, but when he did so he told bad jokes in mangled English, laughing heartily, and poured rotgut red wine with a free hand. To North Americans for whom wine at table was a very unusual luxury, even that seemed an impressive amount of civilization. The second officer, who acted as purser and general factotum to the passengers, extended his creepy smile into every corner of the ship and implied, in good sibilant English, that nothing on board escaped his notice. Certainly, the women didn't. He liked to rest his hand causally on a female shoulder when giving advice or information, and sometimes his hand slid lower. And one of the young women was happy to have his hand go as low as it pleased. She made it clear that she wished to sample on this trip everything the Old World had to offer, capitalist or Communist or anything in between.

On the third night out, the door banging in the dark hours shot Lew upright in his bunk. In the light leaking from the passageway he saw his cabinmate looming large on the narrow strip of floor, his hand clapped over his mouth – an unstable vessel thumping into dock at last. Startled awake, Lew swung his legs over the edge of the bunk, cursing softly and prepared to let fly some choice words on considerate behaviour.

But Everett apologized hastily, blaming his noisy entry on a crack in the flooring and an intake of alcohol.

'You see,' he admitted with a wry face, 'I've been drinking upstairs and the room got emptier and emptier till I was saying hello to four walls. Not the most intelligent walls, either. So I came down to see if you could help me squeeze the bottle.' He pulled a half-bottle of vodka from behind his back and shook it.

What Lew really wanted was a night full of sleep, but that chance was now blown. Everett had clicked the light on and was already rinsing glasses in the corner basin and pouring a couple of stiff shots. So they clinked glasses and stared at each other, Lew warily and Everett with the hopeful grin of the slightly tanked.

Lew took a sip and was surprised that the vodka was excellent. But he didn't intend to let his cabinmate off the hook too easily. 'Okay,' he said sourly, 'tell me something worthwhile to make up for loss of sleep.'

'Hm, stories? This ship has many tales to tell; it's a box of tricks all right. If you put your ear to the deck you'll hear plenty of rustlings. Not shipboard rats either, but another kind of wildlife. Last night, for example, at the dead end of a corridor I almost stumbled on that hairy young man in a bandanna bombarding a large lady twice his age with a fury of kissing. They were tugging at each other's clothes like all-in wrestlers. Seems to be some pheromones on the loose, and the dogs have got their noses adjusted.'

At dinner Lew had noticed the woman, looking large, ruddy and fulfilled, seated almost primly next to her weary neurasthenic husband. Certainly, Lew agreed, the ship was crepitating with whispers and urgent breath.

'And what about our musician,' Everett went on, 'our gypsy accordionist who looks like the king of the hoboes? Except he's no gypsy. He's a Jewish boy from Poughkeepsie. In fancy dress, of course. There's hardly a private space on the boat where you can get away from his dismal squeaking box. Early this morning, trying to enjoy the good air, I found him seated on a bollard, flooding the deck with scales and chromatic sludge. I had to turn tail smartly to avoid the rush of a sickening glissando.'

Everett stopped and they both drank, each cast into his own version of gloomy thoughts. Lew reflected that they were all in fancy dress, to some extent. Got the uniform before we knew what the job was. It seemed ass to front to Lew, but he supposed that identity was now a commodity to choose, to buy and to sell, even without knowing the nature of the self beneath. From the moment the ship had cast off moorings the passengers did so too, becoming pirates, ragpickers, lotharios, whatever one had in mind, riding the freedom of the ocean before landfall boxed them in again.

'For the duration of this trip, we're all on stolen time,' Everett added more cheerfully. Then raising his glass he said, 'But here's to stolen time. I may not be sure where I'm going but I'm sure as hell glad to be going there, wherever it is. The best part of wisdom is to know that you don't learn much on an Iowa campus, where I put in my academic time. And perhaps even less in Harvard Square where human recognition only begins at about the ten thousand bucks a year level. Best thing college does, it gets you in training for the long deadly haul to retirement. By the way, you wouldn't have a joint on you, would you?'

Lew shook his head. He didn't object in any way but he liked to take stock before plunging into too much relaxation. On this ship, he was holding himself a little aloof. Spending as much time as possible alone on deck, he liked to feel the weather in his face and soon found a corner behind a lifeboat where he could sense the tremor in the rigging and trace the complicated play of sky and sea. After a while, the measure of time was the slow pitch of the ship and the slap of the bow wave. The days collapsed into a sort of insensibility from which he was often jolted by the clang of the dinner gong. His appetite for the bad food was excellent.

Lew found himself slipping into a mood of quiet contentment. Seated in a deckchair, or below in the little saloon, he would lose his place in his book, the page sliding over unnoticed while his mind was absent on some dream. There was a lot to dream about.

Costa del Sol

Hardly ever had he known it so bleak and cold. He was used to Canada – had lived there all his life – where yearly the temperature could go down to minus thirty, easily. Here, it was still just above freezing. The difference was, as the Boy Scouts said, 'Be prepared.' In Canada, when winter came, people were ready: the right housing, the right heating, the right clothing, the right transport, the right attitude.

In this village, on the so-called sunny littoral, the walls of the houses were merely whitewashed clay and rubble, the roofs uninsulated tiles with many a chink and windhole, the floors stone flags or glazed tiles set tight on the earth. The putty was loose in the window frames, which had trouble closing, being warped and withered by weather and lack of paint. Often, the warmest place to be was with the mules in the stall at the back of the house, where steam rose from the urine-soaked straw, compensating for the ripe smell with some welcome natural heating.

Lew had rented two upstairs rooms, one of them not bad, with two lopsided windows and a little landing out front. The larger room had a couch that doubled as a bed, a couple of cane chairs, an ornate wooden piece something between a sideboard and a cupboard, as dark and heavy as iron, a rush mat on the floor before a large open fireplace that refused to draw and down which the cold air moaned. The small back room was whatever you could make of it – kitchen, dining room, workroom. At the moment it had a plain deal table and an upright chair, an electric hotplate and a basin with a cold-water tap. The WC was behind a flimsy partition in the corner, but the toilet itself was like nothing he had seen. Set into the floor were two ceramic footfalls into which he stepped and squatted over the open hole between, with an intimate view of his knees. The flush was a bucket of water. From the street door, which no one remembered to close, a long straight stairs led the dark clammy airs of winter up to the landing from where they crept under the loose-fitting door and laid siege to all his extremities.

The negotiation to rent this little apartment had surprised Lew. The landlord had been suggested to him by one of the several foreigners who propped up the local bars at all hours. The landlord, a man of the village respectfully known as the Commandant, held a position concerning harbour regulation further down the coast. He wore a peaked cap with some modest braid, a blue coat with a double line of brass buttons, and he leant on the dignity of his office at all times. They met at a bar, standing stiffly at the counter, keeping a careful eye on propriety, for it would not be quite correct on this first formal occasion to be seated like pals at a table. Drinks were offered, turned aside out of politeness, then graciously accepted. Tapas were sampled, and criticized sharply by the Commandant, who thought them unworthy of visitors. Enquiries as to health were made. In a jumble of Spanish and English they just managed to keep the conversation afloat.

When healths had been drunk the Commandant wiped his mouth with the back of his hand and attended to business. He apologized for the poverty of the accommodation he had to offer, for its gloom, its mean furnishings, its lack of amenity, its dilapidation. He felt ashamed that he had to ask so much for so little.

'But,' he said mournfully, thrusting hands deep into his pockets as if to demonstrate their emptiness, 'we are not the real masters of our property, is it not so? We are ruled by unfriendly forces, by taxes and repairs and maintenance and the need to raise an income from what is ours. A most unfortunate need.'

He looked in embarrassment at his well-shod feet and proposed a seductively low monthly rental. Lew was taken aback. When the summer and the tourists came, he thought, then the price will surely shoot up. He wanted stability and a reasonably long let, so he mentioned that a six-month lease with an option to renew would suit him best, and for this he was willing to pay a slightly higher monthly rent.

The Commandant was shocked. 'But señor,' he protested, 'that must not be. If you are good enough to dedicate yourself to my poor apartment for such a period, then that commitment must be shown in the rent.' He proposed an even lower rent than the one first mentioned and hoped that Lew would 'do me the honour of agreeing to it'.

He had a serious frown on his face and it did not seem within the order of things to cross him. What appeared to be an ordinary piece of financial haggling had suddenly become a different matter, a question of how men stood one to another. So no more was said of the rent, and they shook hands, and another ceremonious drink was ordered before the Commandant judged that matters were as satisfactory as they could ever be with a foreigner and made a dignified exit, casting as he went a further venomous look at the inferior tapas.

So here Lew was in a bitterly cold apartment, on days as quiet and cheerless as the morgue, with an open fire that smoked and wouldn't draw, a brazier he suspected of giving off dangerous fumes, hands and feet like freezer meat, a blanket around his shoulders and a beret on his head, on the table a typewriter that still remained dumb, and a sheaf of paper alongside begging for use.

*

In the spring, everything changed. Softer airs swept in from west and south, picking up African heat, bearing aloft migrating birds, forcing through the new shoots of the oleanders, beginning to unroll the yearly carpet of wild flowers. Lew felt a stirring after the winter lethargy and began to take walks into the hills.

He liked the early morning – the earlier the better on fine days – when the rising sun had bounced up huge and genial out of the Mediterranean. In a knapsack he put a bottle of local wine, coarse bread with dried ham and a lump of cheese, a tomato or an apple, his pipe and a small blob of hash. Sometimes he took a book, which he usually forgot to read. By the time the village mules were heading for the fields, with the farmers hanging on to their tails up the inclines, Lew was gone, 500 feet above the coastal fields in scrub and rock, sweating gently.

In the course of exploration he followed many trails, some animal some human, but found himself most often circling round for a midday rest to the remains of a small mine high in the hills, in remote country where valleys diverged. The scant ruins – a broken wall and a few piles of dressed stones – stood in a slight hollow in front of the opening to the mine, which the collapse of the shaft had formed into nothing more than a shallow cave, a mouth shaggy with roots and the bristles of bushes. In the hollow was a little rocky pool under a solitary pine surrounded by a few feet of rank grasses and sparse vegetation that were just about comfortable enough to lie on. That it was a choice spot he could see by the garbage left around the pool – cigarette butts, the broken glass of beer bottles, scraps of filthy paper. There was even the occasional condom, a sure sign, among a poor Catholic peasantry, of the presence of foreigners. He tore a branch from a bush and swept the leavings into a hole and covered them, for the place was worth preserving from the worst human stains. In the midday heat, with the birds gone quiet, he rested and ate with his back against the pine tree till the arc of the sun sent him to a rock in the cool of the cave mouth. He wanted time and silence and the landscape and the spur to thought.

He had an idea that history was best evident in living structure. The truth of the story of the past was only tested and confirmed in the lives and the land of the living. You read the books and could believe them or not, according to prejudice and judgement. But you trod the land, rested on the hilltops, scrambled up watercourses, translated ruins into what they had been, saw a progression of use and effects, watched the peasant in black coat and black hat scrape a hoe around the roots of vine or olive or orange-tree, noticed the crumbling of the ancient terraces gouged from the inhospitable terrain and the little fields creeping back to dereliction, and you began to *know* something about that thousand-year distance between the Moorish formation of Al-Andalus and the present deformation, from the richest, most populous, most productive, most wide awake and brightest corner of Europe to the present lean, sour, barren, empty, priest-ridden and police-bullied territory, as wretched as any Western land, perhaps with the exception of Albania and Ireland. But that was not the whole story, though maybe a large part of the book story. What sustained and gave dignity to the present and made the place worth living in were the climate, and the tragedy of a landscape slipping from cultivation to natural grandeur, and the enduring resolution of the people who in their lives still demonstrated what they had been, and in their bearing and reticence and courtesy held themselves to be still no different from that, though the rich material things had flown from them and the future was dark enough.

The present is distilled past, and what makes it worth tasting or not is the ageing and maturing of the first ingredients.

He would walk back to the village still getting the facts of the matter, as he saw them, all lined up and wondering whereabouts he fitted into the line. The day was hot and the walk had tired him. Retracing the hillside irrigation channels he gave way to the invitation of clear running water, stripped naked and lowered himself into the current. The channel was just wide enough for his shoulders. The water, about two feet deep, mounted around his earlobes, tickled his chest and spread his pubic hair like a mat of ferns in which his member rested, a small log in the shallows. He hoped there might be a use for that, too, even in a land lacking contraceptives. For a good while he lay there soaking, which was something he needed, for the primitive ablutions in his apartment made a comprehensive wash difficult. The closest he could get to a shower was a bucket of tepid water over his head, standing in the buff in the footholds of the privy.

He closed his eyes, feeling contented and luxurious. His new circumstances had made him shy of judgement and slow to decide. He had managed to get himself to this place safely and he felt settled and at home. But what now? He didn't want entertainment, he wanted to compose his mind. Life was worthless without an ideal, without something beyond a bank account and a house in suburbia. What was worthwhile, or so he thought, what he wanted to put down on the page, was the narrative of his own existence, but only if it amounted to something more than a can of beans.

So it all depended on him alone, as intellectually naked setting out as he was here physically naked in the water channel. He shook himself out of the current, put on his socks, boots and underpants, and stuffed the rest of his clothing into the knapsack. Let the warm evening breeze dry him. Suddenly he felt as if he were in a hurry. He must get about more, make his routine each day more a process of inquiry than a round of idle pleasure, drink not on the paseo but in the bare bars where the farmers and muleteers stood. If he looked and listened hard enough, a direction should become clear.

*

Yet here he was again, not in a backstreet bar, as he had intended, with a naked light bulb and peanut shells underfoot and wine as dark as ink poured from unmarked bottles. Instead he was at an outside table of one of the smarter bars on the paseo.

At the edges of the conviviality those with no more coins to jingle hovered thirstily, hoping to be welcomed but without confidence, wearing the haunted look of people with pressing matters neglected and half-forgotten. At the tables the noise rose with the drink taken, a hubbub shaking the air with plans, conjectures, boasts, complaints, fantasies. The outspewing at the end of another day with so little done.

Lew pulled his beret low over his eyes, ready to be hard-hearted and unfriendly if need be. He had learnt very quickly that the offer of a helping hand carried the danger of being dragged into the swamp of waste and idleness.

The tables outside were filling up and newcomers had to fit in where they could. A couple in late middle age laid claim to two spare chairs at Lew's table. The man had a seamed, worn face, reddened rather than sunburnt, ears like unsecured garage doors, his thin hair carefully swirled around a bald patch. His very thin wife was dressed in violent colours, with rope sandals and a silly straw hat, looking more tipsy than gay. They both appeared to be embarrassed, and always would be, for life had marched out on them and slammed the door. The man leaned towards Lew, clutching the chairback, bent in a sort of benediction as if offering the grace of his company.

'Speak English, I hope?' he said loudly but without conviction. 'Sorry to take up your space and all that. The name's Bright, and this is the wife.'

Did she have a name? Her mouth cracked open, a row of small unsightly teeth between vermilion lips, and then snapped closed, as decisively as a camera shutter. Nothing more seemed to be expected from her.

After ordering a beer for himself – 'not too cold, mind you' – and a coffee for his wife – 'none of that frothy stuff on top' – the man was determined to talk.

'New here, I bet?' he enquired, with the air of an old hand. 'Of course, we've been here about a year. Up the hill. Very nice. But a bit remote, you might say. The natives are perfectly polite but not on our wavelength. Language trouble chiefly, can't seem to get the basic points home to them. The wife is trying to learn some Spanish, from the gramophone records, but she's not making much progress. I sometimes think they deliberately don't understand. Still, I expect they'll come round to our way of doing things eventually. Patience, don't you know? Great virtue. In the meantime we drive down here most evenings. Take the air, stretch the legs, view the sport.'

He stopped and shifted heavily in his chair, this way and that, perhaps in search of the sport. Lew wondered what sport he meant. A village band? Urchins hustling for handouts before the waiters drove them off? Randy Spanish bloods on scooters, whooshing the semi-delighted girls, trying to whip up their skirts in the slipstream?

'It seems pretty peaceful to me,' Lew said, prepared to apply a little needle. 'What sport did you have in mind? Circus performers? Bullfighters? Maybe gladiators?'

Mr Bright looked perplexed, the red face taking a deeper shade. He was not prepared for any exchange that went beyond the normal limits of banality.

'Now, now, sir,' he protested. 'No call for that kind of humour. I just made an observation. No offence meant. But perhaps I can show you the sort of thing I had in mind.'

He craned his neck once more, taking in the whole sweep of the street and the plaza. Emerging from a side street was a lean, loping figure with a trimmed but patchy beard and some unruly hair of conventional length escaping from beneath a forage cap. The forward angle of his body gave his stride, which in fact was not very brisk, a sense of dangerous urgency. In contrast to the tousled head, his clothes were neat and clean. A short-sleeved, open-necked casual shirt revealed arms and shoulders surprisingly meaty for a slender frame, and taut tendons in the neck suggested more years and troubles than one might have expected. Behind him, at the end of a frayed piece of rope, came a middle-sized, liver-coloured dog. The dog looked sick, crabbing along with a bad leg, stopping every so often to strain its bowels, though nothing came out. The muzzle was held low, going to ground, and the eyes, even at a distance, were forlorn and lost.

'Well, just look at that,' said the indignant Mr Bright. 'That hound should be put down. So much disease in the dogs and cats, it's cruelty really, the way they're neglected here. I hate to see it. I can tell you, it wouldn't be tolerated in Burnley, where we come from. That fellow there holding the lead, he looks like one of us, he should be ashamed of himself, dragging around a poor sick beast like that.'

Beneath his beret Lew allowed himself an evil grin. Innocently, he let his gaze light on the loping figure and the dog cutting across the plaza. The man was almost bouncing with good humour, his eyes on some pleasant memory, taking no notice of the drinking at the winding down of the day. His attention was way up, in purer zones, and the groups at the tables hardly existed for him. As he went by, Lew called out, 'Hey, Carter, surely you've got time for a drink?' After a quick glance, the man swerved almost in mid-stride and brought himself up to the table, beaming like a streetlamp and yanking the wretched dog abruptly behind him.

'Carter, I'd like you to meet Mr Bright,' said Lew solemnly. 'Mr Bright has opinions on the treatment of animals in these parts. He thinks that dog is on its last legs and should be put down. He doesn't approve of the unkind way you treat it. He says it wouldn't happen in Burnley, wherever that is. Says you should be ashamed of yourself.'

At that moment, the dog appeared to be going into some sort of fit. Trembling, it hunkered down on its haunches and squeezed until it laid, just by Mr Bright's smart holiday sandals, a small, misshapen turd.

*

They called Carter Brock the Lord Mayor because he had been the first foreigner to settle in the village and live there for lengthy periods, on and off. He claimed to have discovered it, a dozen years before, running south on the coast road with a leather satchel stuffed full of banknotes, in a peculiar DKW car bought on a whim on the Genoa dockside, with a French-Canadian cutie by his side. They were both, he said, 'in retreat, bung full with the profits of colonial enterprise.'

Descending the foothills of the coast range, he saw from a bend in the road the village below him. A cluster of white houses with faded red-tile roofs, sleeping between two beaches separated by a spur of flat land that tumbled at the sea edge over a rocky promontory. He let the car drift and turned to the girl. 'Why not?' he said, and she nodded. They had travelled far enough and fast enough and were itchy from grime and too few baths.

They parked in the shade of the church and spent the afternoon poking around the streets, testing the feel of the place. In the siesta hours it was very quiet. In the silent plaza some dusty trees drooped, wishing for rain. Carter and the cutie took stock of the few shops and the tiny provincial savings bank and the primitive workshop making rugged furniture in chestnut and pine and the covered market on the far side of the coast highway between the walled cemetery and the garbage dump. He paid attention also to the big garage on the highway, a real *taller* with a smithy, capable of putting to rights anything mechanical from a bicycle to a Pegaso eight-wheeler. Carter had a word with the mechanics, handing around Bisonte cigarettes, making sure they understood the innards of a DKW. He was particular about his own wheels, wanting them to run fast and smoothly at all times. All this was warm work, so he and the girl were in and out of a few bars as well.

He made enquiries in correct but stilted Spanish, in lisping Castilian. The men of the village tried hard to understand him. He could see the effort on their faces, and their evident satisfaction when they got the meaning right.

'What is this language, señor, that you are speaking?' they asked.

'Spanish, of course,' he replied, 'as you can tell because you are answering me.'

'Spanish perhaps, but . . .'

He was please both by their confusion and by their determination to get to the root of the problem.

'I think we'll be as right as two pennies here,' he said in English to the girl, and his new friends in the bar, without a word of English between them, smiled in enthusiasm at that too.

They were not suspicious of these foreigners, though puzzled that people of such obvious means should want to live among them, specially in one of the eccentric or tumbledown houses offered to Carter for a pittance in rent. In fact, they took all this as a curious honour to their village, and seeing their pleasure Carter reciprocated with warm feelings.

He chose a gaunt house on the ancient lava-bed just beyond the village limit, a location worthy of a castle, on a barren rise, appearing to overlook a settlement of serfs. The rooms were spacious, with fine proportions, though the dingy upkeep was lamentable. The views over the village and out to sea were magnificent. There was no water – not even a well – and no electricity. Every day he took his car to the garage on the highway and used their hose to fill a water-butt and several large plastic jerries. Even so, on many hot days it was a trick to make the water last. In the evenings, from the cracked and weed-grown terrace Carter and his girl watched the day fade out before lighting candles in the big old rooms. The long shadows bled into the cobwebs of the high corners as they ate. To dine by candlelight lent some romantic grace to what was no more than a hand to mouth existence.

One night Carter, who, as usual, had taken a few glasses, knocked over a candle and set fire to the tablecloth. The flames took hold abruptly, and when Carter ran for the water he found only a few dregs left in the containers. Since he was, or aspired to be, a literary man, he remembered the smart work of Gulliver in Lilliput in a similar predicament, and had no hesitation in opening his flies and letting go the contents of a full bladder. In retrospect, it pleased him to combine quick thinking with practicality and scholarly memories.

In this ruined grandeur Carter lived until the money, for the time being, ran out. The French-Canadian girl had run out a little while before that.

*

Three years later, when Carter Brock returned to the village, having replenished his purse by further 'enterprise' in far lands, he was still well remembered. '*Un hombre, claro,*' they said of him, nodding with approval. They liked his air of confident energy, his brisk progress here and there, the decisive manner in which he did almost nothing day by day. They admired his neat and unusual dress, the flamboyant silk scarf hurled around his neck on auspicious days, the handkerchief peeping from his jacket's top pocket. It seemed foolhardy, the way he threw money around, but generosity was the necessary act of a gentleman, and this they took him to be. He was now accompanied by another woman, to be sure, but the villagers had nearly forgotten the face of the first one, and the bedtime habits of foreigners were accepted on the whole with tact and good humour, so long as licentiousness was not thrust in their faces. Even the priest managed to look away. These outsiders were not Catholics, and it was a matter of local doubt if Protestants were Christians at all.

On his return Carter took a house in the village, and this close proximity laid him open to closer inspection, At first, matters went on as before. He flung his arms wide and enveloped all-comers in a bear-hug embrace. He had little idea just how powerful he was. The wary soon learnt to avoid his affection which had led more than once to cracked ribs. In the streets, he was either so busily preoccupied, so ardently stargazing, that he noticed no one, or so high on the friendliness of life that he buttonholed everyone – dogs and cats too – and barely made it home by the middle of the night. The sellers of lottery tickets laughed with pleasure when they saw him. His favourite, a savage hunchback, deaf and dumb, clamped a hand over Carter's mouth to catch the vibrations of the number chosen. The feel of that filthy tobacco-stained hand was a little disgusting, but Carter did not try to avoid it. He regarded it as a small act of communion, the closest he could get to religion.

In his favourite bar, a cool, dim hole owned and run by a retired workman from the Malaga bullring whose duties had included many things bloody and gruesome, he and the owner stood facing across the bar, looking lean and soldierly, at least until Carter began to buckle. He was more guest than customer and the owner was content to keep on drawing the Malaga *dulce* or Pedro Ximenez from the barrels along the back wall, putting a tick on the beermat for each glass taken, just for the sake of form. Most often, the owner was explaining the finer points of bullfighting, his hand deep in his pocket, jiggling his balls, enriching the good memories. When the time came to pay, the account was often wiped clean, a token of respect and friendship. 'My house is your house,' said the owner gravely. In appreciation Carter would pass a 100-peseta note across the bar, and then the owner vigorously struck the large goat bell which in those days was used to herald a spectacular tip.

But gradually it appeared that there was a darker side to Carter Brock. After a time, you guessed that you were not seeing things as he saw them. He smoked a fair amount of grass and hash, and that made his world either more effervescent and high-coloured or bleakly empty. Up or down, who could tell? He was occasionally violent and quite often tearful. He drank, that was obvious, but then so did most of the other foreigners, more or less. It was not so much that he was drunk – he could hold his liquor reasonably well – but the surprising and convoluted sorties that emerged out of alcohol. Some mornings found him, without a memory of events, in places he did not know, with people he did not recognize. His private life was grievously chaotic; his driving, when the masterful irresponsible mood was on him, was a danger and a disgrace. His perfectly sane plans of a morning were abandoned by afternoon and might never have existed by evening. As for the night-time, he was a genie out of a bottle, too large, too strange, too alarming.

He had a nose for women and admitted to sudden overwhelming desires to fuck, almost anyone available. And so he did, relying on the strength of an animal urgency which seemed to release a musk that hurried unwary women out of their panties and way beyond good judgement. He tracked disasters in and out of bedrooms and bars and on the public highway, and in retrospect what he had done genuinely amazed him. When his exploits were brought home to him, he could hardly believe them. He was not sure that it was he – or at least the real he – so he stood himself aside from his offending double, his ghostly doppelgänger, and gave himself absolution for his many sins.

In time, a shorter time than he had believed possible, he ran out of money again. He began to dispossess himself in order to stay, selling whatever came to hand. His acquaintances were surprised but fitted it easily into a pattern. It was what Carter Brock would do. At the tables around the plaza they were half-pleased by the extravagant consistency.

'He did much the same thing last time,' said the artist Tim Byrne, who had studied Carter as if employed to paint his portrait. 'He said he was going to stay here for ever, even if he had to sell the clothes he stood in.'

'And he did end up,' confirmed Ulf, the tall Scandinavian, a man slow and steady with words, 'selling those very clothes.'

'That's right,' said Byrne. 'And he'll do it again this time. I suppose he thinks he can do it for ever.'

'But he doesn't seem the same this time.'

'He's the same.'

'Did he look like he does now, that old? Haggard – you might even say desperate? I guess I didn't really know him then.'

'The same. You didn't know him.'

'I heard he came back from Morocco,' Ulf said in wonder, 'with a slab of hash big enough to tile a bathroom.'

'And what would he pay for that?'

'Let's see. About a hundred dollars, I guess.'

'A hundred dollars? A man of his low financial standing!'

'Perhaps he meant to sell it, raise some cash. But it would soon disappear with him – fizz! up the chimney. It's a lot of hash, but maybe not the way Carter gets through it – smoked, lost, given away. That much would last me a year, maybe two.'

'A hundred dollars,' said Byrne, getting it in context, for he was always nervous about money. 'That's thirty-five pounds, if you please. No wonder he's now trying to sell his loo and his bath.'

But not even the loo and the bath could save Carter. He was forced back into the unforgiving world of business and commerce, which he hated so much but for which he was so ironically suited, having outrage, imagination and daring at his fingertips, and having at some point mislaid most of his conscience. He was always vague about his position in the commercial world, changing the subject or making do with cloudy hints. A family business, connections abroad, exports, promotions and sales, public relations. It was in any case a long way from his present tenure, the lord of the village with a high heart and the expectation of a sort of *droit de seigneur*.

On the day of his departure he arranged one last exemplary drunk, in the big bar by the bus stop on the highway, attended by as many people as could cram in. As the bus arrived with a blast of its air horn the villagers submitted incautiously to Carter's rough embraces as the rivulets of tears coursed his cheeks and the gouts of snot sprung out of his nose. In the bar, the goat bell bonged loud and long till the door of the bus hissed closed on the fringes of his silk scarf.

All in all, the villagers forgave him and wished him well. They recognized a man of many faults and at least some virtue, coupled with a welcome ability to surprise and amuse. In the dull night he was as bright and erratic as a firefly. They took him as that – a thing of wonder whose ultimate purpose lay beyond their horizon. He was a novelty in their world, generally agreeable, and they were too humane to judge him finally, for they could see quite clearly a man in the grip of strange demons and mysterious suffering.

*

Six months before Lew arrived in the village, Carter Brock came back again. He had yet another woman, a new car, and a new house, but this time the house was purchased not rented; for Carter had found the making of money in the New World much easier than the construction of a life in the Old. With the house, he now had a 'project'. It was something he thought he could put his heart into. He did not like to admit the flight of time, though the small ravages were starting to appear on his face, his twitches becoming more insistent, his beard patchy and uneven. At his age he wanted to tie himself down, a Samson fixing his own knots. His aim, as he put it grandly, was 'a place of repose and inspiration suitable for the work of composition'.

He began to plan and labour with the energy he gave to all new beginnings. So long as the manual labour lasted he could put off that moment of blankness and doubt, when life rests and composition commences. But the unwinding of his building scheme, lurching from crisis to triumph and back again, was an entertainment in itself, and the village held its breath. No one was safe from a call to arms. Builders, masons, plasterers, plumbers, electricians were hired and fired, abused and effusively praised. Red wine for workers was poured freely, and it was time to knock off at any hour the boss might say. Foreigners were not exempt from the pressing demands. Any spare hand skulking towards the beach might be stopped and corralled into the labouring gang.

Carter lassoed Lew one morning in the sun, when Lew hardly had his wits about him, being intent on nothing more strenuous than a haircut. The two had been introduced by Byrne and had spent a fair amount of time together, walking the hills, sinking beers, jousting cautiously about the nature of words. After inspecting faltering ambitions together they had signalled the start of a friendship in almost redskin fashion, sharing Carter's hash pipe sprawled under the stars, a powwow that resolved nothing on the still-warm sands. Lew was too relaxed to argue. The day was open for any sort of reading, so he just followed the drift of it.

They swam and sunbathed and smoked and ate. Then they strolled on the shore, just about as lazy as even a foreigner could get. Lew picked a large bunch of daisies – at least he thought they were daisies – he didn't know why. Driving back, they saw the remains of a car crash, an event common enough on the coast road, where the traffic was brisk, the surface poor, and the Spaniards too often electrified by the novelty of car-ownership. A small Fiat was entangled with a larger station wagon. The Fiat was badly damaged, one side almost torn off, the windscreen gone, and a buckled front seat nearly out of the door. Police and ambulance had done their work and gone, and the scene had the eerie quiet of abandonment. Some dark patches on the tarmac might have been blood. They didn't stop, barely slowed down, looking ahead without comment. Carter was silent, then again he jarred them out of their groove, abruptly swinging north towards the stables. Manure also had its place in the day, needed for Carter's patio plants.

In the stable yard they inspected the horses, lean beasts like hatracks, their shoulder blades sharp humps under the skin. The manure was waiting for them, neatly bagged in jute sacks. The stableman plunged his arm in a sack up to his elbow and brought out a good handful, crushing it in his great calloused hand, and letting it sift back between his fingers into the bag. 'That's horseshit,' he said proudly. 'No straw, no dirt, just pure horseshit.'

They went in the house to pay and to mark the deal, as one should, with a *copa* of *anis*. The stableman brought out some bread and a bar of coarse dark chocolate. Without washing his hands he tore the bread apart, broke the chocolate with a brutal stained thumb, and put the bread and chocolate together in his mouth.

'People think I'm crazy,' he half apologized, 'eating bread and chocolate like this. They've never tried it. You don't know how good it is until you try.'

That evening, sitting in a cane chair before his empty fireplace, eating olives and just getting started on the local *tinto*, Lew reflected on the day, and what he had seen. It seemed too simple, if that was what life had to offer. It had its pleasures, to be sure, and maybe did less damage to mind and soul than the often fearful activities of the bonded and salaried pack.

But beaches and bunches of wild flowers? Manure and blood on the road? Horseshit and chocolate?

*

Lew was in Carter's house, standing with him on the unfinished terrace, looking down on the unfinished patio. In the rubble below he could make out the outlines of the new design. To the left were two small cypresses (Carter had wanted orange-trees but could not find ones of the right size and impatience had overtaken him), and to the right was a large shallow terracotta bowl crowded with the blooms of geraniums. Between the funereal trees and the startling flowers were piles of fresh earth covering an area just about the size of a burial plot. A grave, Lew thought, dug and ready, with all the panoply of death, cypress and the raw colours of grief. But a grave for whom?

Carter was in a melancholy mood, gazing upon the erupted earth. He sighed. So little done, so many compromises, so much still undone.

'I waited a long time to get started,' he said earnestly, 'waited to see what I had to say. And I'm still waiting, some of it forced on me, some strangling me from goodness knows where. Have I waited too long? I get the feeling that everything – life and time – is running out on me, dribbling towards the ditch where all hopes die.'

Just when Lew thought he was getting settled, with some sort of hold at last on the skittish conditions of his life, he saw that he had been warned. The breezy road out of Toronto, clear of baggage, was now suddenly salted with traps, slippage, rockfallls, mudslides.

*

On all sides in the village Lew heard dissent, in English and in several languages that he didn't understand but could interpret by the weary gestures and the rucked-up faces. People were trying to pull back, rearing up like a horse seeing a snake (that would be modern life, of course), yet still in huddles all the time, jamming together in little groups like swallows on the telegraph wire ready to move but nervous about the direction. It seemed that they needed grievance in numbers, all tied up in complaint. Was that what they really had in common? Lew thought it might pay to take a cross-section of those in the huddle, try to find some common element.

It was a reasonable intention but somewhere along the way he went awry. He could begin the day with a clear head and a clean page, but somewhere between the coffee and the churros, and the couple of beers at lunchtime, and the early evening *anis*, and the joint or two in preparation for night and wine and cognac, and then the head spinning and mildly debauched towards bedtime, he fell into the pool of talk. He let it lap over him, floating at ease amid the currents, as abandoned as the best or worst of them.

He could see without difficulty two broad groups: those who applied themselves to some plan or purpose; and those who maybe tried, but failed on most days to discover the wherewithal to keep steady and composed, to keep away from bars and off the beaches and out of each other's beds. They were the ones to be pitied perhaps, but more than that, the ones to be liked. They showed, without accomplishing much, the wildest imagination, the most invention, the loftiest aims and ideals, all of which came tumbling to ground like fallen fruit that rain had not swollen nor sun ripened. There it all lay, discarded, lost jewels, a gleam in the litter of cigarette ends and crushed peanuts. They were showing the most universal and characteristic of our qualities, the flaw of being human.

So Lew got stuck with the second kind, the ones who laid out the feast of talk, who set out an enticement that seduced but maybe didn't nourish much.

Costa del Sol

She sat alone at one of the outside tables, a coffee and a cognac in front of her, long legs crossed in fawn slacks, painted toenails peeping from open sandals. Her hair was long, dark brown and slightly tousled. Her sunglasses were on, even in the shade, and it looked as if her face might be naked without them. She was cool and poised and appeared to be waiting for someone, though perhaps she didn't care a damn if he came or not.

Her name was Vera Gwinn, and she was one of those people whom you saw around for a week or two and then not at all for several months. She did not give explanations, at least not to casual acquaintances. But there she was when you least expected it, sometimes with a man, sometimes not, but always calm and a little distant, as if she had her eye on life and love and work and such things but hadn't made her mind up yet.

At the next table Lew was testing his Spanish with *La Vanguardia* – he had not lost his interest in newspapers – seeing if the subjunctive still scared him. The voice, apparently addressed to him, interrupted a particularly knotty and baroque passage on Real Madrid football.

'I believe we met at the painter Byrne's place,' she said. Her voice was level and quiet, neither a come-on nor a challenge. A mere statement of fact. 'If I recall,' she went on, 'you said you were a writer.'

'An overstatement, I think,' Lew replied, surprised by the sudden approach. 'For many years I was a journalist, back in Canada.'

'So what brings you here?' The question suggested there might be better places to go, things to do.

'Well, I'm taking some time off,' he replied evenly, 'making notes, trying to observe the way things go, see where that will lead.'

'Ah,' she said, and looked up at the roofline, as if the topic was exhausted.

Lew stared at her openly, wondering what more was coming, not sure whether to be intrigued or annoyed. 'Perhaps I could get you something?' he offered, testing her with a world-weary ploy.

Her dark glasses came down a few degrees and rested on him. 'Yes, that would be nice,' she said sleepily. 'A *ciento-tres* please.'

When the waiter brought the drink, Lew indicated that he put it down on her table. She did not offer to join him, and he stayed where he was, a few feet of morning sunlight separating them.

She raised the glass to him, tipping the shot back in one easy gulp, but not in any showy way. A woman, Lew thought, who likes a drink and can hold it. Then she cleared her throat. 'I heard you had some recent trouble on the bus.' Again, a statement of fact, No emphasis, no prurient interest, an agreeable tone. 'Something to do with drugs, I'm told.' Some days before, on the bus from Malaga, there had been an episode involving drugs and drink.

Lew was tense now, and getting annoyed. 'Could be,' he said sharply, 'but I don't know what makes it your business.'

'Oh, peace, please,' she smiled, slipping her sunglasses down her nose for a brief moment, giving him the full force of her brown eyes. 'I'm quite partial to a drug or two now and again. Rather frequently, in fact.'

Partial to drugs now and again? Was that Lew's own position? He had not thought much about it. Marijuana, in North America, had been around for many long years, used by students and professors, musicians, critics of society, drifters, the socially daring, those who needed help to get through the day, the lost curs with no kennels to go to at night. It grew like a weed nearly everywhere, cost little to prepare, and though illegal it hardly bothered the conscience of the enthusiasts or the police. No relaxation seemed complete without a little blow, the equivalent of stripping off the tie, undoing the collar button, getting barefoot in the grass. Suddenly, many things in a grim world appeared manageable, even irresistibly amusing, and connections you might never have made slotted easily into place. As the now popular slogan might well have put it, things went better with grass. To Lew, that was the truth. He had been a reporter, one of that hard-headed tribe who gave themselves a reputation for daring and devil-may-care and didn't mind if noses were out of joint. He had smoked marijuana without a guilty thought, at work and play; he had done his work efficiently and well, and he considered himself no worse a citizen than the next man or woman.

But there was other stuff of course, powerful and toxic hallucinogens that could get you hooked and desperate. A descent into those, in Lew's opinion, depended most on a chance combination of bad luck, bad circumstance and certain traits of personality. There were always those who dared themselves to dive among the rocks in the big sea. But the signs were there to avoid them, and it took no great virtue to do so.

Since coming to Spain, it was true, Lew had become a little loose in his indulgence, but the place encouraged minor experimentation, either to fill an idle day or to fulfil a more creative one. Looking at himself now, he saw someone unlikely to become a wreck. Depravity was too hard and strenuous a game for him.

'I expect you wonder what I'm up to,' she said calmly, tinkling her spoon in her empty coffee cup. 'Nothing, really. When I saw you here this morning I remembered that you'd popped into the conversation last night. With the Scandinavians. You know, that tall diva who looks like a slinky Greek goddess, her husband with the gimpy leg, the solemn redhead, and the rest of that crowd. I'd say there was considerable admiration, the way you handled that business on the bus. It could so easily have turned nasty, with bad vibes for all us foreigners. That redhead, Anders, was particularly warm in your praise. He'd like to talk to you. Asked me to tell you that, if I saw you.'

Talk was free and plentiful; in fact, it was what most of the foreigners did most of the time. But what about? Lew did not think he wanted to talk about drugs, for example. On that, he had no position to take, neither as theorist, user, rebel, hedonist or dropout. Like alcohol or friendly sex, marijuana served a useful purpose, but it was foolish to allow too much to rest on it.

'Anders likes to play chess,' she said, rising gracefully and setting her sunglasses firmly on her nose. 'Thanks for the drink. Give me a call sometime. At the end of Calle Granada, before the market. Ask any local.'

And then she was walking away without looking back, taking easy strides and swinging her hips, seemingly without any artifice in mind.

*

The redhead Anders was playing the Ruy Lopez. It was a simple opening to try on an untested opponent. Lew had no misgivings about that. The various openings, gambits, defences were no more than strange names to him. His chess had not progressed much beyond his first fumbling trials against the laughing foreman in the printing works at Port Arthur. He moved by instinct, ignorance, and an intoxication with unwise dashes across the board. He would begin with high hopes of achieving discipline and logic and usually, by mid-game, had muddled himself into a mess. Then mate was never far off, sneering at him after every poor move. Sometimes, more by luck than judgement, he performed a minor miracle and stunned himself and his opponent with a mate of his own. That made the game even more mysterious and added to its attraction. He could never quite see where he was going, nor understand when he got there. It was, like his writing, an act of faith.

Anders was serious; he took his time, sucking on his pipe, giving himself leeway for thought, even against someone as technically ragged as Lew. Chess was a game, of course, but also an intellectual pursuit. One didn't horse around at the chessboard. Concentrating, he released a cloud of heavy pipe smoke which Lew wiped away with his hand. He didn't need that disadvantage; his game was weak enough as it was. Anders castled safely and began to dominate the central squares. Lew scrambled to get his king castled and lost time. He was tempted into using his queen to capture an unimportant outlying piece and lost position. The potent combo of cavalry and church – knight and bishop – rolled through his misaligned defences. An innocent pawn pushed forward one square. The rival queen hitched up her skirts and looked interested. She strolled down a long diagonal covered by a knight, and it was all over for Lew, bar the celebratory smoke signals from Anders's pipe.

*

The pipe, having played its part in the victory, was laid aside. Another game was offered but Lew was still contemplating his mistakes and needed to get his breath back.

They were seated on the floor, lounging against fat Moroccan cushions, the chessboard between them on a low, inlaid table. In the pause after the game Anders carefully rolled a joint. The room, the best in a small apartment rented long-term by the group of Scandinavians but only intermittently used, was sunny but almost bare. Two Berber rugs in deep reds and blues on the floor, a scattering of puffy cushions, a couple of large brass water jugs with graceful necks, an unglazed fruit bowl in rose-coloured clay, a hookah in the corner, a sleeping bag rolled up against the wall. An open door gave on to a small, strangled garden, largely untended, where some healthy cannabis plants fought it out with myrtle and laurel and honeysuckle and fig, and big pots of camellia and chrysanthemum and aster.

'I see you play to win,' Lew said, adopting a rueful tone, though defeat meant nothing to him. But he wanted to get a gauge on his opponent.

'Of course,' Anders replied, looking smug. His English was good if sometimes a little off-key. Sounded to native ears like the English of the academy, not the fluid lingo of the streets. 'To me, to play is no joke. Always, I make it a test, to overcome dangers and the unforeseen.' He lit the joint and took a long pull, then handed it to Lew, letting smoke out with satisfaction.

'Perhaps it is unfortunate,' he went on, 'that this is my nature. Maybe it is better fun if I play like you. With lots of ignorance but with a smile and – how you say it? – with a shrug of the shoulders.'

They played another game, just for the hell of it, and Lew lost as heavily as before. He enjoyed the game very much.

'I must say you take defeat very well,' Anders observed, some wonder in his voice, a little irritation too. Too much lightness could diminish his triumph; victory, to the victor, is often a solemn affair. 'Well, that's good. I think you are very firm in foundation, so life can surprise you without too much hurting. I see something like that in what you did on the bus the other night.'

'What did I do?' Lew protested. 'Nothing more than give a helping hand to a companion who was going through a bad time.'

'I hear rather different,' Anders replied with a knowing look. 'It is not so much that you help – that is normal – but the calm, quiet way you do it. No panic, no aggravation. What could not be avoided had to be endured, but patiently and with good judgement. Excellent decision. When I hear what you do, I think it has things to teach me.'

He lay back on his cushion, eyes closed, taking a puff at the joint, no doubt contemplating those mysterious things he might learn. Then he passed the joint to Lew with a significant look, as if handing on something shrouded, undefined but valuable.

The bastard wants to manoeuvre me into something, Lew thought, but damned if I know what it is.

*

He called on Vera Gwinn on a Sunday, and then twice again in the following week. Their talk was a little stiff to begin with as her remote manner did not invite a rush of confidences. But gradually they surprised each other with the things they had to say. It was not, from Lew's point of view, that Vera was very forthcoming. She dealt in hints and obscurities and rambles round and about a subject, sliding from a past of patches and misdirections to an unresolved present. But the view on the way was picturesque even if veiled. Perhaps dangerous, too. There were too many gaps for Lew to fall into.

Her experience was extensive and unusual, but experience of what exactly? She had been, briefly, to a convent school, though she didn't think she was a Catholic. She had started, at some early stage, a medical training and then stopped. The task was not as amusing as she had hoped. She had waited tables and cooked at a seaside café on the Yorkshire coast. She had been remanded in Holloway Prison for an unpleasant week on suspicion of possessing a small amount of cannabis; the case was dropped. She could not remember losing her virginity, though she supposed it was important. Her name was familiar to the Guardia Civil, for reasons unknown. From time to time a Guardia would accost her informally, materializing suddenly in the street, in a bar, at a bus stop. He would ask questions or, more usually, make gnomic observations whose point she could not be bothered to work out. In any case, there was very little she could tell them that they did not already know. She suspected that the real purpose was to examine her breasts in the skimpy tops that foreign girls were then wearing without bras.

She had travelled much, in Europe and America, for reasons she did not elaborate. In New York she had worked at a Playboy Club, one of Hefner's Bunny Girls. She had learnt the Bunny Dip, that graceless bob used by the girls when serving drinks, designed, as Vera said with a sardonic snort of laughter, 'to keep the tits out of the customer's plate'. The memory amused her greatly and she insisted on giving Lew a demonstration. It was a comic turn: the tripping walk in heels impossibly high; the legs as long as possible encased in shimmering nylon; the dreadnought bodice with twin barrels threatening a poke in the eye; then the bob like a poleaxed beast, the twitch of the butt for good measure, the pull against gravity to get gracefully upright, and the demure smirk as she tucked the dollar notes of the tip into her cleavage.

Lew, highly entertained, almost choked on his drink.

Men and boyfriends had come and gone like autumn leaves. She was frank about these matters, as much as her oblique method allowed. She liked the pretty and pleasant things of life, and she did not mind if they were handed to her. But no commitments. So she had never married. 'A couple of times,' she admitted darkly, 'I came perilously close.'

*

Lew borrowed a car and they went up country, into the hills and valleys, by remote lakes and desolate villages. They stumbled upon a lonely place that particularly pleased them. In a steep hillside village they sat in a bar set above a precipice. There was a window on the void open at the end of a room without decoration or comfort. High on the edge they watched the swifts below them screaming and twisting in their evening adventure. As the sun lost heat a raw mountain wind blew the length of the room. Once, in peculiar weather, the rain swept perversely up the cliff and in the window, flying towards the ceiling. In other squares in other slumbering villages they ate and drank in pinched bars with grave, suspicious locals and in fly-speckled rooms that barely earned the name of restaurant, served poor food by silent waiters.

Then they were back on the coast, finding that in many ways it was a relief to be where the crowds were, and the standards higher. At a beach jammed with holidaying townspeople from the interior, with hardly a foreign tourist in sight, they ate on a terrace on the edge of the strand, with a drift of warm sand from the beach tickling their toes. They had almond soup with rose-petals floating in it, fresh tuna with olives, a green salad, and orange flan. Lew ordered a Valdepeñas, which was rather thin, so they compensated with another bottle of a better Rioja while they watched a swarthy huckster with a little trained monkey on a chain try to conjure money out of their pockets. It was a sad sight – the tiny puckered face with old man's whiskers looking like a headhunter's trophy – and Vera was reluctant to let it pass. She waved some pesetas at the trainer, and when he came to collect she suggested to him sharply that he and the monkey should change places, so that he might learn to endure the practice of cruelty. It was, she added to Lew, a lesson humans too often neglected to learn. The man, who possibly understood her poor Spanish not at all, raised his red fez and grinned like a lighthouse.

They had drunk a little too much in the sun and fell silent and preoccupied on the way home. Lew attended carefully to his driving. The last thing he needed was an accident in a borrowed car. She was withdrawn, turning her enigmatic dark glasses on the dying light gilding the always enigmatic sea.

Then Lew did not see her for two weeks or so. They seemed to stand at some divide that would take a little courage from both to step over. But the next weekend, a movie was advertised at the makeshift village cinema, and they agreed that it was something worth seeing. The film was *Cape Fear*, with Bob Mitchum exuding sleepy-eyed menace against dithering Gregory Peck, the action shifting unnervingly on the open-air screen that billowed slightly in the night breeze. The film was dubbed and each of them, with only a loose grip on the quick-flowing Spanish, constructed a separate story. Later, Lew was surprised by the twists and narrative perplexity of her version.

After the film they walked on the beach. Feathery clouds were drifting over a full moon, and they tried to assess the madness such a moon can bring. Then arm-in-arm they took a roundabout route to her street door, where she gave him a little kiss, and at the top of the stairs a more fulsome one.

In her room she yawned and stretched and sighed with some feeling that may well have been contentment. He was never quite sure.

'A good evening,' she said in her subdued mumble, 'but now I'm so tired. I'm going straight to bed. But you're welcome to come and join me. Make use of my body, if you wish. I might even enjoy it.'

TANGIER

They were playing, this time, in Lew's front room. Months had gone by, the season now on the swing, the hard glitter of summer and early autumn giving way to moody weather uncertain where it was going. After the game Anders stood at a window, looking into a dirt yard below, watching spurts of wind tangle the washing on a line. 'That, I think,' he said seriously, as if examining the entrails of important history, 'is the fiftieth game of chess we play.' Lew was surprised, though he could rely on Anders to keep a tally.

He went to make coffee. Fifty games? Was it only that many? Sometimes it seemed like an unending series, through months, through years. Had he done much else in the last six months? Not always with Anders, who had a habit of fading away, taking himself out of circulation without warning, then arriving back in the same arty corduroys and in the same smart Volvo car, but with a couple of thousand extra miles on the clock. When Anders was away Lew had played with others, those who had the fortitude to batter on his front door in the empty spaces of the day, climb the stairs with a few slivers of dope in a matchbox, a bottle of wine under the arm, and a book that needed discussing. He played with Ulf, whose quick careless moves, so unlike those of his fellow Scandinavian, were usually sound and sometimes inspired; with Carter Brock, who came with killer moves of startling complexity that nearly always misfired; with Vera, who could play well, if she chose, but thought it amusing to alter the permitted moves of the major pieces; with the painter Byrne, who played hopeless chess very slowly, with such an eccentric view of the board that he easily lost, even to Lew.

In the apartment there was silence, both men preoccupied as the metal coffee-pot began to bubble on the hotplate. Then Anders came back to the theme of chess, calling into the kitchen, 'And I find that we have several draws, but I lose to you only one.'

'You were unlucky there,' Lew called back, 'because that was when I was not trying.'

Anders smiled politely; he was never sure when a joke was worth a laugh. He took his time putting the chess pieces back in the box, waiting for Lew to bring the coffee.

Then he said, 'Do you think sometimes that you are bored, perhaps that you are wasting your time?'

Lew was startled, and not pleased. It sounded more like an accusation than a question; even a moral judgement. No, he did not think he was bored. If you worked at it there was usually plenty to do. Each day was like opening a shop and never knowing who might come in or what transaction might develop. Some days, he might even get a few words down, not exactly words in the sense of writing – coherent prose that was going somewhere – but jottings, notes, character sketches, scraps of conversation, descriptions of people and places. He spent long, quite happy periods shuffling his notes, staring at certain passages to try to see where they had gone right or wrong, wondering where they might fit in some larger whole. Then dreaming began, and sometimes he nodded off, catnapping on muggy afternoons in his cane chair.

And there was always chess, an alternative to the often wearisome fraternity on the plaza and the suspect chumminess of the bars, where for brief moments you were arm-in-arm with the world and rolling towards a befuddled bedtime. Chess, at least, allowed you to select the company and keep the brain in gear.

But wasting time? In forlorn hours when sleep wouldn't come, or when the hangover pressed like thunder, he wondered if his pace was too slow for the world. Money, too, was beginning to be a small worry. Life was cheap enough, but there were always ways to spend, in particular if there were hours to fill. For a long time now he had reached into his pocket without much thought until the sum he had deposited in a Malaga bank ceased showing nice fat noughts at the end of the number on his statement, shrinking to something much less healthy. He was not bust yet, not by a fair distance, but he needed to take a more cautious approach to the expenses of the day and even, if possible, earn a little income.

'I asked,' Anders went on, for once unsure of his ground, 'because I thought you might be pleased to have a small diversion. A little holiday, in a way.'

'Oh yes?' Lew replied. He knew that Anders was much trickier than his stiff and proper manner suggested.

'Yes. Carter Brock is planning a trip to Tangier and is looking for someone to go with him. To keep him in order, I expect. I hear that he wants to buy some hash – a substantial amount of hash – to sell when he gets back. Trying to trade his way out of chaotic life and desperate finances. All that is nothing to me. Brock is Brock and I have found that, good company though he is, it is wise to step back from him a little. No, what I'm interested in is whatever dope he manages to find. He has a way, you know – a peculiar personality, a strange charm that draws people, an irresistible pull towards danger. And of course, he speaks good Spanish. I have a feeling he might make some discoveries that others might miss.

'Now, you would be doing me a favour if you accompany him. He likes you. Have a good time but just notice what he gets up to. Where he goes, the people he sees, and most of all what he buys and the price he pays. I'll give you some money to cover the ferry and the hotel. Also, some money to make a purchase, at your discretion. If you find good hash, take a cut for yourself and bring the rest to me. Then we shall see.'

The proposition had its attractions, and Lew thought he could handle it well enough. He had been to Tangier a couple of times, an idle but snoopy visitor, with his nose deep in strange aromas and his eye captivated by a brilliant palette. He needed a break, and to him Tangier was a better place than most. And if he went he saw no betrayal of his friendship with Carter Brock. His task was to observe only, not to interfere. To be a ready prop, if that were necessary, in Carter's wilder moments was more like an act of charity.

*

The arrangements for the journey were easily made. In fact, Carter's pleasure that Lew was coming along made Lew nervous. With Carter Brock, it so happened that much heartache often started out with radiant smiles and a joyful rubbing of the hands.

They left in the night, to make the morning ferry from Algeciras. In the dim street glow Lew was surprised to see fresh bruising on Carter's face. A bloodshot eyeball squinted from a painful purple spreading over his left cheek. He had been at work on the chassis of the car, rabbiting out a hiding place for what he intended to buy. The work was laborious and difficult, so when he chiselled off the last spot-weld to reveal a cubbyhole clear and accessible he had tossed the heavy hammer in the air in triumph. The hammer flipped and the handle whipped over and caught him in the eye. Lew looked at him dubiously. Carter certainly knew how to make himself distinctive.

They had plenty of time, and for once Carter drove soberly. The exhilaration of the departure was running away fast. The car, a decrepit former bread van misused by all its owners, was poorly tuned, the heater didn't work, the rumble of a defective wheel-bearing came from the rear. The red light on the fuel gauge was winking but Carter did not notice. Already, he was beginning to get jumpy about the trip. 'Think we should go back?' he said anxiously, but then he noticed the blinking fuel light and drove on to find a garage. The first was closed, the second, some five miles on, was also closed, with a cop directing traffic away from it. Carter put on speed, staring ahead.

'Did you see the cop?' Lew said.

'I make a point of not seeing cops,' Carter replied, and it was as if not seeing the policeman had made him bold enough to go beyond the point of no return.

On the outskirts of Malaga, with the engine stuttering for lack of fuel, they found a garage open and pressed on. The night was clear and cold. When they stopped to urinate Lew saw a rash of stars over the mountains, the Big Dipper standing on the tip of its handle. Now the going was easy, the coast road swaying by the seaside towns where the tourists were buttoned up tight with their dreams. On the left, the great dark shoulder of Gibraltar was dotted with a few winking lights, suggesting wakefulness and caution. Then Algeciras broke into their reverie. They were much too early, stunned by cold in a car with no heater.

Cold and hungry they drove around looking for an all-night bar. In the plaza by the port they saw a man in rubber thigh-boots carrying a fat fish – a cod? – perhaps a metre long, two middle fingers inserted in the gills. The man said there were two fishermen's bars open down in the port, so they parked the car and walked through the gate. Two Guardia, in grey cloaks down to their heels, eased themselves out of a dark guardhouse and stopped them. The cops were remote, indifferent.

'The fisherman,' Carter said in his most correct Spanish, 'says there are two bars down there. We're travelling through and we're very cold and tired. May we go and look?'

'There are no bars there,' said the younger guard, sounding as if he didn't care one way or the other.

'Could we go and see, just to make sure?'

'Of course, if you know better than we do, go ahead.'

The way through an empty dockland scarred by brutal sheds and incomprehensible machinery seemed interminable. They took wrong turnings and came abruptly to dead ends. The cold had made Lew tighten up miserably and his groin ached. After five minutes they saw a slow figure approaching.

'Excuse me, señor,' Carter began, 'can you tell me . . . '

'*Si, si,*' the man replied before Carter could finish, 'right ahead for a hundred metres and then turn left.'

They came to a big shed where men were dragging blue-black carcasses of tuna off a boat and across a rough wet floor. In the corner of the shed was a primitive bar, hardly more than a plank counter and a few shelves behind, with a metal sink and an old chipped refrigerator closing off one end. Some derelicts stood at the bar, several of them stoically drunk, each of them paid a few pesetas to unload the night boats. Lew and Carter had a couple of quick cognacs, watching a man put a sugar-lump on the toe of his boot and offer it to a trembling brown dog, all ribs and nose. Was it the man or the dog that was teaching the other tricks? The dog looked diseased. A drunk who tried to pet it looked diseased too.

Any further stay in the fisherman's bar was too sad to contemplate, so they decided to look for an early breakfast and then see if they could get the heater fixed.

In another part of town they found a breakfast of a sort, standing in a workmen's bar in the pre-dawn. They ate stale churros and washed them down with cognac and coffee while hasty customers gulped black coffees and dropped the sugar-wrappings on the floor. Then they drove out of town towards Cadiz to try to borrow a pair of pliers to force open the stopcock on the heater. A cheerful chico manning some petrol pumps lent them some and they wrestled with the heater.

'Perhaps there's no water in the system,' Carter suggested. 'Sometimes this old heap goes for ages without any water.' Then suddenly the heater was working, although they were not sure what they had done.

'The history of your life,' Lew said sardonically to Carter. 'Things happen by voodoo.'

Still with time to wait for the ferry they pulled off the road into some scrub under a sparse grove of pines, on the downward slope of a hill. From there they could watch the port and the sea and look over the great arid mass of Gibraltar.

They hoped to get a little sleep, but in the east the sun was coming up, vesting the world in changes of gorgeous clothes, from fire to gold. Then all at once the thought of sleep was gone, the new day pricking at them like pins and needles. The Rock of Gibraltar looked like the profile of a man laid out, a toothless old man with his chin hard on his chest. The slow dart of a plane winged by very high up, dragging a vapour trail at first sharp then growing fuzzy. No wind. The sea was as level as a table, the colour of gunmetal. A fishing boat making for harbour etched a broad vee on the quiet surface, towing a tender so low in the water it looked swamped.

An old white dog, filthy dirty, came from nowhere, nosing at the car door, moaning for something. Along its grubby white back was a slash of scarlet paint, burnished by the rising sun into the imitation of a wound. Then the sun roiled entire above the sea and climbed into the stirless heavens. The moment took away the breath, like a plunge into ice water. Yet it was so much better than that.

*

Off the boat, Tangier and the hungry men were waiting. At the ferry-port gate the hassle began. Inexperienced Western tourists, anxious for fun but wary of excess, were overawed by men in too many wrappings. What sort of nature could possibly lie under all those billowing clothes? The local guides were hawking for customers, making sudden forays into bemused groups of strangers and causing nervous souls to back away. Pedlars more burdened than pack-animals thrust anguished faces from the midst of their crazy piles of trinkets, bawling out 'Get your jonk here. Get it all here.'

Carter eased the car carefully through the press of people and parked by the old city station, hoping that it would still be there when he returned. They unloaded their bags – Carter hindered by some unnecessary bundles – then he and Lew retraced the path to the steps by the Grand Mosque and mounted into the medina. And here, in large and small ways, the focus of the world changed. Words sounded more or less the same – the natives of Tangier, Mediterranean traders since dark ages, were masters of many fractured tongues – but where did those words lead? Movements, gestures, looks, the half-glance, the hang of the head, a garment partly drawn over the face, what was permissible to be noticed, all were evidence of another vocabulary generally unknown in the West.

In the Socco Chico they booked a room at the Hotel Beccera, a second-floor room with a dangerous little balcony overlooking the public space. After a wash, and an inconclusive discussion on how to proceed, they could think of nothing better than to sally forth and see how things might go. Lew was ready as he was, casual but clean and tidy. But Carter dressed smartly in his gent's outfit, white shirt with loose silk cravat, blue blazer, grey trousers with a sharp crease. He gave his black shoes a quick buff on the bedspread. With slicked hair and unruly beard, with his eye puffy and still purple with bruising, he would be hard to miss. And at the last minute Carter rummaged in one of his bundles and pulled out an ancient tennis racquet, which he tucked jauntily under his arm.

'What the hell is that for?' Lew asked in amazement.

'Kind of a flank manoeuvre,' Carter said insouciantly. 'Get them thoroughly puzzled. Throw them off the scent.'

'Don't you think you might be overdoing it? This isn't the land of the country club. You look about as inconspicuous as a performing seal. Get rid of that damned bat. Puzzlement is one thing, dying of laughter is another.'

Carter looked a little hurt, but he pushed the racquet under the bed, and they managed to get away looking less like a vaudeville act.

They took seats at the Café Fuentes, sipping mint tea slowly, looking out of the window at the human traffic. Carter was conspicuous enough and some startled glances came their way, but no approaches. They watched people watching them. The surprised look, then the eyes shooting away and the half grin. The many hippies about – harlequin clothes, flying hair or ponytail – smiled in derision, an insulting judgement in the circumstances, which they were glad to escape. So they took to the street and strolled towards the Socco Grande, letting it be known by their genial pace and wide inquisitive looks that they were potentially in business.

In the big open space by the municipal market the urchins and the corner boys began to pester them until a grizzled man in a shabby grey djellaba took two handfuls of dirt and drove the kids off. 'You want good *kif* you follow me,' he said, first in French and then in Spanish, and though they wanted hash, not *kif*, his manner was serious and dignified and worth investigating. They followed him, walking about a dozen yards behind the grizzled head, which did not look back. He led them away from the jeers of the urchins, into the maze of the medina. In an alley like a funnel a youth in his mid-teens pushed himself off from the wall and greeted their guide solemnly. They exchanged a few words in Arabic, listening to each other courteously, with all the time in the world. Then the youth gave a small nod and the old man and the youth set out again with Lew and Carter still following. The four of them went deeper into little streets, past open doorways where boys sewing pale-coloured garments sat cross-legged on mats, past the bright eyes of females hidden within the private envelope of their all-encompassing dress. In a short while the elderly man dropped away and the school-age youth took over. He beckoned the two foreigners forward with a smile. It no longer mattered that they might all be seen together. He was confident of his reading of the situation, confident that he could do the tasks of manhood.

'You speak English, I think,' he said. 'I speak too. You want *kif* or hash? I know very good black hash. Very wonderful, price okay.' It was pointless to pull back now, so they all went on.

The downstairs room of the small house, indistinguishable from others to right and left, was bare of furniture but lively with women and children. The noise stopped while the new party went upstairs, then the novelty was erased and the serious business of being young began again. The upper room, no larger than the one below, had a barred hole in the floor, roughly circular and with a thick, raised lip of beaten clay around it. It looked down on the play of sounds and shadows below. In a corner of the upper room a sheep was tethered by a hind leg, and a ghostly figure, completely covered by a djellaba, lay motionless against a wall.

They sat on the rim round the hole in the floor while the youth fetched a bag of *kif* and ceremoniously made up a joint. After a few puffs they gave each other cautious smiles, and then the youth began trying to sell the *kif*. 'No, no, you don't understand,' Carter protested. 'To smoke *kif* is very nice, but we want to buy hash.' He said it in English and repeated it in Spanish, so there would be no mistake. The youth nodded in good humour, said it could be arranged and left the room, promising to be back in fifteen minutes.

He was away for a lot longer than that. Sitting on the clay rim they watched the sheep in the corner snuffling along the floor until the tether on its leg jerked. The figure against the wall gave a sudden start, came upright, gathered his djellaba around him so that everything was still hidden, then departed without a look or a word. A woman's head peered around the door, withdrew hastily, followed a little later by a timid knock. The woman entered with some strips of cardboard and a large wooden bowl of grain. Shyly, she offered them the cardboard, indicating that they might like something to sit on. Then she began to pick through the grain before setting the bowl in front of the sheep. Her fingers, red with henna, sifted the grain deftly, finding little lumps that looked like rat's droppings, squeezing them to make sure. But the sheep had no doubt that it was good food, nosing into the bowl, knocking it about and spilling the feed. The woman, bobbing her head and smiling tentatively, left and was soon replaced by a little girl with a twig broom who whisked the floor around the sheep, kicking the animal briskly on the rump when it tried to compete for the fallen scraps. She and the sheep seemed to be on good terms. She left and they sat without speaking, aware of the steady grind of the sheep's jaws.

After nearly an hour the youth returned, looking crestfallen, with a small chunk of hash. He put a match under it and wafted it under their noses, but at the same time he was still trying to sell them *kif*. Lew was getting annoyed and Carter looked offended, but it appeared that some little obstructive ritual had to be completed before they could move on. The youth sighed.

'Okay, you miss good chance with *kif*,' he lamented, 'but now we get best hash, like this one you smell. Now you come with me, you see my friend Mustafa.'

Once more they dodged in and out of alleys, all sense of direction lost, and came to a slightly superior house with a small courtyard where girls with plastic buckets and metal jugs were drawing water from a standpipe. Between the fillings, the tap was left running and smaller children dabbled toes in the wash of water tumbling down steps. In the house, again they went upstairs into a long room with walls painted in a pale dirty yellow. It had a wide alcove at the far end with an open window letting in a faint breeze with the weak evening sun, a welcome breath of air after the vapours of the close streets. Standing by the window Lew saw that the house seemed to be set into the west wall of the medina. Below, there was an area of trampled earth and ill-kempt greenery that might be a park, and from beyond he heard the braying of donkeys and the barking of dogs.

Mustafa was waiting for them, and it looked like he had been at the mirror, petting a sleek head of hair and regimenting a Charlie Chaplin moustache. He wore a shiny brown jacket that was very new and might even be leather, or a good imitation. His manner was both fulsome and confidential, suggesting he had secrets to tell and they were the ones favoured to hear them.

They sat on hard couches along the wall. Mustafa clapped his hands and called in Arabic through an open door. Then, while they all waited for whatever was supposed to happen, Mustafa began his pitch. Seated cross-legged on the couch, as sedate as a fakir with a basket of snakes, he began, in fluent Spanish, to tell them that he had always liked and respected the *faranji* and knew them well.

After ten minutes a man came with a brass tray on which were four glasses of mint tea and a small block of hash. They drank the tea, still sweet-talking each other, and tried not to eye the hash. Then the hash was heated and sniffed and a pipe was prepared. Lew and Carter took the pipe in turn, inhaling slowly but not overdoing it, and lay back feeling the world was just right. Mustafa put aside the pipe, which neither he nor the youth had tried, and watched his guests begin to lose their grip on the day.

Then the man who had brought the tea reappeared with several blocks of hash in different sizes and shapes – a square kilo block, two long half-kilos, two oval quarter-kilos – each one tightly wrapped in clear plastic. Mustafa slammed the blocks one after another on the tiled floor to show that they were solid. To help his guests to a decision he pulled a porcelain bowl of hash fudge out from under the couch.

'Try this,' he urged. 'Same hash I show you here. It make your soul fly most happily.'

Lew took a couple of pieces, finding the fudge spicy and gritty. He wished he had taken some more. He noticed that Carter and Mustafa were now doing business, discussing terms. Carter seemed to be losing his usual firm hold on Spanish. There was too much hash, much too much, and the price was anything but clear. It had crept up, drifting higher until they suddenly found themselves talking of a sum they did not recognize.

'You like this hash,' said Mustafa, looking hard into their faces. 'I think you want it very much.'

'Too many decisions for one day,' Carter replied, his teeth getting in the way of his tongue. 'Boring matters, should sleep on them, wait till tomorrow. As you say, all this is too good to miss. We'll be back. But now,' he concluded grandly, turning to the youth, 'take us away, young man.'

For a long moment the ball skimmed the rim of the wheel, then dropped and the tension broke. Mustafa gave a slight nod, and the youth rose and led them away. In the daze of the medina, now muted by the tones of late evening, their bodies seemed suspended in air, and the paving as soft as rose petals.

At the hotel, all solemnly shook hands and the youth agreed a time and a place to meet at mid-morning the next day. Lew and Carter ascended the stairs, double-checking with each other the floors as they passed and then the number of their room, before subsiding gratefully into a night of long dreams.

*

They woke in the morning with clear heads and good appetites. They had not been deceived; the hash had been of excellent quality. They walked to the Boulevard Mohammed V for coffee and croissants, read *The New York Times* and *The Manchester Guardian*, as any contented tourist would do, until it was time to meet their guide.

Back in the house by the west wall of the medina business was soon concluded. Everyone was very brisk now and had a firm idea how things would go. Carter bought a kilo and a half at a price slightly more than he had expected, and Lew took a quarter kilo, paying with Anders's money.

There was no reason to stay. Mustafa wrote down an address, where a friend of a friend would know how to reach him in future, then the youth escorted them to the car, the blocks of hash hidden under the schoolbooks in his satchel. The car, rather to everyone's surprise, was untouched, so they drove out of town beyond the Kasbah, on the Atlantic road. Some miles out Carter tucked the car into the lee of a ruined wall of an abandoned building and made the transfer from the satchel to the prepared hiding place in the chassis. The youth, who had been kicking stones and looking gloomy, refused a ride back to town.

'It is not good you know me,' he explained. 'I not say my name because I am a schoolboy and this business is secret. Perhaps I suffer in my future. So I walk to next village, it is not far. I say now – how you say it? – best of British luck. Goodbye.'

He gave a wave of his hand and walked slowly towards the sea, a bright young scholar, proud of his English.

Lew and Carter had been lucky, and they knew it. Within the labyrinth, the ball of twine had held and had led them, without knowing where they were going, back to the solid world. On the return drive to Tangier, Carter Brock let out a long exhalation of relief.

*

They were wandering around the little shops and the cavernous storehouses within reach of the Socco Chico, killing time before the ferry left. With lazy interest they studied piles of kilims and Berber rugs, shelves of djellabas and handsewn cotton garments, lacquered slippers and leatherwork with intricate decoration, pottery, glassware, utensils in copper, iron and brass, the endless profusion of an Aladdin's cave. They had no money left with which to buy, and the choices were too many in any case. They were stunned. There was good work and not such good work, some done from love and some in haste to sell quickly, but what sort of peoples were these who ached to stamp some beauty on everything under their hands, even to the meanest artefact? That, too, was a lesson for Lew to take away.

At a table outside a teashop, a game of dominoes was under way. They watched a man who looked like Sinbad lay down a tile and then screw his fez to a new angle. He had no front teeth, two fangs at the side, and a forehead furrowed like a ploughed field. But his hands moved deftly, small, soft and graceful. The game was getting fast and rowdy, with much banging of pieces, and then it suddenly stopped. It was obvious, without further moves, that Sinbad had won. But his Spanish opponent began to complain.

'Go on, play,' he said hotly. 'Let's just see how it all comes out.'

Sinbad looked at him, shifting his fez around. '*Hay bandera*,' he said with quiet contempt, '*ya esta.*'

'What's *that* mean?' Lew murmured to Carter.

'He's saying something like, "I've taken the flag, now that's the end of it."'

When fate rolls over you, there's no point in bitching about it. It was a thought that made Lew uneasy.

Maghreb

The Mountain

They left in the dawn light with full rucksacks. Whatever path they might follow, they intended to make a day of it.

Anders was driving his smart, powerful Volvo – leather seats, carpets and FM radio. Lew, purring along in bourgeois Swedish comfort, saw the day rise on another world outside the car, hard and elemental and disturbing. From his interior viewpoint, the land seemed more bones than flesh. But Anders drove with quiet satisfaction; the new day looked just right to him, the perfect setting for whatever it was he had in mind.

After ten miles or so on the coast road Anders turned inland on to a dirt track, heading into a rough, narrow valley spanned by an ancient aqueduct. He parked in the shadow of the high arches of the aqueduct, a slim and graceful structure that might have been Roman or Moorish or Renaissance, depending on whom you talked to, but in the local opinion it was completely Spanish. Then they pulled their packs from the back seat of the car and started into the country.

Climbing out of the valley they laboured up a steep hillside, picking their way over rocks and loose stones and through a thin cascade of detritus that had been dumped from the ridge above. This outpouring appeared to be not so much the garbage of everyday consumption – the throwaway of society overburdened with things – but rather the leavings from a past that had once meant something but was now irrelevant. Lew noticed objects he had almost forgotten: an old garment that looked like a torn frock-coat, once black but now ripped and green with age; a single shoe for a man, in cracked patent leather, with a high blocky heel and a pointed toe; the broken lid of a small leather case, with metal corner-pieces and faded gilt initials; large fragments of a china basin still showing the delicate design of pale blue flowers; an old-fashioned silk umbrella reduced to spiky ribs and a bamboo handle. The midden of a time regretfully abandoned.

A footpath lay along the top of the ridge leading to a monument of some sort. It took the form of a stout wooden cross, about six feet high, sheltered by a tin canopy with ornate metal supports. The bottom half of the cross was encased in iron-sheeting set in cement. A metal plaque was fixed to the sheeting, giving the reasons for the added security of the ironwork. It stated that Marxist hordes had torn down the cross at the beginning of the Civil War, but the holy symbol had been rescued and repaired by Franco's forces in July 1937 and set in cement to protect against future outrage. So that was another bit of the past for the people to think about, as they struggled through a landscape still set in Franco's Spain.

From the cross Lew and Anders began a long angled ascent into the high country, the Swede leading the way at a good clip, as if there were something in the timetable he might miss. Lew did not want to be pressed. There was no need to race, and he saw plenty to observe and reflect on. As they climbed, and more and more territory became open to view, he judged that the burden of the land, even in the best of times, was almost too heavy to bear. Nature was tight-fisted up here, giving out little and making you pay in drudgery, weariness and diminishing hope. Over time, for lack of a foothold the population was slipping down the hill, coming to rest on the narrow coastal strip, becoming the dispossessed servants of the new economy where land meant little more than a base for an apartment block or the grounds of a tourist hotel. Only the animals were holding out, not much minding whether man was there or not. In the sparse cultivation that remained, chiefly olive groves, Lew admired the lonely mules, big and intelligent and self-contained, pricking their ears at interesting noises, favouring the world with a sneer from blubber lips and wicked teeth. From higher up, he heard the evocative jangle of the goat bells, and the occasional yap and flurry of the herdsman's dog as some stubborn animal was forced back into the flock.

They walked for about three hours, at first steeply uphill, making them sweaty and silent, but then reaching a high level that Lew imagined to be the rim of the world, the Sierra Nevada behind and old civilization below. And with a little more imagination he thought he could make out Morocco beyond, over the rounded hump of earth. Perhaps he was right, for there seemed to be a faint bluing in the distant air that might well be the line of the Rif Mountains. Though the walking was easy enough along the spine of the mountain, the rucksacks seemed heavier with each step. At mid-morning they had paused in their climb for light refreshment, taking advantage of the shade thrown by a large algarrobo tree. They suddenly heard, instead of their own crunching footsteps and heavy breathing, the sombre 'chook, chook' of a partridge down the hill and the demented celebration of a lark right overhead. Birds so abandoned to their nature enchanted Anders, and he insisted that they get a better view, boosting each other up into the branches among the long beans of the algarrobo until they were perched like two crows, eating bread and chorizo and sipping a few mouthfuls of wine.

But their rucksacks, though a little emptier, in a mysterious way hardly lost weight. The heaviest thing was the liquid – water and wine. The water easily diminished, with frequent stops for a drink. They looked at the two heavy glass litre-bottles of wine and tried to balance the present burden with the future pleasure. They held out for future pleasure. So they plodded on, long past their early morning zest, when they had chattered like jackdaws. At last, when the sun was a little over the zenith, they reached an untidy cairn of stones marking the summit of that part of the mountain range. Lew took off his heavy damp shirt, risking sunburn at this altitude, and wiped his face and his glasses with his Basque beret. They sank to the ground by the cairn and Anders prepared a little smoke before taking charge of the picnic. While Lew had a few grateful puffs Anders neatly laid out olives and raw carrots, rough hunks of breads, *jamón serrano* and chorizo, manchego cheese, apricots and oranges; he had plastic tumblers for the wine, and even a large white cloth to keep the food out of the dirt.

They were a long time eating and drinking, and almost as long having another smoke, flat on their backs, squinting into the sky and rearranging high clouds into strange beasts. Then Lew's eyes were closing. They had seen plenty, but now they wanted a rest. The last thing he remembered before sleep overcame him was his departure from Canada and his reason for it. He was happy with that and did not think he had made a mistake.

*

When Lew awoke he noticed the sun well on its way to the west and saw Anders sitting on top of the stone cairn, gazing southwards. He heard Lew sit up and stretch. Then Anders turned his solemn face and said almost shyly, 'Well, what do you think?'

'About what?' said Lew, wiping away a yawn with the back of his hand.

'In general, about all this,' Anders replied, with a gesture that introduced the whole spread of the world before them. 'But in particular about that little journey you made to Tangier on my behalf.'

'I don't see the connection.' It was sometimes hard to settle on the right track with Anders. He was a university man and a little metaphysics was not beyond him.

'Oh, but there is a connection, you know,' he replied confidently. 'What we are looking at was once a unified world. That bit down there, to the south, whether we call it Morocco or the Maghreb, was intimately linked, despite the narrow waters in between, with this bit we call Spain. Religion, thought, culture, agriculture, commerce, trade, language, they were all shared. A complete way of life, properties in common for the use of everyone. That, I think, is what we call civilization. The recognition and expansion of human qualities impartially shared. Then came the break. A rupture, dispersal, good things despised, neglected, now lost and gone. A long degeneration leading to today. We may argue about the reasons. Hunger for land and power, ideology, bigotry, ignorance, greed, envy. The familiar villains. But those are human qualities, too, the dirty side of civilization.'

Anders is well away now, Lew thought. A latter-day Kierkegaard, working up a thesis. Lew did not see yet how he came into it, though he expected that Anders would drag him in by the back door. No doubt that was why they were on a mountain; the Swede did few things unplanned. But Lew was not quite ready for conundrums and decisions. At the moment, his mind was wandering. His attention was grabbed by a small weathered skull half hidden in the scrub. Was it a cat or a rabbit? He might get up and look at the teeth.

'I'm not quite with you,' he admitted, trying to keep things within bounds.

'Look, man,' Anders said with some annoyance, giving up on the grand exposition. 'There's nothing much we can do, socially or politically, about the mess of the present. But I can give you, both of us being mere individuals, some part of an ideal – or near ideal – from this past I've been talking about. We both like to smoke hash and see nothing wrong with that, beyond some half-arsed rules only half believed and half enforced in the West. In the Maghreb what we do is seen, and always has been seen, as a sort of communion. And in a way that is how we look at it. One of the good things of civilization, in moderation. It is, strangely enough, one of the glues of our community, successfully used for more than a thousand years, and I'm damned if I can see why we should be deprived of it.'

So here it comes, drug-runners as social therapists and the linkmen of history. It sounded too grandiose – even ridiculous – put like that, but it was not something Lew fundamentally disagreed with.

'Your trip to Tangier,' Anders went on, 'was a success all round. Some pleasure for you, some profit for me, and no harm done. So I want to offer you all the strangeness, the interest, the resources of the Maghreb, to make what you want of that, to incorporate it into our narrow, parsimonious and blinkered worldview.'

'Sounds a bit dubious to me,' Lew said; 'too plausible and easy.' He was suspicious but did not want to let go of the idea entirely. 'How do I know you're not setting me up to be a fall guy?'

Anders protested. 'No, no. That would be inhuman. I set value by friendship. There is some risk of course, because of stupid laws and regulations. But our aims are modest. We touch nothing but hash. And we are not a normal capitalist enterprise, set up to maximize profits and expand markets. I see myself as a representative of a wide group of northern youths in the Scandinavian countries, who want looser bounds, a wider experience, more fraternal feeling, a more intense pleasure. I and the people I work with need to make a profit but we are not in it primarily for the money. We are sensible, co-operative, and very cautious. We work on low margins, so as not to get rash and greedy. We help each other every step of the way, and our combined experience – now rather considerable – is put to common use. If you throw in your lot with us you will be looked after as far as possible. No rush, time to learn and make judgements, dangers minimized. If you want to back out at any time, just kiss your hand and leave.'

The sensible thing would be to do that right now. Doff his beret and flee down the hill. Lew got to his feet and drifted among the rocks, a blank look on his face but his mind in some turmoil. Just to be doing something, he picked up the small animal skull. Seemed to be from a rabbit after all. Where had death come from, up here on the mountain? A bird of prey, a night predator? This small nervous mammal, it must have felt secure, to be out in the open under a huge sky, with so little cover around. In every destiny, however safe it might look, there was likely to be a joker.

He began to repack his rucksack, adding the rabbit skull as a memento. 'Time's getting on,' he said, feeling a chill in the air. 'Better get down the mountain soon.'

They went down fast, almost carelessly, skittering and sliding down slopes, grabbing hold of bushes to put the brakes on. They didn't talk much, and then only of immediate or inconsequential matters – the best way round a small ravine, or how grit invariably got into your socks. In difficult places, the taller, stronger Anders waited to give Lew a hand.

Reaching the ridge above the aqueduct and the parked car, they heard the final evening blast from a nearby limestone quarry. Lew took it as a signal of what he knew and welcomed – the first drink in the bar, the conversation around the table, the expectation of the evening meal. They hurried down the last slope to the valley floor, knocking aside the discarded junk they had seen in the morning. At the bottom of that dross the last thing they saw was a large male doll, as big as a six-month infant. It lay naked on its back and had an erection, a penis such as one might see in the Bosch paintings in the Prado. Lew burst out laughing; he couldn't help it. But Anders seemed shocked. He gave Lew a dark look and kicked some dirt and rubbish over the offending member.

As he stood and watched, Lew still couldn't help smiling. Anders was all of a piece, a natural moralist of his own kind and making. Though his words sometimes wandered around the block, you had a pretty good idea how he would think and act. Suddenly Lew felt a warm glow of affection for this drug-running friend, champion of a lost time and a lost world.

TANGIER

He had taken the boat from Malaga to Ceuta, the Spanish enclave on the Moroccan coast, hoping by this slight detour to have the benefit of discretion. On the boat he put himself in a corner with a Penguin paperback, anxious to keep his head down. He hoped that Flaubert's *Salammbô* might keep enquiries at bay. The boat was noisy with a party of cheerful young Spaniards in suits. From snatches of their conversation Lew judged them to be junior members of the colonial administration in North Africa, making the most of the short freedom of the seas. They had smiles and a warm embrace for everyone, smoking pungent cigarettes and looking rather glazed, as if they were at the end of a mild debauch that had gone on just a bit too long. The motion of the boat tipped the young fellows here and there, and when they swung in a body towards Lew he met their jolly advances with a blank look and some puzzled English. He hoped that they would take his Canadian for an American accent and note him down as an example of dumb Yankee incomprehension.

But one of them, more reckless than the others, was determined to take this chance to try his English. All life was an extension of the schoolroom. He had noticed the Penguin book in English in Lew's hands, so he came over, a warm beacon fuelled by alcohol, and pulled up a friendly chair.

Laboriously, he began to set out his little stock of English. This book, he insisted, it was very difficult, yes? Lew did not think so. It is about this Africa of the north, yes? A long time ago. The world is different now, yes? Yes.

The young Spaniard beamed. That seemed to be as far he could go for the moment. He was shuffling further English idioms about, trying to find something serviceable, when an announcement began on the loudspeakers, warning of disembarkation. With relief, the young man looked at his watch, then he rose at once and shook hands warmly. 'I must go now,' he said. 'I think you very smart, you read this book.' Lew did not deny it.

He hated these occasions of stilted banalities. His own Spanish was by now good enough to do better than that. But he was still not sure how he should stand, what clothes he should wear for native eyes. He was reticent by nature and increasingly saw that as a worthwhile virtue. He thought he could reproduce most safely the innocent abroad from the wide American West, with a camera strap around his neck and a folder of American Express cheques in his back pocket.

On the bus to Tangier he tried to work out a simple plan. Nothing brilliant came to mind. Mustafa, on Lew's previous visit, had jotted down the name and address of a friend of a friend – a series of gatekeepers no doubt – but at least a place to start. In Tangier, he began to search, trying to remain as unobtrusive as possible. He went to the Tourist Office and inspected a city map but could not locate the address. It was possible that the transliteration from the Arab name was wrong. Or was the street a tiny cul-de-sac in the medina? Or a new street in the spreading tentacles of the suburbs, a raw slash through what had been orchard or field? He began to ask the townsfolk, the officials at their posts and the citizens in the streets, almost at random. The address he had been given was written in English script, which the respectable could read but not place, and most of the locals not read at all.

At first, he was energetic and hopeful, quartering the main parts of the city at a good pace, with cheery greetings right and left. Then it appeared to him that people were giving him strange looks, watching him speculatively until he turned the corner. His presence became an anomaly in whatever part of town he happened to be; even his footsteps on the pavement sounded too lonely and too loud. Some desperation crept in, and he had hardly started.

On the evening of a weary day, chasing down yet another possible lead, Lew was eating in a tatty, fly-blown restaurant far down the avenue that ran alongside the beach. The waiter spoke English and was friendly – too friendly – but needing whatever help he could find Lew told him something of his woe, and the waiter, though he did not know the address himself, took the piece of paper and offered to ask the other customers in the restaurant. Most looked blank, but a taxi driver who worked that part of the city was interested. He rubbed his head, as if to stir up memory, and thought – no, he was certain – he knew the place. It was out in the direction of Cap Malabata. If Lew would be kind enough to compose himself with a coffee while the cabby finished his meal, they would look for the place together.

It was not hard to find. For ten minutes the taxi wound around shabby roads then turned on to a rutted ribbon of track in an in-between landscape, not yet town but not quite country. An agrarian past was being abandoned in the ache for a better present. The cab dropped him at a spot that seemed no better and no more relevant than any other and juddered away down the dirt track. As the headlights receded, darkness gathered in the surroundings. No lights appeared, the low houses few and indistinct, bleeding off into an obscurity that Lew was unable to read. At some distance a dog began barking, hysterical for a brief period, then silent, then starting again. He felt lonely in a way that the vast spaces of Canada had never made him feel. He did not feel any danger, just a nullity, detached as he was from that small portion of reality with which he was familiar.

The arrival of the taxi had been noted; no doubt a car at night was an uncommon event. A door in the nearest house opened, creaking in the silence, and a lantern emerged with a shadowy figure behind. After an apology for the lateness of the visit, Lew explained himself in Spanish as best he could and mentioned the name of Mustafa and also the name Mustafa had given him. A man's ghostly face appeared above the lantern, nodded without expression, and gestured with the lantern towards the door. They entered, Lew following the soft flip-flop of the man's slippers. A short dark passage led to a door, open a crack, with some low-wattage light stealing out. The guide pushed the door and pointed Lew inside, still without a word. Inside, in the far corner, was a pile of several thin mattresses with a man reclining on them. The man was fully clothed, with a bulky, loose turban on his head; his face was old, seamed, weathered, with a fierce nose and a stubble of grizzled hair on his chin. He was drawing placidly on a water pipe and seemed to be contemplating the world about the ceiling. A battered little radio, turned down low, was giving out Arab music, a strident female voice sounding as if she were in agony and enjoying it.

The old man, who admitted to being Hamadi, Mustafa's friend, waved casually towards a mat and some cushions and suggested in Spanish that Lew might like to sit. The music continued for a minute or so while the old man sucked on his pipe, all the time fixing Lew with an unblinking stare. When the song stopped he snapped off the sound and spoke abruptly.

'I am Hamadi,' he said, in a voice that sounded like stones rumbling in a torrent. 'You want hash.'

It was a declaration, not a question. Lew was silent. Had some message gone before him, from Mustafa perhaps? Or was his purpose written on his clothes and his face, a text that the whole world could read? Then he collected his wits – why else would a foreigner be out here, in the nether reaches of the city, in the night, asking for Hamadi by name, if not for hash? Hamadi, misinterpreting his silence, now looked a little more anxious.

'You speak Spanish?'

'Oh, well enough if we go slowly,' Lew replied. 'Keep it simple.'

'Mustafa gave you my name? That is okay. So he has confidence in you. It is not necessary you go back to him. I can sell you whatever you want here.'

The old face went from fierce to kindly in a twinkling. It was a trick of the eyes, at one moment hooded and aggrieved, and then startlingly wide open, radiating a tranquil beam from within. I wouldn't like to meet him, Lew thought, in troubled times on a mountain pass; he would skewer me in a moment, without compunction. But now it was time for smiles. The old man set aside the flexible tube of the water pipe, reached under the top mattress of the bed and pulled out a small slab of dark hash.

'This is from Lebanon,' he said. 'There is no better.' He threw the packet forcefully on the tiled floor, where the dense block clattered and almost rang, before skittering over against the wall. Then the silent man who had guided Lew into the house and the room, and who still crouched against the wall unnoticed, suddenly laughed.

'You want hash,' he said, 'this is the best place. My father knows hash. He smoke it for fifty years. Look, I show you.'

He retrieved the slab from the floor, carefully unwrapped one end of the packaging and broke off a small piece which he gave to his father. With the Lebanese hash, the old man prepared a pipe, using the meticulous procedure of a lifetime now become so ingrained as to be unthinking. When he had the pipe going he handed it to Lew.

'It is a gift,' he said. 'Try it and you will see.'

Lew drew in gingerly, and then more happily. For a while he smoked slowly, attending to whatever tales the pipe might whisper to him. The old man watched him. 'Go on,' he said, 'finish it. I have more to show you.' Even in Lew's contentment he thought he heard a command, perhaps a hint of threat, in the voice. Then it didn't matter, and he was chuckling quietly to beat the band. The world was more hilarious than a burlesque show.

He had never had such good dope – not that he was very experienced, or knew much about different kinds. The old man and his son, who had been watching keenly, relaxed. They were pleased with Lew; he would give no trouble. It was time to get down to business. Hamadi nodded to his son, who pulled an ancient suitcase from between the mattress and the wall, tossed it on the bed and opened it. The gesture was well-practised, intended to impress, and it did; for the suitcase was packed full of slabs of hash in various shapes, sizes and weights.

Hamadi tossed blocks on the bed and began to sort them. 'I have Lebanese, I have Syrian,' he said. 'Not so good but cheaper. How you want to pay? Dirhams no good, pesetas not so good either, dollar best.'

Lew was prepared. He had dollars. Had they asked for gold bars or diamonds he might have agreed, but dollars were good enough. The price for the Lebanese was 150 dollars a key, which was steep, but they were in harmony now, and another pipe was being prepared – this time Syrian – and the old man refused to haggle.

'Best is best,' he said sharply, drawing his brows for a moment into a thunderous look. 'I give you Syrian now, so you can see the difference, but you will not even want to know the price.'

The Syrian was good too, a little camphorish but subtle and strong. And while Lew was savouring this he forgot about price. He gazed fondly at his companions. He was safe. Their business was business, and he could let such worldly matters lie in their hands while his mind made the grand tour of light and sound. He felt universal sympathy. Hamadi was like a father, he would not deceive. The faces watching him were impassive now, Hamadi once more drawing calmly on the water pipe. The radio was back on quietly – Lew had not noticed. The thin, plangent chords of an oud sighed in speechless melancholy. Lew saw complicated, teasing shapes in the cracks of the wall plaster.

Somewhere, an agreement was struck. So much Lebanese for so many dollars. Lew handed over big notes and hardly looked while Hamadi grubbed in a worn leather bag to make the change. The sums now meant nothing to Lew. He waved all commercial thoughts away. Then the old man's son began to sort out the slabs, gathering together the weight that Lew had purchased, a considerable bulk which for ease of carrying the son divided into two piles. Carefully, he wrapped each pile in newspaper and then in cloth and tied the parcels firmly with string. He went then into another room and returned with two stout fabric bags of the kind that had contained several kilos of rice or maize flour. He put a parcel of hash into each bag, so that Lew could carry them one on each side, the load nicely distributed.

Then Lew was trying to say something in Spanish important to the world. He couldn't make it, the Spanish words slipping away from him. He tried in English and that was not much better. But he felt everything was there intact, his thoughts in order and eager to go, if only his tongue could reach them. Hamadi began to look anxious, though there was commiseration in his eyes too. He knew from long experience the tricks and turns of this ride, where the fun and the gaiety stumbled off. He spoke softly in the local dialect to his son, who went out again and returned with a thick woollen djellaba and a couple more cushions. He helped Lew into the djellaba and spread cushions on the floor against the wall.

'I think you like to lie down now,' Hamadi said gently, indicating the cushions. 'It is too late to go back to the city.' Then he added, to sugar the pill, 'Too dangerous. Many bad men about in the night.'

Lew was not thinking about danger. He knew he was sinking. It was sleep he wanted. He drew the djellaba tight about him and pulled the hood over his head. He lay down gratefully and soon was asleep.

*

He woke suddenly in the dark with an overwhelming sense of dislocation. The room was black, closed-up, stuffy, rich with the ripe fudge-like smell of good hash. He tried to look at his watch but could make out nothing; perhaps he had forgotten to wind it. Hamadi and his son were gone. The silence was intense and Lew could hear his own laboured breathing. He was close to panic, most of all because he could remember so little. He was surprised to find himself in a djellaba – a smelly one at that – with his clothes on underneath and his shoes still on his feet. Then he remembered – not everything, but fragmented pieces.

He began to feel a deep sense of failure, a calamitous drop in his understanding of his own competence. He had fallen into the bog of self-indulgence, and that at the first hurdle. He panicked again. O Lord, the hash – where was it? He groped on the floor and along the wall, and by the cushion where his head rested he touched a bag, where Hamadi had placed it. The old man was honest, which was one of the things he wanted to believe. Grabbing the bag he clutched it to his side, beneath the capacious folds of the djellaba, and hurried from the room and the house. In his haste, the djellaba fuddled around his feet and nearly tripped him, but he did not take it off. Hamadi, after such a good sale, could well withstand the loss of a garment. Lew needed it against the cool night air, and perhaps to cover himself from his own introspection. Like a hurt animal, he wanted to hide.

Dawn was not far off when he stumbled into the road. At once, the dog whose barking had greeted him began another noisy assault, an adieu that Lew could have done without. He wanted no observers. He discovered, in any case, that there was only one track to the tarmac road. A dim glow announcing sunrise was beginning to leak into the day, but the earth track was badly cut up, and a couple of times Lew nearly fell. Then, instinctively, he clutched the bag to his heart.

In about fifteen minutes he had reached the road and was walking along the dirt verge on the edge of the blacktop towards the city. Behind him he heard the sound of an old engine with a stuttering heartbeat. As the vehicle approached – one-eyed, with a defective headlight – Lew waved it down. It was a little Italian truck, very worn and rusted, with a battered cab and open bed behind, carrying produce to market. The driver had stopped for a hooded figure in a djellaba whom he naturally took to be one of his own. When the two Moroccans in the cab saw and heard a foreigner by the road, at this time and in this place, their young faces showed consternation mixing with the age-old desert impulse to help a wayfarer. But at this hour they would not abandon a person in need, so Lew climbed over the tailgate of the truck and settled down amid melons and sacks of onions. The truck limped off at a comfortable pace and soon Lew was dozing.

He jerked awake as the arms of the city began to close in, with a new realization gripping him. Had there not been *two* bags of hash? The second bag had fallen through the holes in his memory, an orphan of the disordered night. When he groped along the wall for the first bag, had there been another? He didn't know, but he now believed that it had been there. He reached suddenly into an inside pocket of his jacket for his money and passport and found them safely in place. If Hamadi had wanted to defraud him, he would have taken everything, robbed him blind. Why take one sack and leave another? It made no sense. Hamadi had his own standards; he was a man who relied on an agreed exchange. Robbery belonged to another kind of man. But that kind of man was hardly more contemptible than the fool that Lew found himself to be.

He stood and banged on the roof of the cab, and the truck swerved to a stop with squealing brakes. But already Lew recognized that it was too late. All that happened was lost in darkness. Could he find the lane again? He doubted it. Would he know the house, that shadow of a dwelling clothed in night? He doubted it. And to make a fuss searching would only draw attention to his own place in the story. Hamadi and his son would be long gone by now – he knew it. They neither knew nor cared who Lew was, and they had no means to reach him again. Lew's muddled brain – his negligence – had made them a present, which they would gladly accept, though it would be mysterious to them how or why it happened. They were the kind – their trade demanded it – who took the world as it comes and would not worry themselves for the sake of Lew's conscience.

When the truck stopped the driver put his head out of the window and looked back with a frown. 'It's nothing,' Lew mumbled apologetically. 'I made a mistake. I thought I had lost something important. Please go on. If you go near the main Post Office, drop me there.'

The truck dropped him at the Place des Nations and departed, the smiles and good wishes of the driver wreathed in oily smoke. It was still too early for anything to be open, so Lew started walking, working over events, sending himself angry missives and recriminations. He still had to meet Walter, the courier, whose specially prepared car would carry the hash northward through Europe. But no explanation was required there; their tasks were deliberately separate. Walter took what he was given, no questions asked, and went on his way. Anders, however, was another matter. Lew had squandered half his money. It was strange that Lew could feel such loss of honour in what was, after all, an illegal enterprise. He wanted to embrace Anders, assure him that he was not like that. But like what?

To puzzle that one out he found an early-morning café in the smart part of town and ordered coffee and a brioche. The patron looked at him with suspicion – an obvious foreigner in a dirty grey djellaba with a bag of swag. And at this hour of the morning. Lew was not too bothered, for he knew that Tangier was a haven for eccentricity and louche behaviour. He took his coffee to a dim rear corner and worked his memory backwards, trying to sequence events, to classify and assess. For all his effort, nothing much emerged except shame. Tired and despondent, he soon nodded off over his coffee.

When the patron shook Lew, the sun was well up. Customers were going in and out, impatient for newspapers and cigarettes. He paid and departed, walking along the boulevard more secure in the surge of work-bound people. He turned into the PTT office, feeling like a shaggy Father Christmas with a bag of goodies, trying to remember where in Stockholm Anders would be.

*

The telegram from Morocco came while Berta was getting breakfast. In her small house in the suburbs where Anders came and went she had opened the door for the messenger and the weather had done its best to crowd in too. A dirty day outside, a cold Stockholm drizzle that made you miserable to be alive, the sky low enough to be punctured by the TV aerials.

Methodically, Berta slit the envelope, took out the message and read it impassively. Never any hurry with Berta. She read it again and then passed the flimsy paper to Anders, who was sitting at the head of the table in a dressing gown, peeling an orange. Anders laid the telegram by his plate and slowly wiped his sticky fingers with a napkin. Vera Gwinn, seated opposite him, took off her sunglasses to watch him. Nothing would be said until Anders was ready.

A flurry of rain rattled the kitchen window and Vera looked up sharply. 'Well?' she said.

'News from Morocco,' Anders replied, as if it meant nothing to him.

There was a long pause while Anders began to quarter his orange. 'How's the weather down there?' she asked, to get the ball rolling, to stop the suspense teetering over into indifference.

It hardly needed answering but Anders gave it some consideration. 'He doesn't say,' he replied.

There was a spot of trouble, that was clear, but it did not seem to need discussing, or perhaps not while Vera was present. The other two were unruffled. Anders finished his orange, wiped his hands again and folded the message away in his pocket.

'How do you think he'll make out?' Berta said at last.

'Oh, I expect him to do very well when he gets some experience,' Anders said placidly. 'I have every confidence in him.'

'Bit of a slip-up at the moment, though?'

'Yes. These little problems come and go. We know we must expect them. It's no great matter.' There was another pause while Berta went back to the kitchen stove. The coffee-maker had started to bubble. Anders, still relaxed at the top of the table, was looking at Vera, something sad and speculative in his eyes. At once, she felt uncomfortable and replaced her dark glasses.

'You know,' he wondered, looking just over her head, 'you could go down there and join him.'

She thought about it. 'I might do that,' she agreed, looking through a rain-streaked window at a distorted world, 'I might just do that.'

Berta glanced up from the stove with approval. 'Steady him up, if he needs it,' she said softly. 'Hold his hand.'

Vera knew it was what she could do. Hold not just his hand but make a claim on his person too. And perhaps his heart.

Anders lowered his eyes to the level of her own and smiled enigmatically into her dark lenses.

The Northern Coast

When he was young Lhassen used to walk the distance once a year, the two hundred hard kilometres out of the mountains to the city on the coast. He thought then that it was nothing much; he was young and strong, thanks to Allah, and what are feet if not for walking? His wife Fatma – hardly more than a girl – went with him and they travelled as fast as nature and the road allowed, sleeping sometimes among friends, pushing on, walking often at night through territory where there were few friends and many ancient enmities. At night, they kept to the highway, but in the day they avoided towns and people as far as possible, taking tracks known to the goats and herdsmen. Though she had flat packs wrapped in plastic strapped to her body beneath her clothes Fatma walked easily and without complaint. She was carrying the best of their harvest for sale in Tangier.

The harvest was cannabis from which, in those days, *kif* was refined, for the preparation of hashish was not well understood in the Rif Mountains. That came later, when strangers passed through with new ways of doing things. Even then some grumbled that the growers of the Rif still hadn't got the hang of it. But as the strangers preferred hash, and thus the profit from hash was higher, the farmers stumbled on with more hope than attention, with primitive equipment and a process that was more exacting and fussy then they cared for.

In Lhassen's mind, the growing of *kif* or hash was the fact, the law and the rules against that cultivation were the mystery. No family memory could recall a time when the cannabis plant had not been grown in those high altitudes. No local community had ever considered the use of it as anything other than a normal part of the daily activity. Over many years Lhassen, and his father and grandfather before him, had thrown everything they had in the way of work and money at the few lean parcels of land – you could hardly call them fields – that the family possessed, conjuring out of the scrappy ground at best a mere subsistence, and by far the largest part of that subsistence was realized by the growing of cannabis. A hardy, undemanding crop, it did well enough on poor land and raised an income sufficient for bare needs. Lhassen had nothing else to offer society. He was surprised that society, or at least the official, coercive part of it, should look on him as some kind of outlaw.

His Western friend Jeff Gartree – also his best customer – had tried to explain it to him. It was complicated but seemed to have something to do with modernism, national respectability, fear in the West, and with the horror of the USA in particular that their fresh young folk might be contaminated by the world-relieving balm of the plant. Lhassen was surprised that they were willing to forgo such simple pleasure and thought that they might be a strange and saintly people. Later, he knew better; they were at heart rather like himself. Unfortunately, their society also had an official and coercive part.

According to the rules of power, pressure was put on Morocco, then in a fragile state between ex-colonial instability and nascent monarchical government (and needing all the friends and money it could get), to abate this social malaise before the brutal posse from the Wild West arrived, as it did in Mexico and Colombia, with rifles and helicopter gunships, and fire and corrosive chemicals to eradicate the crop for ever, and rub out entirely an age-old peasant life that was meagre in the extreme but sustainable and steady.

It didn't come to that – no fire and brimstone. A compromise of some oriental subtlety was devised. The people of the Rif were granted a licence to grow and consume cannabis, but they could not take it outside the mountain region, and the rest of the country was declared to be clean. This arrangement was policed with a suave lack of fervour. Foreigners were frequently hassled, a trouble easily overcome by a quick and well-placed bribe. The only native growers or traders likely to be picked up were those against whom the police had a personal grudge. Then six months in jail, a foul enough experience but easily endured by mountain men on the edge of poverty. Otherwise the traditional life went on, *kif* being the favourite relaxation, making rough days smooth, for peasants and townsmen, merchants and shopkeepers, policemen and government officials, and not least politicians and ministers.

Yet the early years under the new law had been hard. The closing of the region, the extra cost in labour, time and money in the long tramp to the city market, had taken a toll. For many farmers, familiar poverty ebbed towards destitution. There were too many mouths to feed from marginal land. In those days, when the farm was still under the control of his father, Lhassen had a strong back but an unnecessary appetite. The solution, of course, was to offer his brawn and desperation elsewhere, to become a migrant worker in the fruitful fields of European exploitation.

On a certain day he announced his departure, and then he had to go. The village expected it of him and looked forward to the money he could send back. His mother did not cry. She took him by the ears and gazed intently into his eyes, her face a few inches away, as if she might not know what strange beast would return. His wife Fatma said nothing; there was nothing to say. Their first-born, a small simian baby, was splayed on her back, tied under a shawl. Sitting behind the dirty window of the bus, waiting to depart from the ragged brown muddle of the village, Lhassen counted the villagers he knew; he knew them all. An infirm old man on sticks raised a hand, something tentative between a wave and a blessing. It was a great-uncle whom Lhassen knew with certainty would not be alive when he returned.

He became an illegal immigrant in a country he knew nothing about. The journey was hazardous but at that time, before more recent maelstroms of world-displacement, not difficult to arrange. A fishing boat took him and five others across the strait on a stormy night. He had never been on the sea before, he could not swim, and he was seasick. He recognized it as an education of a sort. And though he didn't know it then, pain would be the constant element in all the lessons of his exiled life.

The country he landed in – southern Spain – looked more or less familiar, not unlike his own tortured hills and harsh light, and many of the poor people in the streets had the same hungry look. He soon learnt that there was a fraternity of the luckless and dispossessed who looked after each other. They guided him into channels of relative safety and propelled him at last towards Madrid, the big city of casual jobs and anonymity. An agency that specialized in illegal North African labour (owned by the son of a minor judge) found him a night-time job helping to clean Atocha railway station. He was no longer properly human; he was a unit of labour, a machine – with a humanoid appearance to be sure, though of the wrong colour – for sweeping, wiping, cleaning, polishing, delivering a quantified amount of work in a quantified time. He became a cipher living with six other Moroccan ciphers in a small grey room. His soiled skin took on the look of an underground, nightmare thing. Working at night and sleeping most of the day he almost forgot the sun, though this had the advantage of rendering him largely invisible to the world and perhaps to himself.

He worked in this way for three years, maintaining a simulacrum of life at the lowest level.

Compared to many he was lucky. First, he survived; second, by scrimping and niggardly living – and in this he was not lacking in cunning – he was able to send enough money home to help keep farm and family going; third, he learnt a limited but fluent demotic Spanish. After three years he returned home and became a man again. Before he left home he had been physically tough and resilient, but now he had studied the way of the world as well. He was no pushover.

He was lucky, too, in one other respect. The time of his return coincided roughly with the influx of a new kind of business for the Rif growers. Young Western strangers began to arrive in the hills in battered cars and vans, in parti-coloured clothes and with long hair and eyes that begged for understanding and sympathy. And they had money in their pockets. They wanted hash and lots of it, to use themselves and to transport to other lands. They were in fact those fresh young folk whom a mother country yearned to protect and for whose safety the laws were chiefly promulgated, or so it was claimed. But no one had asked them their opinion, and they felt that their maturity, their sense of being, was insulted.

Lhassen, though he would not have phrased it like that, sympathized with them. He was warm towards them and their aims, finding them on the whole friendly, unaggressive, respectful of local life and tradition, entertaining, and a little lost. Rich, too, by his standards, and he had to remind himself to resist the impulse to cheat them. One of their troubles was that they smoked too much, and the strongest stuff at that, and then their wits often disappeared. Lhassen considered himself a realist, with a living to make. He was disturbed by innocence.

Even so, with his easy Spanish, and some understanding of how the world went, Lhassen began to make contacts, establish relationships, and work up good business. Slowly, he grew quite prosperous, not least because he judged it wise to take the long view, make settled connections, even friendships.

He was on his way now to Tangier and then to Asilah, to visit the most solid and enduring of his foreign friends. There was business to do.

ASILAH

Lew Holle was looking for a house with a garage, somewhere to close the door against prying eyes. He had a car to prepare. Jeff was expected soon, wily Jeff Gartree, full of experience, master of the tricks. And maybe Vera Gwinn would arrive afterwards, which was something he tried to put out of his mind for the moment, lest he lose balance. The matter in hand was difficult enough.

The town of Larache had served their purpose in the previous year. It was the usual business: the outlay of a hefty rent, haggling only for appearance's sake, because the right house and garage were so important that almost any fee was acceptable, however outrageous; agreement of a lease of any length, no matter how long, since in a few weeks the place would be abandoned, if necessary in a midnight flit, no refund of rental demanded, the house bare and scrubbed, as if the nameless tenants had never been. Prudence, however, dictated that the trick should not be repeated in the same place too often, though in practice serious trouble was rare, owing to the conspicuous avarice of landlords and agents.

So Larache was out. This more or less left Asilash, a nervy place at the best of times since it had a rather European look which carried a false sense of order and security. Lew did not like or trust the place. In Larache, he had been conscious of being seen; in Asilah he was conscious of being watched.

He found a place that was possible but by no means ideal, a house detached but close to others, a garage that fronted straight on to a road with too much traffic. He did not wish to begin work on the car, partly for lack of privacy, partly because he was not too sure how to go about it. He needed Jeff to set him straight. There was nothing for it but to wait and brood.

*

Asilah was no town for walking in the winter months. The Moroccan cafés were cold and unwelcoming. There were few foreigners in the streets; native eyes chivvied him around wherever he went, making Lew feel both idle and furtive. He found an English bar, which served excellent food, but the owner and most of his customers were gay. A clan of suspects feeling safer on an outcrop of Europe. One to one, Lew had nothing at all against homosexuals but found a pack of them less than alluring. Looked like a club for plump matrons expecting the Avon Lady. The first night he ate there, the gay group at the next table had pulled up two chairs for their poodles – little balls of springy hair attached to sweet-coloured ribbons. Amid much cooing the owners fed the little beasts with choice titbits from their plates. Lew did not wish to go there too often.

The days were bracing, chill and blustery, but the rain held off. Getting away from the town Lew walked by the sea edge to the deserted beaches south of the medina. He liked the exercise and thought he needed the time to think, or at least to worry. Heavy Atlantic swells romped up the beaches driven by dark towers of cloud. In a cove clogged with driftwood the carcass of a jackass slowly decomposed, jostled into a new contortion with every passing tide, the flesh wearing away to expose yellow teeth in a fearful grimace. Returning by the rampart walls in early evening Lew was usually in time for the rowdy gathering of a species of garrulous sparrow, pecking and shoving atop the great stones of the medina walls. Further into town, on a bastion overlooking the water, a convocation of silent men, arms withdrawn under their djellabas, set themselves against the sea and sky, looking like another flock of birds, this time tall and stiff and flightless.

Back in the house – the not-quite-satisfactory house – he filled in time reading, dozing, daydreaming, or he idly watched the charwoman whose services went with the property. She was a stout, middle-aged woman, nearly as broad as she was tall, with the flat, brown, crinkled face of an Eskimo. She crabbed through the house, slow and sideways, groaning, puffing, grunting, and occasionally sighing as if punched in the stomach. She spoke a little Spanish, mainly to say she'd had a hard life. Her husband was dead. Her only son had gone to work as a cook in France five years back, promising to send money. Since then she had seen no son and no money, not one sou. A photo or a postcard might have helped, though she couldn't read.

'Suerte,' she sighed, holding up a hand turned in from the wrist, making a slow fanning motion. 'Suerte.' Luck, chance, fortune, fate – it was all one, and all bad.

Her hands were broad, thick and red, like two swollen rubber gloves. One day Lew asked her how old she was. Her eyes slid up towards a corner of the roof, her lower lip drooped. She spread the fingers on both hands to try to count her years. She appeared astonished to have so many fingers, studying them, perplexed, front and back. The calculation was beyond her and with a despairing groan she gave up. She returned to the only thing she knew, which was work.

Bent low, with her prodigious rump in the air, she backed out of the room, dragging a damp tattered cloth over the tiles, rearranging the dirt.

When he was not walking beyond the town limit Lew kept to the house. A European with vacant days pacing the seafront or the main streets raised too many questions. The best remedy would have been work on the car, but he was in a dither how to start. He wished he'd taken better note when another car, some months previously, had been stripped and channelled. He was in a dither about Vera, too, wondering how emotional needs fitted into the dangers of an illicit enterprise. He wished he'd taken more careful note of just what it was they expected from one another.

Yet he found a certain solace in the back and forth of indecision. He gave himself credit that he was examining pretty keenly what might be possible, though on the bad side all that turmoil of mind gave him indigestion.

Otherwise, he found pleasure in reading. The owner of the villa, an English academic, visited it hardly at all, keeping it for an occasional holiday and perhaps for rental income. He left for his tenants a small but select collection of books, from Brecht to Camus, from Faulkner to Graham Greene. Lew became miserly of his reading time, stuffing as much of it as he could manage into each day. In the morning he was out of bed and had his eyes on the page before even coffee and breakfast were made. Eating was a pleasure too, something to conserve carefully. But to read and eat at the same time, as lonely people did, was to attend properly to neither.

He came across Anthony Powell's *The Soldier's Art* and read it for the first time, could not get enough of it. The title was taken from a poem by Robert Browning. Lew was very surprised and impressed by the book – sly wit and social buffoonery, written with malice and delicacy. One line, which explained the title, arrested him in particular: 'Think first, fight afterwards – the soldier's art.' It seemed a mode of action for which he could fit himself.

Between the soldier and the smuggler there were some striking similarities. Both followed a campaign trail, all too aware of the danger. Death was a possibility, more so for the soldier, but Lew had heard of fatalities among his own kind. Jeff Gartree's closest colleague had been gunned down and left to die, a major artery uncorked and bubbling blood on to the dirty slush of a mountain path near a village whose name he did not even know. A drug-smuggler, when about his business, lived his life within the lines of the enemy camp. And then he and the soldier shared, in nearly equal proportion, the dreariest of all burdens, waiting.

*

From cool nights and chancy days, the weather turned nasty, snarling at the land as a low-pressure Atlantic front sent the barometer into sudden freefall. Then the storm rolled ashore, as fast and dangerous as a runaway truck.

The first thunderous crash and the shooting wind had sprung the French window in the living-room, barging through like a drunken hitman, sending broken glass sheeting over the tiled floor. The electricity flickered and went down. Furious wind and rain followed, upending a cane table, grabbing books from the shelves, pulping them in cold floodwater. Soaking wet, Lew struggled to contain the invasion, which seemed to be entering by every door and window and even sneaking through the roof. Wrestling with a heavy mirror that was about to jump off the wall, Lew fell and wrenched his knee. It hurt so much that he could only hobble up to bed, leaving the house to the four brutal winds and the tumbling rain. He lay under the covers, wet and naked, listening to the howl of air, the groans of the house, and the small cascade of water streaming down the stairs.

Man against nature, he thought. No damned contest.

Next morning, in restive dawn light with the trees still flapping their arms, he saw that the house was close to wrecked and half the roof had blown off the garage. After painfully sweeping broken glass he retired back to bed. His knee hurt and he was too miserable to attempt a clean-up. He would leave that to the Moroccan charwoman, presenting her, at her rate of progress, with weeks of work.

He saw now that his position in Asilah was hopeless. A broken house, only half a garage. What now? He shied away from that puzzle, didn't feel like booting that horse over the fence. A troubled sleep got him through the day and into the night.

At a late hour he heard a regular banging from below and limped down the stairs kicking debris out of the way. The front door, a big double door, about the firmest thing still standing in the house—though any stranger could have climbed in the broken window a few feet away—revealed two men in shadows.

The electricity was still out, but Lew had a flashlight and he put the beam on two faces wide-eyed and grinning, taking note of the rare spectacle of the damage. The first man, the white one, tall and loose, was Jeff Gartree, whom he already knew; the other, a North African whom Lew didn't know, spare and slight, with a gaunt face and a week's worth of stubble beard, had a head of very dark half-curly, half-matted hair. He looked like a tamer sort of Hottentot.

*

The first thing Lew did, he began apologizing, a jumble of words, hardly knowing where to start. The town, the house, the storm, the mess, his limp, no electricity. The car, unprepared, in the garage with the busted roof.

But Jeff, still grinning, held up a hand.

'I see we catch you at a disadvantage.' He said with a chuckle, surveying what he could see of the wrecked house, against which their plans might also crash. But flexibility was second nature to Jeff; he recognized no catastrophe from which some good could not be salvaged. He liked to be tested, to run along the dangerous edge. He thought of it as a kind of flying, without the burden of wings.

He shook hands warmly with Lew and gave him a hug. Then he waved to the stranger by his side. 'You've heard me speak of Lhassen,' he said. 'Well, here he is. Looks like we've got some problems here, but I don't doubt we can work something out together. I brought some wine for a little celebration, but now I think we need it to fortify ourselves.'

Lew offered his hand to Lhassen whose handshake, like that of many non-Europeans, was soft, cool and limp. They did not understand the deep message of the manly grip.

Then they followed the beam of the flashlight and stepped cautiously to the kitchen, at the back of the house, which had survived rather better than the front, seaward rooms. Lew found candles under the sink, snapped his lighter, and began to take stock of Lhassen, about whom he had heard many enthusiastic things. At first sight, he did not look impressive. His eyes, in a narrow grubby face, were lively, but Lew thought that they were wandering too much. Who knew where the point of his interest lay? His hair was a ragged bird's nest. He had discarded native dress – those robes of some elegance – and wore Western jeans and a plaid shirt and zippered jerkin that were none too clean, and looked as if they had been slept in. But Lew knew that Jeff trusted and had a fondness for Lhassen, so he decided to discount the Moroccann's appearance, his hair, his whiskers, his clothes, even his soggy handshake. Lew was still learning the meaning of difference, the signs that didn't matter, and those that spelled danger.

A bottle of wine was produced and promptly emptied. Lhassen drank rapidly and shoved his glass forward for refills. Another bottle appeared out of Jeff's shoulder bag. Somewhere down this diminishing bottle Lhassen grew lively, laughing at shadows, broken glass, books on the floor, the whole fantastic mess. He rumpled Jeff's hair and clapped him on the back. They had difficulty with language, for though Lhassen spoke fast and easy Spanish, Jeff had only a few dozen words of tourist Spanish. They made up for words with nudges, winks and a sort of clumsy horseplay. The closest Lhassen got to Jeff's name was the Spanish *Jefe* – chief or boss – which showed that they understood each other well enough.

In a while Jeff prepared a pipe from a sample Lhassen had brought and Lew found it very good, though he was surprised that Lhassen waved the pipe away.

'I do not like to smoke hash too often,' he said. He tapped his brow. 'When I smoke hash, I think too much. But when I drink I don't think at all. I like to drink. It is something I learn to do very well in Spain.' He pushed his empty glass resolutely towards the bottle.

By now, with the wine comfortably inside him, Lew was trying to explain – and to excuse himself, maybe. But what it came down to, and Lew saw this clearly enough, was a hopeless case of wrong choice and bad decisions. The house and the garage were in the wrong place, too close to people and too close to the road. The din of metalwork would bring neighbours running. And now the garage itself was half open to the sky.

'I feel rotten,' he admitted ruefully. 'I certainly fucked it up. Waste of time, waste of money, and nothing done. I've been stumbling around here like a fool, and now this storm has dealt me the final knockout blow.'

'Come on, man, cheer up,' Jeff rallied him, giving him a friendly punch. 'Take a cool look. Even if everything had been perfect, once the storm hit the garage we were out of business here. But there are other garages, even in Morocco. In fact, Lhassen's been telling me he knows a pretty good place – decent house, isolated garage. While he looks into it, let's go up in the mountains to Lhassen's place and cut loose for a couple of weeks. Sort ourselves out. We're not time-and-motion men.'

*

Going off to the mountains – Lew was pleased with the sound of that. Sounded like winter sports in Val d'Isère or St Moritz. Before he went, though, Lew had money to change. This was always a tricky moment, changing handfuls of foreign currency, often in some hick-town bank, so suspicious that the jumpy guard with a rusty .38 might shoot you, if the bank teller who could barely count didn't rob you blind first. Large notes, which smugglers liked to carry for convenience, laid you open to doubt and fraud. The US 100-dollar bill was the favourite, universally recognized and used, but also widely counterfeited. There you were with fistfuls of assorted notes, and who knew when someone – usually a bank – might have slipped you a counterfeit? Clerks in the booth pawed through notes, looking as if they knew a thing or two, and occasionally they did know enough to pick out a forgery that you had missed through ignorance or haste.

Recently, that had happened to one of Lew's colleagues, a Czech who had reasons for reticence and obfuscation, having hopped over the Iron Curtain possessing only very dubious French papers. The job of drug courier, given what life had taught him, was about the best business he could find. He had been changing a large amount in a Tangier bank among which there was a fake 100-dollar bill. Arrested, he spent several days in a cell before a natural talent for subversion and double-dealing, well practised among the student opposition in Prague, found a way to bribe two senior policemen and an Interpol agent. It was a lesson well learnt, although it cost him plenty.

On this occasion Lhassen offered to go with Lew to the bank, to sort out language problems, but even more to show that they were both working in the same field. Two slovenly militia guards slouched in the doorway, fingering automatics in holsters. Lhassen brushed them aside with a stiff shot of sharp-sounding Arabic. Gave them something to make their ears tingle. At the counter Lew pushed his money – this time it was West German marks – into the cage where a youth with a long face and a mouthful of rotting teeth presided. For several moments the youth switched his eyes between Lew's face and the money, his hands crawling towards but not yet touching the wad. Then he looked at

Lhassen, recognizing a fellow countryman, and said something in Arabic.

'Don't you speak Spanish?' Lhassen answered in that tongue. 'You can see that this gentleman is a foreigner.'

'Why should I?' the youth answered sulkily but in Spanish. 'We are not in Spain. Who is this man?'

'A customer.'

'He has lots of money. Foreign money.'

'So what? You make a profit on the exchange. It's business for the bank.'

'None the less . . . It's a headache, all that counting and checking.'

'So get on with it,' Lhassen said contemptuously. 'Just do it.'

The youth looked behind him to a desk where a little fat man, like a stunted Oliver Hardy, worked at a ledger that went the full width of his desk. The fat man did not look up, so the youth sighed and started on the money. He counted it carefully, losing his place twice, and made jottings of currency and amounts. Then he completed a form in quadruplicate, using a carbon that had almost disintegrated. He tested his calculations nervously and wrote in the final amounts of the exchange. Taking the money, the paperwork and Lew's passport he sidled over to the fat man's desk, approaching at a tangent as if fearing a frontal assault, even a gunshot. But the fatty did not pause in his ledger entries, and only when he came to the end of a column – you knew that he would never be really finished – did he reach for the papers.

He examined each one slowly, counting the money, scrutinizing the forms, turning each page of the passport, while the youth, back in his cage, re-checked his figures. Fatty did some mathematics, which must have agreed with the youth's calculations. The boss grunted, initialled each copy with a flourish, shoved it all to the edge of the desk, and returned to his ledger. Not once had he raised his head, or even looked up.

Now the youth was beaming, showing too many decaying teeth. He gave Lew a thumbs-up. They were on the same side now. They had both been sweating it.

KETAMA

They took a taxi from Tangier, an old grey Mercedes, extremely neat and clean and smart enough to set out on a plinth, though the interior smelt of that kind of deodorant you spray in the toilet. The driver had light coffee-coloured skin and a round handsome face that reminded Lew of Joe Louis, the old Brown Bomber. Lew didn't see much of the face since he sat behind the driver, with a view of tight curly hair and little tidy ears flat against the head. Outside, in the fading evening, the road was entering a contest with the mountains, heaving itself through cracks and rifts of harsh country until night closed off the more scary slides and precipices and all Lew knew of the journey was a further two hours of lurching and jolting and the low-gear groan of the engine.

The taxi passed through Ketama without Lew noticing it. Then, about four kilometres beyond, Lhassen in the front seat indicated a turn-off, and they followed a narrow, muddy track for another couple of kilometres. The taxi driver was muttering; the main road was bad enough, but this unpaved lane of mire and muck and holes did his beautiful vehicle no good.

They emerged from the car into a clear, chilly night, under a sky friendly with stars trying to crowd out a half-moon. From somewhere below came a sound of running water. They descended a steep, slippery switchback trail, placing their feet cautiously behind the beam of a flashlight. In the pale moon the landscape was indistinct, humps and swells rising out of darkness in which gleamed a few luminous patches that Lew took to be pools of water and discovered later, by daylight, to be moonlight on corrugated-tin roofs. From far below the bobbing light of a lantern came to meet them. Lew heard the flat tunk-tunk of a drum and the occasional riff of voices carried upwards. A dog barked, the pack joined in, and then suddenly stopped, as if a plug had been pulled. Lew caught the vagrant smell of woodsmoke, an aromatic smell of burning cedar.

The lantern arrived, carried by a boy who, without a word, fell in at the rear of the little column. The path straightened and the slope eased to level ground, and then, quite suddenly, Lew realized that they were within walls. Lhassen pushed open a door crying out, 'Ah-Fatma! Ah-Fatma!'

They entered a long narrow room, sparsely furnished, lit by two paraffin storm lanterns and a couple of incandescent pressure lamps. The light was wavering, the pressure lamps hissed, and the shadows shifted uneasily. Four men and three women rose to greet them, but only the wife, Fatma, came forward. She smiled at Jeff, whom she knew, and offered Lew a welcoming gesture, the palm of the hand opened, the eyes lowered and then suddenly raised in a full look. Nothing brazen, but a look that was steady, candid and serene. She stood, dignified, yet somehow pliant and easy. To Lew she seemed to be saying, 'Here I am, my husband's woman, mother to my children, mistress of this household. It is enough.'

Lew looked away quickly. He was surprised by such candour, in this time and place. He thought he might be blushing, and he was glad the dim light veiled him.

And before he could quite recover himself one of the other women in the room, a tall, bony servant in careworn middle age, dropped to her knees, grasped his hand and brought it to her mouth. For one tangled moment, such was his anxiety, Lew thought she might lick it or bite it. She kissed it gently, with rough chapped lips.

Lhassen was giving orders now, a much steadier man than he had been before, at home at last and very conscious of his place. The wildness had gone out of him, though he still had his eye on his foreign guests and some part of the haughty manner was put on for their benefit.

'*Jefe*, give them your shoes. Look how wet and muddy your feet are. Throw your bags and coats over there, behind the bed. Here, sit close to the stove. Soon we will eat.'

He barked out some orders in his local Berber dialect and his people snapped to it.

The far end of the narrow room was almost blocked by a big bed with a cradle beside it. Behind the bed was a sort of platform or loft, up five steps of a little ladder, which seemed to be used as a store room or junk room. Jeff tossed his coat and bag on to the platform and reached out for Lew's things. Lew gave up his coat but was reluctant to let go of his shoulder bag, which was full of money. Jeff took it from him firmly and threw it on the pile, his reproachful look saying there was neither distrust nor suspicion within this household. Everything was safe. Once more Lew blushed, at the treachery of his own instinct.

They sat on a low couch covered by a Berber rug in warm rosy colours.

Sheepskins lay under their feet. A barrel stove with a long tin pipe angled through the wall kept the room comfortable. Once more the aroma of smouldering cedar. A baby slept in the cradle and a child stirred on the big bed. Fatma and two servant women squatted around a single-burner camping stove. The younger servant, a hefty, pretty girl, with skin as clear as a fresh snowfall, went up and down the ladder to the storeroom with the agility of a cat. As she went, Lew kept half an eye on his shoulder bag. He scolded himself for doing so, but he couldn't help it.

Jeff began preparing a pipe on a small brass table while an aroma of dark coffee crept over from the stove. The coffee arrived in steaming glasses, the liquid hot and excessively sweet, brought by the teenage boy who had met them on the path with the lantern. After the coffee, he came back with dishes piled with little cakes and biscuits, a bowl of tangerines, one of raisins, and another of mixed almonds and walnuts. Jeff passed the pipe around, though all but Lew declined it. The men turned their faces away behind upheld hands. Too strong, they said, it dissolved the brain.

Lhassen's eyes missed nothing, taking note of the preparation and service of the food. Now that he was the master at home he was calm and serious, but ready to make the whip sting, if necessary. He was still joking with his pal Jeff, but with Lew he was attentive and almost courtly.

'Señor Luis, are you warm enough? Then some more coffee? Here, try another of these honey cakes. No? Perhaps a proper meal is what you need, something with meat.'

Lew thought he was gorging himself, but if he paused between a biscuit and a tangerine Lhassen leaned towards him with a frown, 'Eat, please eat, Señor Luis. You don't like it? Eat.'

Lew was doing his best, though he didn't like to stuff himself. He was conscious that all eyes in the room, save for those of the women around the stove, were on him. The stares were open, unabashed, critical and prolonged. A trial by scrutiny. When he met a look full on, the man did not glance away. Lew decided he was in strange territory between impertinence and guilelessness, a no man's land for Western conduct. And just when he was getting red and flustered, a bearded elder, who was giving him unwavering attention, laid on him a gold-toothed smile of sweet benevolence.

Later, when he had got his nerve back, Lew realized that his eating habits had been amiss, even offensive. There he was, with the coffee glass in his right hand and eating titbits with his left. The left hand, he should have known, was for other, unclean business.

People began to come and go in the room, curious but mostly silent. Come to see the new specimen from the barely comprehensible world, making a spectacle of himself. Some shook hands, stiff and formal, as if in some old ritual whose form was important but meaning obscure. After the handshake, some touched their fingers to the heart, and some kissed their fingertips before touching the heart. They did not speak to Jeff or Lew, it was not their place to do so.

Who was who was never clear, men – no further women – coming in and out of the shadows. Only two were brought forward to meet Lew. One was Lhassen's father, a lofty figure in a beige djellaba and a puffy white turban that added inches to his height. He had a patrician look, remote and above the fray, weighted with years – he was, Lew learnt, only about sixty – one who made justice work and reaped respect. His welcome to Lew, translated by Lhassen from Berber dialect, sounded like rhetoric from a lost senatorial age; his smile displayed teeth you would be keen to avoid.

The other man introduced was a much more approachable figure, a tall soft-looking character in a knitted skullcap. A man with a smiling face you could hardly look at without smiling yourself, a round moonface with a slight oriental cast and a faint resemblance to Chairman Mao. This was Slhemen, Lhassen's brother-in-law, a great favourite with Jeff who claimed he was the peacemaker, the intermediary in feuds before they went mean and murderous, as happened too often among the mountain tribes. He was also the best craftsman for miles around, patient, careful and exact among workers who tended to lose heart at difficulties and saw mistakes as the inevitable judgment of Allah on human presumption.

Slhemen also spoke only the local dialect. Lew found immediately that it did not matter. Who could doubt the intent of that open and companionable face? Slhemen took his long-stemmed pipe and a little packet of *kif* from the hood of his djellaba and smoked. Then he refilled the pipe and passed it to Lew. Jeff was watching with approval.

'What do you think, Lew?' he said. 'Could anything be better?'

Jeff was sailing free, and the voyage was good. Up ahead, some harbour of fraternity awaited him.

Lew, though new to this scene, was inclined to think that he too was on a similar journey. He drew on Slhemen's pipe, which tasted sweet, almost perfumed. He knew that strictly speaking *kif* was just marijuana – the resin-producing flowers and seed-pods of cannabis, finely chopped until almost a powder. He was giving this *kif* some serious attention, seeing how it stood up against the much stronger hashish.

'Learning some discrimination at last?' Jeff said, watching the thoughts cross his friend's face.

Lew grinned, 'About time, eh? I was thinking that we live for moments of revelation that are not easy to come by. I see now that good *kif* is like the best champagne while good hash has the punch and subtlety of a fifteen-year-old malt whisky.'

He found that made sense, at least for the time being. But now he was noticing the neat and dexterous way that Slhemen, when the pipe was finished, blew down the stem and made a little live coal leap out with a plop. That seemed part of the secret too. He began practising on the next pipe, much to Slhemen's delight. It did no harm to Lew's mood.

*

In the long shadowy room, men kept coming and going, joining and leaving a conversation that never ceased, talking quietly in their dark tongue. Lhassen's father had a soft, gravelly voice, like a distant stream in a rocky chute. The old gentleman had kicked off his slippers and sat crossed-legged, fondling his toes and pink heels. Looking at those extremities Lew had no doubt that Lhassen was his father's son. Their toes were identical, in particular the big toe, which was like a flattened light bulb.

Lew allowed himself to slide forward from the couch to the sheepskins on the floor. The warm floor seemed all he needed for his well-being. Immediately, Lhassen showed concern.

'Señor Luis, you are not comfortable? Do not fatigue yourself, please.' He clapped his hands for the teenage youth. 'Here, this boy will bring you pillows.'

'No, it's no bother.' Lew stretched himself luxuriously on the sheepskin. 'I prefer the floor. The world from down here is just perfect.'

And surveying his surroundings Lew could think of no improvement. Furniture and possessions were few but there was nothing mean or ill-considered about them. None of the confusion and pointless excess, the bric-a-brac and jumble of so many Western rooms. The warm glow of the barrel stove was a focal point, the humans at ease gave the room meaning.

Then Lew was suddenly conscious of himself, reclining indolently there, in a strange house with a strange people whose language he understood not at all, everything more alien than anything he had ever encountered before. Yet he was completely relaxed and more at peace with himself than he had known for a long time. More than an hour had gone since he had thought of his shoulder bag and his money. He was safe and so were they. He could think of no other situation that had given him such a feeling of contented security as being a guest in this Berber home.

He saw Jeff yawn and rub his eyes. He nudged Lew with his foot and they rose together, making no commotion other than a quiet murmur of thanks to Lhassen. Jeff, who knew the way, took them into a courtyard and then into a cold chamber with a pile of woollen and goat-hair blankets as thick as carpets. They rolled themselves into two bundles and were asleep within minutes.

Trans-Europe Express

Now that she was on her way she was no longer sure why she was going. Anders drove her down to Copenhagen, to catch the train south, talking most of the time with his studious, invincible logic, as if human conduct were simply a matter of levers, cogs and pulleys – a Newtonian model. Pull the correct handle and the bells jangled, the lights flashed. Bingo, jackpot!

After a while she was no longer listening. She stared out of the window, looking at nothing much, Swedish countryside, trees, lakes, moorland, fields, rocks amid which the people so successfully secluded themselves. To her – an outsider – it seemed so lonely, almost heartbreakingly so.

It took Anders a while to notice. He glanced at her and saw that she was as far away as the horizon. 'Vera,' he said then, with reproach, 'I fear you are not listening.'

She gave her head a guilty shake and forced herself back to the present. 'I'm sorry,' she sighed, 'I've not been very polite, have I?'

She began trying to think how she could address Anders's many cares and problems. Most likely, he needed nothing more than a friendly nod, a light touch on the arm. But on the matters that worried him she saw that she had nothing to offer. No advice, no suggestions, not even a smile of encouragement.

'I'm thinking about Lew,' she said at last, 'and my thoughts are not very clear.'

Anders, confronted by an army of sullen facts, was busy in his mind shuffling practical measures – stratagems, tactics, methods, transports, routes, payments, bribes. Vera could make out very little in that territory. What she saw mostly was Lew Holle, a figure of shifting attributes whose intentions, motives and desires she could not quite fix. She did not want to be in the way, for Anders or Lew, but on quaking ground she was afraid she might stumble and sink. She might need to be rescued herself, an extra burden that nobody needed.

She gave up the struggle for anything relevant, or even intelligent, to say. 'Forgive me, Anders,' she mumbled, 'I'm rather tired. I think I'll sleep for a while.'

*

Then, finally on the train, she found that she was tired. The train timetable ahead looked interminable – she almost said inevitable, which was even harder to face.

But now sleep eluded her. The compartment was full and stuffy. She thought she detected in her fellow travellers – no doubt an average spread of average people – a bourgeois peace and satisfaction that worried and annoyed her. There were reasons to protest in this complacent world, though she herself knew none of the words of revolution.

On the long leg to Paris she dozed on and off, barely aware of the changing faces of the other passengers. When she was awake she was as close to dreaming as made no difference. A brisk lady, smartly dressed, questioned her in several languages, in which she caught only the word *Paris*. Speaking neither German nor French, Vera waited for English to come up; yet when it did she was so muddled by what had gone before that she could only gape, her mind vacant. Paris did not seem to register in her lexicon. The brisk lady, staring puzzled into Vera's dark lenses, gave her up as an imbecile.

From Paris, she might have taken the night train, but she wanted a bed with sheets, and a pillow under her head. On the Metro to Montparnasse, where she hoped to find a cheap hotel by the station, she was surprised by the number of dark faces. Brown faces from Algeria and North Africa, black faces from French territories *outremer*. She judged by their clothes that obviously they were not rich, and perhaps not happy, but most had an air of patient resignation that suggested hope and endurance. An inner strength, she thought, and wondered if it might be misdirected. Some of the coloured youths – both brown and black – seemed prickly enough.

In the morning she was up early with plenty of spare time before her train. Her cheap hotel, where she'd shared her room with some inquisitive bugs, was no place to hang around, so she walked at random out into a mild day. She went towards the river, trying to join patches of green space together, by way of the Luxembourg Gardens to the Jardin des Plantes. Somewhere in her wanderings she came across a big mosque, and the Islamic tilt it gave to the surrounding life was another surprise. Arab script on shopfronts, bookshops displaying covers with sensuous squiggles, a café with a bubble pipe in the window, travel agents with trips to places she had never heard of. She wished she had questioned Lew about these ethnic drifts, why these Arabic-speakers were up here in Paris, and he was down there in Morocco. Then she just wanted to talk to Lew, period. They'd had some good days – and nights – in their short time together, but what in fact had they spoken about?

That realization began to depress her and she wandered some more, seeking diversion, which she found after a while in a crowded student café off the Rue Mouffetard. At a long table students jostled each other in a friendly ribald way to make space for her. She did not mind; it was what she needed – the impersonal cheekiness of the young in which she knew she was safe.

As it turned out, she found herself sitting next to a Tunisian. About twenty years old with soulful doe-eyes and a forlorn smile. They struggled into conversation, he trying French, which was hopeless, then discovering that they could both manage a simple mix of English and Spanish. He seemed to have nothing in mind except friendliness – perhaps he was as momentarily bereft as she was – and when the conversation stalled he offered her a joint. In this place, with many openly smoking it, marijuana was hardly off limits, so she took it.

Soon she felt better. She began to reorder her thoughts, seeing that the flip side of insecurity and doubt might be her own necessary development, and that heartache was often the coin you paid for rare and intense moments. She took another long draw on the joint before handing it back to the young Tunisian.

She felt ready now to put another question to the absent Lew Holle. What would he say, she wondered, to this thought, that they were just a couple of simple dope-fiends, taking refuge from life in fright and flight, running towards the overwhelming ocean in which they might float, or drown? 'Surely not,' she said aloud, unable to stop herself, and then she laughed.

She shook herself, like a dog shivering, and found that all the responses required to get her through this journey were now in place. She walked peacefully to the station and settled into the train, ready for the dark shore beyond and what it might bring.

KETAMA

Lew walked out next morning into pure light, pure air. For a moment, it stopped him dead. He had known nothing like it since the fleeting days of his youth, watching the great tides rip in the Bay of Fundy, and the wind jiggling nervously above. Or later, in the Rockies, when the Canadian Pacific train halted on an early summer morning at Revelstoke, and the sun was announcing itself solemnly over the eastern peaks and airs as chill as icicles coursed off the slopes ruffling the young leaves of the birch trees. Now again he saw mountains on all sides, their flanks forested with cedar, and the far ranges capped with snow. It made him reel a bit, the weight of the memory, and the sudden realization of what he had forgone for so many years.

The house stood on the edge of one of the many irregular fissures that split the coastal range. Lew was in the yard in the angle of the two low wings of the house, his feet in the churned muck of the cold months in which misallied poultry pecked for cannabis seeds. In the small canyon below, a rushing stream turned sharply north, battering seaward over a rocky bed. To the east of the stream the slope was rugged and precipitous; to the west was a more gradual but still steep rise from which a pattern of little terraced fields had been gouged. Dotted about were the dwellings of tiny farms, earth-coloured, unwhitewashed, so married to the humps and rocks of the land that they looked like humps or rocks themselves.

All around was a dense, lush winter green, on the high ranges the sombre hue of the cedars, in the fields from where the harvest had been cleared, the lighter green of the grass and weeds displacing the rich emerald of cannabis, Ketama's chief and most profitable crop.

*

Each day in the mountains began with a simple routine. He rose early, stepping out into cold air, his skin tingling, holding soap, towel, toothbrush and toilet paper, and then he headed upstream, following a path along an irrigation ditch. Shards of ice still glazed the puddles, though the night frost was melting away leaving the path slick and slippery. The path led to the bed of the canyon where the stream was hurrying and the bottom-land, scoured by flood and run-off and winter violence, was rough with boulders and scrub. Behind every boulder large enough to hide a crouching man was evidence of temporary occupation and the detritus of the bowel. It seemed as if strange sheep had pastured there, toilet paper clinging to bushes like tufts of wool.

Treading carefully Lew dabbled by the water edge, brushing his teeth, then he stripped to the waist and dashed handfuls of the snow-fed current against his face and chest, sending all his pores into shock. He stood there gasping and chattering but even his damaged jaw felt braced and better for it; it was like the beginning of the world, a new baptism each day. He drew in the air, cramming his lungs, deep breath after deep breath. Way below, clustered around a flat rock sticking out of the water, women were already up to their knees in the stream, beating washing against the rock. Seeing that earthy, almost primal labour, then he too was ready for the day.

He returned to the house with a good appetite for a breakfast of coffee and fried unleavened bread, or batter, or a heavy, sweet, honeycomb-textured pancake soaked in oil. And the rest of the day was partitioned by great bouts of eating accompanied by the insistent refrain from Lhassen, 'Eat, Señor Luis, please eat.'

All through the day the human traffic came and went in the main room of the farmhouse, men and boys come to satisfy their curiosity. These visitors rated no special attention, spectators at an intimate mystery whose enactment they did not understand but whose forms and colours somehow pleased them. They sat silently against the wall, in the outer circle, and scratched and yawned and smiled and went away. From time to time important men of the neighbourhood visited, and then all present were drawn into another rite of eating.

'Must we?' Lew groaned to Jeff, rubbing his distended belly.

'Yes, go ahead.' Jeff replied firmly. 'Refusal is out of the question.'

The nuts, the fruits, the little bits of sticky pastry, the many glasses of coffee – that was just the light workout, to tone up the system for the main events. These took place at lunch and dinner. Then Lhassen went around the men with a basin and a dented kettle, pouring water over the hands of each person.

They gathered around the table on which was the single large bowl of the meal, with as many side dishes as the women cared to provide, the number of dishes rising with the importance of the guests. The custom was that the men ate alone, and then the remains in the bowl, from which the choicest bits had been robbed, were passed back for the women and children, a practice known as *baraka* or blessing, a term that sounded cruelly ironical to Lew. But at Jeff's entreaty, when he and Lew were present at table, Fatma was allowed to join the men, sometimes with her youngest child – a baby of about a year – still bound in a shawl on her back.

The big communal bowl contained stew, or couscous with scraps of meat and chopped vegetables, or there was a large dish of braised or roasted meat, mutton or goat. The couscous was usually millet, coarse and grey, often a little gritty between the teeth. Lhassen divided round, flat girdle cakes of barley or millet. Fatma's baby, with a dreamy eye on busy mouths, slobbered on her shoulder.

The dogs slobbered too, a couple of rangy beasts creeping forward tremulously to catch bits of bone or gristle or fat tossed their way. A swift kick sent them yapping if they strayed too close. Cats, if they were discreet, were permitted under the table itself. Sometimes Lew felt them there, rubbing stealthily against his shin.

'Eat,' Lhassen cried from across the table. 'Señor Luis, eat meat!'

Lew was uncomfortably replete and his mouth was always full, yet he could not avoid this reproach for lack of appetite.

*

To escape the painful duty of eating Lew and Jeff took long walks, most often up the ravine in which the river ran, climbing steadily on to more open mountain. It was the easiest course in this gnarled terrain, if they wished to avoid the human paths and the frank looks of surprise and wonder that followed them there. It was an instinct with Jeff, which Lew was still learning, not to be noticeable. Be one of the crowd, or if there were no crowd, no more than a line in the dust. Not easy to do, in these circumstances, where foreigners stood out like freaks in a circus.

After a couple of hours of tough hiking they were tired enough to rest, collapsing on the ground and congratulating themselves that they had sweated off some of the excess calories. To the north, the view had opened up, the long sweep of the coast and the fractured waves of the Mediterranean biting the sands.

'What are we doing here?' said Lew thoughtfully, hurling a stone towards the distant blur of the sea.

'You know as well as I do,' Jeff replied.

'Yes, but this is nothing like the thing I know as trade or business. These people are after money, of course, but something else is going on.'

'You've seen that, have you?' Jeff smiled, with heavy irony. 'The feeling that humans matter more than the money in their pockets? I'm no professor, but Anders laid it out for me a while ago. What we have here is a different kind of commerce – Anders called it "pre-capitalist relations". It means humans count more than their cash. But don't kid yourself. Cash matters too. These are hard men, reined in and humanized by tradition, culture, religion – a long-held way of life that supplies sufficient reasons for doing things. Keep to the rules. Step badly out of line and the relationship breaks, and then all the cash in the world won't save you. They'll blow you away as soon as look at you.'

They stared at the far sea in moody silence. Lew was still feeling a rumble in the gut. Then Jeff sighed.

'I suppose we'd better go down,' he said with some desperation in his voice, 'and eat some more.'

*

Along with the feasts, there were obligatory visits. They were invited to Lhassen's father's house, another jumble of terracotta-coloured buildings, squatting about a hundred feet up the hillside above Lhassen's own house, earthbound, but looking dangerously likely to shift moorings in any violent storm. Lhassen's mother, a small, thin, bony woman with a hatchet face and a sharp tongue, served them the coffee and the sticky hits of unnecessary food they had come to fear. She was fit and energetic and never idle, and Lew saw at once how her son took after her, the same narrow purpose, the same determination and restlessness. Often, during his walks on the mountain, Lew saw her patching fences with backloads of branches and brushwood that she carried down rough scree and vertiginous paths. In the multi-coloured flounces of her Berber dress, her back hooped and straining, she looked like a harlequin set to hard labour, consoled by the jangle of her large earrings and many bracelets.

Lhassen's father – the patriarch – shared his house with his daughter, Lhassen's sister, and her husband, the genial moon-faced Slhemen. Another invitation, more eating. The sister was a timid creature who had given Slhemen no children. She set a tray of silver tea utensils in front of her husband and returned to the shadows, as if invisibility was the penalty for a barren womb. The first taste of fresh mint tea was always delicious. From there, the taste cloyed fast, and by the last dregs Lew was nearly ready to retch.

When the civilities were done, and a few polite belches had been squeezed out, Lhassen came up the hill to join them. He and his brother-in-law led the way to a dim back room, entered only through the chamber where the patriarch slept. There, collected together at last, was their hashish, the merchandise on which Jeff had already made a down payment, the rest of the price to be handed over when the assignment was weighed and the quality assessed, and the final delivery completed. It was piled like cordwood, in plastic sacks each about the size of a gross German sausage, containing roughly a kilo and as hard as stone.

*

In these lazy days Jeff Gartree was giving Lew some tuition. Coloured the picture for him, though the outlines had been clear enough for some time. Lew knew what his job was and that he could do it.

According to Jeff, people in pursuit of certain desires and satisfactions faced, historically, problems of practice. In overcoming these they converge upon solutions that were similar, though subtly different in different times and places. To know and understand these practices, Jeff implied, meant taking notes on the definition of culture. Lew was interested.

Here was how it went. In general, extracting hash depended on the nature of the cannabis plant, which varied widely from one land to another, and upon local tradition.

In Morocco the method was to rub the resinous parts of the plant lightly on the surface of a cotton cloth stretched tight over a wide, shallow bowl. Quality depended on the weave of the cloth – not too loose – and on the force of the hand – not too heavy. Above all, the process called for patience and delicacy.

And here Jeff shook his head. 'The trouble in these mountains,' he said, 'is a lack of useful tradition. These are great people, men you can deal with and grow to like. Experienced heads, too, from far back. But they are users of *kif* not hash. Hash is relatively new here, introduced about the beginning of the fifties by enterprising Europeans who wanted the stronger stuff. It's not much used by the native population. For ordinary working stiffs, who rely on *kif* to get them through the day or to smooth out an evening, hash is too potent and too expensive. Only the better-off urban classes can afford it. With *kif*, one decent-sized plant might provide a week's smoking. It takes about ninety kilos of plant to make just one kilo of top-quality hash, the kind called *zero-zero*.'

Jeff didn't like to criticize people who had become his friends, but he was in business and that had forced him to recognize their limitations.

'It's like this,' he said. 'We might as well ask ordinary peasant winegrowers to make a fine cognac, though they don't even drink brandy. We could help them out, maybe, if we were tactful. But Lhassen gets his resin from many other farmers, over a wide area. We can't meddle there. The vital step, the sifting of the resin, is way outside our control.'

*

In the dim back room, a room smelling sweet and sweaty, they were ready to get down to business. But first Lhassen went to fetch Fatma. Over the years Lhassen had become a fair judge of quality, but his wife was nearly infallible. In the room Jeff chose a few of the plastic packages at random. One by one he split them open, crumbling a little of the hard-packed content into his hand where it lay almost as fine and light as a buff-coloured face powder.

Cupped in the closed hand, the powder went soft and sticky from body heat and could be kneaded into a ball. When it was cold the ball was hard enough to drop on the floor without breaking and the colour was now a deep reddish-brown. Over a match it took fire at once and burned with a blue flame, the smoke pungent and smelling a little of camphor.

That was the first sign – the aroma. Jeff was rocking on his feet, his eyes closed, sniffling deeply. The connoisseur, out of this world. And the others were wrinkling their noses in his wake, like dogs taking it in turns at a gatepost. Then Jeff's eyes snapped open, and he seemed unfocused for a second or two. A shy pleasure spread over his face, the signal for everyone to smile. Lhassen was almost laughing with relief, nodding his head, the child who had put his hand up, tackled the tough question, and got it right.

But Jeff was not quite satisfied. He broke off a little piece and passed it to Fatma. By tradition, she – a woman – was not permitted to use cannabis. But her senses were all the keener for that, not dulled by familiarity or overuse.

Fatma was delicately made in most respects, with the face of an unblemished icon, but her hands were large and coarse – working hands, rough and busy. It was her habit to handle things with thumb and forefinger only, the other fingers stylishly raised, a gesture that lent grace to large hands. She took the sample as gently as a bishop fingering the communion wafer. She turned it about, squeezed it for texture and consistency, touched it with the tip of her tongue, sniffed it several times. She bided her time, a slight frown on her face. Then she handed the piece back, a sudden smile breaking, illuminating the path to take.

'*Zero-zero*,' she said.

Lhassen had been holding his breath and now he could let it go. 'You see?' he grinned. 'Always she knows. If it is no good she makes a bad face and spits.'

*

In the evening they walked an hour to Ketama, to celebrate with a drink. Lhassen stayed behind, though he dearly liked to drink. He was leery of the place, knowing it to be an invitation to grief.

Ketama itself was nothing – a dangerous nothing – little more than a crossroads and a slatternly, government-built hotel, with a garage across the way, and dirt blowing in four directions. Everything that was bad about the trade in cannabis had congealed there. The malice, deceit and brutality of the suppliers, the ignorance, stupidity and arrogance of the buyers, and the greed of both. Jeff Gartree was well aware of the reputation, but he was an old hand and understood the workings of the place, the swirls and undercurrents of viciousness and banality. In these waters he kept his little ship of business tight and seaworthy.

The hotel bar stocked some good and unusual North African wines and a bottle or two of decent scotch; and that, in this Muslim land, was a large attraction. But you took your chances. If you were unlucky you were always likely to meet someone you would regret. For Jeff, that was part of the fun: the chase over rough ground and evil-looking fences.

'Oh, it's a menagerie of monsters in here,' he told Lew cheerfully as they went in the door. 'Double-dealers, undercover cops, informers, provocateurs, mountebanks, fantasists, crooks and just plain cutthroats.' He intended nothing showy. 'We'll just have a couple of drinks, and then escape out the back door.'

On the second glass of wine their luck ran out. A little creature crept up on them with a melancholic European in tow, his clothes in the regulation distress of a hash-head. The little man – just about five foot tall – made a living as a middleman between the Rif and the city, luring Western prospects and delivering them at the doorstep of the larger growers. He was a Berber, originally from a Rif household, and he had some residual credit in the mountains for that; his miserable frame and pinched, appealing face also won him some local sympathy. Moreover, he was a virtuoso of languages, speaking several Romance tongues, a fair bit of English and a smattering of German. His name was Ahmed. He had his uses, and he was reasonably honest, but he was a pest. Lhassen had used him from time to time, and he had brought foreigners to Lhassen's farm. Jeff, who liked to keep his own deals well away from the light, distrusted him completely.

But now Ahmed obviously had a client, this sorry-looking European with a lugubrious face that didn't seem to know where to turn. He stood diffidently two steps behind the Berber, his sad eyes like a sweeping periscope above the little man's head.

As they approached Jeff took one look at the pair, turned back to his wine and said abruptly, 'Go away.'

'But I come to see Lhassen,' Ahmed protested. 'I hear you stay with him, but he is my friend. I have someone – one of you people – he like to meet. This man here, he is a Frenchman, he say his name is Olivier,' – a chuckle here, implying that might not be the case – 'and he wish to buy. I think my friend Lhassen will be interested, yes?'

Jeff was silent. He was almost certain that Lhassen *would* be interested. Despite his close connection with Jeff, Lhassen was not the man to spurn the chance of a sale. Jeff glanced again at the Frenchman and saw nothing further that he wanted to know. The man whose name might be Olivier stared blankly into the distance. He did not need this embarrassment.

'Okay, I can't stop you coming to the farm,' Jeff said reluctantly. 'We're going back soon and I'll tell Lhassen you're coming. Stay here in the hotel tonight. It takes a while to get used to the idea that you're going to be around.'

*

They came the next day, about midday, trudging up the path, a lopsided duo, a long Quixote following a perky dwarf. Lhassen had been warned and he was not wholly pleased. He wanted to sell, yes, but at the moment he had his best customer, Jeff, on his hands, and several busy things to do before he could send Jeff away satisfied. The *zero zero* had to be weighed, pressed and packed. And now that this European circus – Jeff and Lew – was about to depart for another year, latecomers were hurrying in for a view. It was, Lew reflected, more or less a harvest festival, the community rejoicing in Lhassen's good fortune, knowing that money would spread around in this rigorously poor place for another year. They wanted to touch the good fortune, figuratively and sometimes in practice, an unknown hand sliding over Jeff's sleeve or the hem of Lew's coat.

So the main room of the farmhouse was often as crowded as a roost of starlings at sundown. Fatma's brother had arrived bringing with him two mountain men from a Berber tribe of the High Atlas. The young brother, as handsome as his sister, smoked *kif* at a fierce rate, read the Koran, followed the Prophet's teaching, abstained from alcohol and pork. He was a quiet lad, an uncomplicated Puritan, hardly more than a ghost in the corner under a pall of pungent smoke. One of the mountain men, who smoked *kif* but had never tried hash, was offered Lew's pipe, which he accepted as if it were mischief of a high order. He was very animated for while, then his eyes drooped. He climbed on to the big bed, pulled the hood of his djellaba over his head and was heard from no more. He and his companion were itinerant masons, summoned (now that Jeff and Lew were almost ready to leave) to install a stove in the room where the foreigners slept. In half a day the job was done and they strode off in a light rain, each with an old sack over his head.

Amid all this press of people Ahmed and the Frenchman felt out of things, unable to get a toehold in the events of the house. The mood was high and lighthearted and they were floundering along behind, in interior gloom. They looked unhappy; it was hard to think that the Frenchman had ever been otherwise. Lhassen had little time to spare them, especially when he learnt that the Frenchman wanted only 10 kilos of second-grade hash, on which he hoped to make more profit than on 5 kilos of the top quality. Lhassen would sell to them, when he was ready, but Lew could see that he despised this European for his forlorn face, his runny nose and his lame ambition.

Everywhere, the Frenchman – Olivier – seemed to be in the way. Little Ahmed, anxious that his client might lose heart and skip, kept tight on his heels, whining about the effort he had put into this deal, about his poverty and the purity of his motives. 'Not for myself,' he lamented, 'it is for my mother. She is so old and poor. I try to make some money for her.' Even Olivier had the sense to look dubious.

He annoyed Jeff and Lew, looking for reassurance, having little better to do. He was in constant fear of being swindled. He asked Lew for a British or an American coin, to stamp each block of his hash, so that it could not be switched on him before delivery.

'What do you think?' he asked Jeff pathetically. 'Would they do that here? Switch the blocks? Cheat me?'

'In principle, yes,' Jeff replied confidently. 'But if you wish to trade here again you must make a judgement and take a chance. You must trust Lhassen, not insult him. He's better than you think.'

Lew was not sure that it was that simple. What would have happened to himself, he wondered, if he had come to the Rif alone, nervous and a newcomer, without the protecting hand of Jeff?

'I hear such strange stories,' Olivier moaned, 'It is hard to be confident. I must be cautious. Here in the Rif – maybe not on this farm – an Italian bought sixty kilos. He found it was mainly camel shit. He knifed the middleman, luckily not dead, but causing much trouble for everyone. Another time, I hear of a huge deal, ten thousand dollars worth, packed, transported and safely delivered in New York. It was nothing but henna. I can't afford to take these chances.'

'Chances?' Jeff said, turning on the Frenchman a speculative eye. 'What do you think you're handling? Lollipops, or dried figs? Make up your mind, are you a drug-runner or a pussyfooting accountant?'

'I think,' Lew put in quietly, 'he genuinely doesn't know.' He said it with some sympathy.

*

Once the quality had been assessed, and the price and quantity confirmed, the end of the stay was in sight. Now that money was safely stowed in the small brassbound chest under Lhassen's big bed, within the jurisdiction of Fatma's all-seeing eye, life was temporarily a carnival. It would get tough again, when the bad face of poverty turned towards them, but this was a good moment.

The pressing of the hash was done by a merry, incompetent crew in a small stable-room, usually home to a domestic mule, a close space now smelling powerfully of the resin warming in a big eathernware bowl over a charcoal brazier. A jolly teenager, loosely related to Lhassen, carelessly spooned the warm resin into cellophane bags until each contained about a quarter kilo and then checked the weight on a filthy battered scales that looked like a find from Roman archaeology. The bags, sealed with cellulose tape, were then pressed in two small book-binding presses that had also been gently heated over a bucket of charcoal.

Very soon after they began work one of the presses jammed and stuck. To the crew, this was neither a disaster nor even annoyance. '*Suerte*,' they shrugged amiably, ready to throw the press in the corner. Machines were made to misbehave, and no one in the household, apart from Slhemen, who was as careful about work as about preparing tea, had the slightest interest in or understanding of machinery. But Lew, who was impatient to get going, gathered whatever tools were to hand and in a couple of hours had the press working again. The crew, who had gladly stopped work to watch his progress, was impressed. 'I see you are very talented,' said Lhassen, with real admiration.

Admiration did nothing to improve performance, however. The presses were still allowed to get too hot, the cellophane bubbled and the hash was scorched. If a block was out of shape, too thick or too thin, no one would think of re-pressing it to a uniform size unless Jeff or Lew complained tactfully to Lhassen, who would then issue some sharp orders in dialect, often accompanied by a cuff on the ear. Even then, the blocks looked stubbornly misshapen, though on average each was about six inches square.

'Pretty shoddy job all round,' Lew grumbled to Jeff, surveying the completed work. From his earliest days Lew had a feeling for craftsmanship.

'Yes,' Jeff agreed, 'it's usually this way. It's part of their charm.' Hearing a light note in his voice, the crew beamed. Looked to each one of them like work well done.

That evening was a celebration. Fatma and the women prepared a special meal, something in imitation of the grand *meshwi* that used to be provided for the caid in the old days. Half a sheep was roasted, the frail ribs of the carcass and the seared head lying next to beautiful mounds of soft wheat *dshisha*. There were side dishes of wild artichoke, and olives in oil, and the cooked stems of mallow, and the tubers called *bquqa*, and roots that had no word for them in Spanish and perhaps not in Arabic. Two elders of the clan were there as special guests. The other diners waited politely, and a little anxiously, while the two served themselves. They took the flat bread and with three dainty fingers of the right hand enfolded a chunk of meat and ate. In a moment, all was well. The tension broke and many hungry hands made haste towards the dish.

Afterwards, an ever-changing press of men sat cross-legged on low couches or reclined on cushions in the suburbs of the room. The Westerners shared a hash pipe while about a third of the others pulled on long *kif* pipes. Lhassen's father, like many elderly Berbers, didn't smoke but took snuff. He kept it in a delicate silver flask wrapped in a handkerchief in the sleeve of his djellaba. He sniffed prodigiously and when the explosions came he looked surprised and wide-eyed, the child who gives a delighted 'Ah' every time the ball bounces.

Talk was constant and general, rising and falling according to the passion of the speaker. The foreigners, though they understood nothing of the language, were tacitly drawn into the hubbub by smiles and nods, and the choicest sallies were translated into Spanish by Lhassen, if he could make sense of them. If not, the shrunken linguist Ahmed proved his use by giving a fuller account in Spanish, French or passable English. The conversation jumped from group to group, almost as if it were a team game, until some orator more persuasive than the rest took over the topic and gave it a shake. And when that subject had been wrung out, and each had had a turn, all sat back, content to have spoken, and quite happy that no agreement had been reached.

While all this was going on, the women of the household sat off in the shadows behind the stove. They kept an eye on the preparation of the coffee and the little after-eats to sweeten the mouth, but they had their own matters to discuss, with the fluttering of henna-stained hands, so that the noisy presence of men beyond seemed like an encumbrance on lives set towards quieter goals and better purpose. Hamel, the big-boned young servant girl, glided around the room, fetching and carrying, chewing bubblegum and rolling her big cow eyes at Jeff. When their eyes met she ducked her head and giggled, and snapped her gum. This annoyed Fatma's brother, the fervent *kif* smoker. Gum-chewing, he said, was a filthy, alien habit, disgusting to look at, and should be banned.

So Jeff took another, longer look at Hamel. In her large way she was a mighty handsome girl, with eyes that seemed to promise unusual sins and skin like burnished copper. She came from somewhere in the High Atlas. Seeing the way she looked at Jeff, Lew asked Lhassen how old she was. About fifteen, he thought, but others in the company had other opinions. In most ways she was certainly mature and well-developed, so back and forth among the men the argument went, taking into account the theoretical nature of womanhood and the ideal stages of growth. As usual, no agreement was reached. And no one thought to ask Hamel herself. If she heard their discussion, she was not bothered. The long-winded guesswork of the men did not disturb her serenity. She snapped her gum, and in her passage around the room edged as close to Jeff as she could get.

'A man could do a lot worse,' Jeff said privately to Lew, as the discussion ended and Hamel swayed her substantial, pleasing butt past Jeff one more time, 'than to buy and marry a girl like that. Then settle down here to raise kids and hash.'

*

On a cold brittle morning they descended out of the mountains in Lhassen's quite new but much-dented Ford. It was the third car Lhassen had owned in as many years, the other two having been wrecked when he drove drunk off the hillside. He was not ashamed and told the stories with relish; they confirmed to himself his standing with Allah, or at least with Fate. A charmed life.

When they left, their hash had been packed and marked, and stowed in the windowless chamber behind the patriarch's bedroom, waiting to be collected by Lew in his prepared car – still sitting in Asilah – and then the final payment would be made. Lhassen was driving, taking Slhemen and Fatma's brother with him, both on the loose for a weekend in Tangier. Lew regarded the dented car with disfavour, wondering if Lhassen's driving was safe, and how they would all squeeze in for a long, uncomfortable ride. He was inspecting the car, too, to try to judge the shapes and construction of modern cars, to see what he might have to do to make his packages fit in his own car. Recalling the irregularity of the pressings they had just completed, he was not encouraged.

'We should have measured the channels in the car-floor in Asilah,' he complained. 'I have a feeling that most of the bags up here aren't going to fit.'

'Then we'll have to cut,' Jeff said with an easy shrug. 'We always have to cut.'

Lew flushed with annoyance at himself. Why did he allow himself to show so often this rigidity of mind and anxiety of temperament? The game required better, more intricate footwork than that.

They dropped out of the mountains going rather too fast but without mishap other than the rapid fall, which caused a blockage in Lew's ears. He held his nose and blew mightily but could not unstop his ears, and he was still snorting around the problem when a uniformed figure stepped into the road and flagged Lhassen down. It was the police where they were so often, lying lazily in wait where the road left the Rif. It was the road – the only main road – the drug-runners used.

There were three of them, a sergeant who had got himself up to look mean and dangerous behind expensive blue-tinted sunglasses, and two rural cops, tough enough but awaiting orders. The sergeant waved them all out of the car, just a casual gesture as if he didn't care one way or the other. All this hide and seek was just too boring. Cases and bags were taken out and piled by the roadside. Feeling dizzy, Lew clutched his nose, still trying to clear his head for the little play of wits that would surely come.

The two Europeans were separated from the Moroccans, their luggage identified and handed over to one of the toughs to be searched. But gently enough, merely a hand thrust down the sides and the ends, the top layer of clothes respectfully lifted and let fall. Lhassen and his two companions were not so lucky. They were pushed into line, and Lew thought that the Arabic addressed to them had an edge to it. Then, under orders from the sergeant, they took every item from their bags, held up each one to be inspected, which the sergeant did with the barest hint of a sneer, as if amused by the things a man might carry. Then the three cops prowled the car, lifting seats and mats, poking in secluded places, rapping bodywork. Even then there was something perfunctory about the whole business, as if they had had no tip-off and were just routinely filling in time.

And just when they seemed to be getting clear the sergeant noticed Lew's shoulder bag and sprang upon it. 'Now things will get lively,' Lew said to himself, having in mind the large wad of money he had secreted under the lining of an inside pocket. He redoubled his efforts to clear his ears. The cop dived his hand into the main pouch and rooted around, then fumbled in a zippered pocket where he found a notebook. A text scrawled in illegible Roman script meant nothing to the sergeant and with a grunt of dismissal he returned the bag to Lew, who stood with tears in his eyes from his continual effort to unblock his ears. Now that the work was done the sergeant allowed himself an expression of sympathy. He laid a hand on Lew's arm and indicated that he could sit in the car, which Lew willingly did, still holding his nose, a gesture that might have been open to misinterpretation.

But the sergeant had turned his attention to Jeff. 'You smoke?' he said in Spanish. 'You like hashish?' He seemed detached, interested only that this might be a possibility.

'Certainly not,' Jeff replied, with a haughty stare. 'I don't even smoke.'

Lhassen had to look quickly at his shoes. It was a most superior lie, told with sweet conviction. Lhassen had never known anyone who smoked as much hash as Jeff, though it did not seem to affect his judgement and his canny way of doing things.

When the cop waved them away, with a little salute that appeared to acknowledge the arbitrary games one had to play, and they drove off, Jeff leaned back in his seat and undid his belt. He was grinning like the kid who had plucked the best plum from the pudding. Next to his skin he wore a slim money belt, and in it was a slab of hash as big and dark as a chocolate bar.

MARTIL

Lew had hoped – had been confident – that the time on Lhassen's farm in Ketama had done something important for him. Cleared from his mind the trash of cultural and historical misconceptions, if nothing else. Also deepened his trust in a part of humanity that was strange to him, if that was not too fanciful. He did not want to fall back now, losing grip on the handholds. Yet he couldn't help a sense of foreboding. That wrecked house in Asilah, leaking weather like a colander, that unprepared car in the bust-up garage . . .

So Lew returned to Asilah and waited for news from Lhassen and Jeff. The house he had abandoned more than two weeks before had been swept and cleaned and tidied but was still broken, with no repairs in progress. It had the look of a place going neatly to ruin. In a few days Jeff arrived and confirmed that they had found a house and a garage near Tetouan that had all the features they needed. Lhassen was making the final arrangements.

Lew returned his keys to the agent in Asilah, a silent, tweedy German who showed no surprise and bade him a brief farewell. At no time had Lew been asked to sign a lease nor, so far as he knew, had the German bothered to discover his name. He wished all agents and landlords were as careless.

The new house was eleven kilometres from Tetouan, in a little town on the Mediterranean coast called Martil. In the main, this was a newish town of raw, low houses, their roofs entangled like a barbed-wire encampment with power and telephone lines, and with TV antennae. In winter, the place was more or less deserted, with property to let; in summer, it served middle-class Moroccans as a beach resort. Along the coast, sands stretched in both directions, disfigured by great congealed globules of marine diesel oil.

The house had two storeys, a spacious apartment on each floor. Jeff had rented the top floor – plenty of room for everyone, and a gallery at the back with a flight of wooden steps leading down to a scruffy garden. At the rear of the garden, approached from a dirt lane, was the garage, half covered with rank growth. It could be entered from the privacy of the garden, overlooked from the back of the house, so the only immediate danger was the curiosity of the ground-floor tenant.

Once they had seen the tenant, however, they felt more inclined to laugh than to worry. Jeff had discovered that he was a Frenchman, a teacher, perhaps even a professor.

'You've got to see this guy to believe him,' Jeff told Lew on the way to Martil. 'A very queer duck. About thirty, a sickly beard, sunglasses with rimless oblong lens, and a taste for weird headgear. Already, within a couple of days, we've seen him in a beret, in a flaming red toque with a blue pom-pom, in Moroccan knitted skullcap, and in a World War One leather flying helmet buckled under the chin. He seems to lead the idle life, gets up about midday when his hunchback houseboy arrives with a big round loaf clutched to his misshapen breast.'

'No danger, then?' Lew asked, determined to be cautious.

'None at all,' Jeff replied airily. 'This guy is so in love with his own eccentricity that he'd hardly notice the colour of the sky, unless it clashed with the colour of his hat.'

*

Vera Gwinn had phoned Anders, giving him the day and the time of her arrival in Tangier. 'Please pass it on,' she said and then added tentatively. 'It would be nice if someone could meet me.'

Why did she phrase it like that? Anders wondered. They all knew who that 'someone' should be.

Lew drove to Tangier in the Peugeot station wagon, with the back seat taken out and floor pan already stripped of carpet and underlay, so that the interior metal box banged and boomed on the bad roads. Despite the noise he felt composed and even a bit detached, and did not become agitated until he saw Vera step off the gangway from the ferry.

Once, years ago in Canada, he had caught a glimpse of a young nun boarding a tram in front of a notorious brothel. That mysterious conjunction of fair and foul had seemed to suggest as much sexual innuendo as a man could hope for. But now that he saw Vera sweep her hair back with her hand, an anxious look on her usually calm face, and her dress momentarily caught between her legs by the sea breeze, he was not so sure.

Suddenly timid, he was not sure how to greet her; after all, what did they really know of each other? He managed to give her a peck on the cheek and a prolonged hug. She clung to him for a moment and then gently broke away. He picked up her case and walked her to the car, wanting to lay his hand on the sweet curve of her buttock but restraining himself. They were both more than a little tongue-tied, and the bangs and rattles of the car on the way back did nothing to help conversation.

In Martil, Lew found the apartment locked and silent in the gathering dusk. But Jeff had left a little note pinned to the door saying that he and Lhassen had places to go and would be back late. Lew was surprised but pleased; he did not know that his cavalier friend had such tact in him. He uncorked a bottle of wine and gradually he and Vera headed back towards where they had been before their last parting. She slipped off her shoes, tucking her feet under her on the couch, and he was suddenly laughing, though he didn't quite know why. In a while Vera stretched and sighed. She stood and held out a hand to Lew. 'I feel much steadier now,' she said in her warm mumble. 'I'd like you to show me where the bedroom is. There are some things I've almost forgotten.'

Later, lying in darkness, she found that she had remembered after all, though she still couldn't decide whether she was safe or not.

*

Next morning Lew and Jeff got down to serious work on the car. The seats were out and the bare metal exposed, ready for the attack with angle-grinder, chisel and tinsnips. But Lew was still cautious; he suggested that they keep the bonnet raised, so that any inconvenient visitor would think that they were servicing the engine, not rearranging the bodywork.

On almost any day the landlord was likely to enter the kitchen and peer around in an abstracted manner, as if someone would soon tell him why he was there. He would drift towards the main room until he was cut off and it was made plain to him that he had no business there. He was snooping. Perhaps he guessed what was happening; if not the full picture, at least the outlines. He looked intelligent enough, and the facts of the foreign drug trade in Morocco were hardly a secret. But he would do nothing unless events or the police pressed him. A good rent in the winter months was worth much to a landlord in Martil. Luckily, he gave plenty of warning of his approach. He drove to the house in a big lemon-coloured Buick, creeping along in low gear with the engine roaring, blowing his horn loud and long at each intersection.

With these interruptions work on the car went on nervously, by fits and starts. They ran into unforeseen problems. The internal structure of the chassis puzzled them; they could not quite work out what went where. Their tools seemed inadequate to the delicacy of the task.

'Damn it, we've got to begin somewhere,' said Jeff, who had a degree in metallurgy. He punched a jagged hole in the metal, and matters rolled dangerously downhill from there. 'Hell,' Jeff continued to mutter with hopeless enthusiasm, 'we've got to press on. We're falling too far behind.'

Jeff was always impetuous, but Lew's habit, when things went baulky on him, was to stare at the problem in the hope that the answer would reveal itself. He studied the car-floor for a long time. No solution offered itself to him.

*

They were all getting jumpy. Jeff stopped humming or whistling as he worked. Lew scowled in preoccupation, tapping the bodywork with the wooden handle of a hammer, trying to assess the hollow spaces within. Vera, after the first abandonment, had withdrawn quietly to the kitchen or the gallery, to look after the cooking and shopping or to read a book. There was only so much that men wanted at any one time and she saw that she didn't figure in the present worries. She tried to keep cool and look unconcerned, which was her natural stance, and she earned some part of her keep by maintaining a lookout for the wandering landlord.

But Lhassen was causing the most concern. He had always liked a drink, and having nothing to do except wait around while two puzzled Westerners aggravated their problems, getting snappy in a language – English – that he didn't understand, Lhassen liked drinking even more than usual. He was buying brandy, drinking more than half a bottle a day, plus an unknown quantity of wine, and he was often drunk. Nor was he a good drunk, being subject to unpredictable swings of mood, voluble and aggressive, or silent and sulky. Too often, Jeff had to take time out to soothe his drunk, ruffled friend. It was clear that a drunk Lhassen was a liability they did not need, capable in his cups of sinking the whole enterprise. How were they to handle him?

'If he doesn't lay off the booze.' Lew said gloomily, 'I might as well shoot the bugger.'

Jeff smiled, even seemed to be considering the possibility, but laid it aside. They pondered some more, drawing Vera into the problem, getting further depressed.

'I wonder,' said Vera out of the silence, 'if we should ask his wife to come and join him here. She might bring him back in line.'

The two men looked up sharply. Yes, that might be the answer. Both had seen Fatma, seen her in action, taken the measure of her strong character. And immediately Jeff began to build on the idea, making it work further for their benefit.

'That's it,' he said rapidly, seeing it all. 'She can bring her youngest child, and she can bring our hash too. We're so far behind here, it would be a blessing not to have to go to Ketama to collect it. Lhassen can get a message to Slhemen. He can set it all up and send Fatma on her way. Vera,' he went on, 'I tip my hat to you. It takes a woman like you to see a new approach, to get us unstuck.'

But Vera was looking at Lew. She caught the glint on his glasses, and the broad grin spreading underneath, and she knew that he didn't dissent from Jeff's opinion.

When the plan was put to Lhassen, he scratched his unshaven chin with a grubby thumb, wondering where the catch was, then slowly smiled. He had been thinking about what he missed in this nest of foreigners, and his family was certainly one thing. So he accepted and set about arranging it with his old energy. He got word to Slhemen and within a week that careful man had worked out the details. Fatma arrived one evening in the back lane by the garage, in the cab of a small limping truck, the door held shut by a length of rope, her baby on her lap secured like a bundle of washing.

In the bed of the truck, hidden among various loads of vegetables, were three burlap sacks containing fifty well-wrapped kilos of *zero-zero* hash, the smell overlaid by the friendly stink of onions.

*

After the arrival of Fatma, Vera gave the domestic duties over to her. It was not that she wished to take advantage of Fatma, but she thought there was a delicate point at issue. Though Jeff was paying for the apartment, Vera felt that it was, if only temporarily, Fatma's home, in a way that it could never belong to her, even less to the two Western men.

If this responsibility was a burden Fatma showed no sign of it. She hitched up her long skirt and got to work, out shopping or in the kitchen all day. Even so, it was obvious that she had no use for town living. The imposition of an advanced technology between her and nature was, from the sneer she gave electricity and piped water, quite unnecessary. In her own household, when she needed water she sent a maid or a boy to the stream with a bucket. And who was to say that she was wrong? Her bucket always came back full, but in Martil the taps too often ran dry.

In the kitchen she scorned tables and counters, just squatted on her heels in a corner, working on the floor with a single hotplate – a charcoal stove would have worked better – one pot and one pan. When her baby let out one of its furious howls she stooped, hardly pausing, grabbed the baby with one hand and slung it up behind her where it landed on her back, four little limbs spread, like a lemur in the trees. Then, still stooping, she was already about her business, with shuffling steps, slinging a towel around her back, settling the kid into it as if she were drying herself after a bath.

The meals came out as they had done on her mountain farm, native feasts of unusual splendour. Lhassen was content and almost stopped drinking.

Then a great moment was approaching, the Islamic celebration of Eid al-Adha, the Feast of the Sacrifice, in remembrance of Abraham's travails with God on the mountain. Custom called for the slaughter of a sheep, and Lew sat at a pavement café in Martil watching the future feasts dragged home. Rich men proudly led rams as bold as military brass; the poor staggered with dazed, half-dead wretches across their shoulders.

Lew was not aware when Lhassen bought his ram, but on a certain afternoon, going to one of the two bathrooms in the apartment, he opened the door and there it was. Standing in a spread of hay and its own dung, fodder hanging from its mouth, a big black sheep with an introspective eye.

On the morning of the feast day, a small elderly man appeared in the kitchen. He wore a green-and-white chequered headcloth, Arab style, and was drinking a bottle of pineapple juice. His little face was shrunken, with a thin scrub of whiskers. His right eye was green and lively; the left was sunken, opaque and blind. He shrugged off a tattered burnous revealing a faded blue shirt and a pair of knee-length knickers. He began whetting a large knife, and the household followed him into the garden.

The black ram was very docile. It did not struggle when Lhassen upended it, holding the hind legs high with one hand, parting the wool on the throat with the other. The old man slashed the knife deftly, slicing through gullet and jugular, and not till then did the animal give a twitch. Lew, a farmboy who had witnessed plenty of animal slaughter, had never seen a beast die so placidly.

After the ram was bled the old man made an incision in one hind leg, gathered himself together with a deep breath, put his lips to the incision and blew so hard he almost tottered. To the surprise of the Westerners, the skin inflated like a balloon.

The animal was now ready to be butchered. The old man set to briskly, according to the prescribed rites, muttering prayers and invocations in Arabic. He gutted it with particular ceremony, carefully unfurling the entrails, cutting out each organ singly, examining it, then holding it out for a general view with sing-song words. It were as if the sheep itself would have approved, the delicacy, the dignified respect. To Lew, the auguries of ancient literature came immediately to mind, the fates determined by the fall of birds, by a reading of the guts. He wondered what this divination might have to say about his own future, Was he at the mercy of strange gods now, whose faces he did not know, whose language he did not understand, whose prayers he could not say? As the Arabic went on he composed his own silent petition, to the unknown powers, whoever they may be.

When the work was done, within an hour they were all back in the kitchen, squatting around Fatma who was handing out kebabs of braised liver and kidney. So the gods were kindly thus far.

Later, after eating, Jeff and Lew were lounging in the main room, drinking beer. The little man came in, neat and lively as a sparrow, crinkly with smiles from his one good eye. Jeff offered him a beer.

'Beer,' Jeff said, pointing to the label on the bottle. '*Cerveza*. Understand? *Cerveza*.'

The old butcher nodded. He looked eager. Jeff poured him a glass and he took a mouthful. Then a violent shudder ran through him, his mouth pinched up, he ran for the gallery and hung over the railing, gasping and retching. Jeff was aghast, realizing suddenly what he had done, offering alcohol to a devout Muslim, one with ritual duties, and on the occasion of the Eid ceremony. Jeff hurried to the kitchen, to fetch Coca-Cola in the familiar bottle. Then he poured a glass in the old man's view, apologizing, patting the scrawny shoulder in the faded blue shirt. A cautious tongue poked into the glass of Coke, and then the old fellow relaxed. He collapsed in a chair, pale and sweating, and drank thirstily.

When they told Lhassen of the incident he looked disturbed. He, a too-frequent swiller of alcohol who regarded most misfortune as *suerte*, and even as a cause of amusement, frowned and shook his head. He seemed to indicate that sometimes he despaired that these foreigners would ever learn sense and decency.

The carcass of the ram was put into a little storeroom off the kitchen, slumped across a chair like a drunken man. A puddle of blood dried on the floor beneath the severed neck. Lhassen carved off a leg for dinner that night, and over the next week or so the carcass dwindled day by day.

*

Time was going by and the three burlap sacks of hash remained on the top shelf of a broom closet, the door locked and the key on a string around Jeff's neck. At Lew's suggestion an extra hasp was screwed to the closet door, fastened with a padlock, the most rugged padlock they could find in Martil. Even with this security, each time Lew thought of that burden behind the door he nearly had kittens. Every new day invited catastrophe. The landlord still visited, less frequently and still fortunately announced by horn blasts and straining engine noises. They thought the Frenchman downstairs safely mad, but who knew what wild notion might enter his creepy mind? Jeff decided that the apartment must never be left empty – at least one of the three Westerners must be present at all times.

They had worked on the car long enough, and they would have to be satisfied with what they had done. The wrinkles and rough edges of the floor plate were hammered out. Holes in the chassis were sealed from the inside, with sheet metal glued over them, then sprayed with black paint from the outside. The spaces were cleaned and, as far as possible, a thick layer of rubbery underseal was laid down on all interior bare metal.

'That's it,' Jeff let a long breath out, as a cool evening breeze dried their sweat. 'It's not a good job, but we could work on it till doomsday and not get it much better, given the conditions we work under. Only the packing and loading now. We'll start on it as soon as we've had a beer and a bath.'

They were in a hurry to get the job done – the main room, with hash spread around, looked like some disorderly warehouse of vice – but the task needed precision. After the first blocks, which went in easily, Lew despaired of fitting all the rest. Jeff worked doggedly and without complaint, sipping beer and humming along to the tunes on the radio he knew. He had been here before and knew eventually that feet touched ground. Jeff did the cutting and shaping, and Lew, who needed more activity to override his nerves, went from apartment to garage and back, fitting and measuring, telling Jeff what was required. Jeff watched him get a grip on his nerves and let it all go. He didn't mind playing second fiddle. He had seen this tension, many times, and knew the hammering taken by a cautious mind in a state of uncertainty. If it seemed like Lew was calling the shots, then that was fine by Jeff; Lew was the one who had to drive the car.

'It's a bit like making love,' Jeff told Lew calmly. 'It's often hard work and sweaty. You're excited but you're never sure you're going to get there. Then you do, and for a moment the world is singing.'

'Damn it,' Lew replied, 'I'm as keen on a good fuck as the next man, but if you make these comparisons I'm not sure my heart could take this kind of stress two or three times a week.'

*

In two days of concentrated labour they got the car packed, and then came to real grief. The floor pan above the spaces was so sprung and bent – Jeff, the metallurgist, muttered knowingly of 'broken molecular structure' – that it refused to lie flat. With painful slowness, using a system of weights and wedges, they brought the edges into line inch by inch, bonding each tiny gain with epoxy-resin glue. The glue was strong but set very slowly, particularly in the cool winter days and cold nights of the garage. A butane heater helped but was a danger in the garage, amid volatile fumes of paint and sealant and glue and oil and petrol. The heater had to be watched. Taking turn by turn they babysat the car, watching the glue dry.

Ten days to close that floor. Ten utterly blank days. The weather held fine but still cold. The wind off the sea blew all the colour from the sky. The glue took an implacable time to set. For reading matter, to fill the weary hours, Lew was down to one copy of *Time* and one of *Newsweek*, both for the same week. He read them with minute attention, to the least of the advertisements, which turned out to be more enlightening than much of the prose. He read every word, even to the fine print as small as that on an insurance policy. He read the lists of publishers, managers, editors, agents, PR people and – as if in an afterthought – contributors and writers, some of whom he had known and worked with in his newspaper days.

*

'Why is Lhassen still here?' Lew asked. The hash had been safely delivered, the final payment turned over to Fatma for safekeeping. There was no reason for Lhassen and his family to stay.

'I haven't puzzled that one out,' Jeff replied. 'I suppose he might regard this as a holiday, or a chance to get to know our foreign peculiarities even better. An aid to better drug-dealing. And then, of course, there's the booze.'

'You won't throw him out?'

'Oh, Lord no. He's welcome to stay as long as we're here.'

'Then there are the relatives. We see a lot of them now.'

'We certainly see a lot of them.'

Two sisters, Lhassen's distant cousins, lived in Tetouan. Just where they fitted into the family, Lew never discovered. Both were educated, lived the life of the town, having come far from the peasant farms of the Rif. Lhassen liked to see them, inviting them often to the hospitality of the house in Martil, perhaps with a kind of pride, to show off the foreign colleagues of his enterprise. Jeff was paying, Fatma was doing the cooking; it seemed a fair exchange, though Jeff and Lew sometimes begrudged the times it took them away from urgent work on the car, and they were forced to suffer the presence of sister Nina's husband, who was a tedious oaf. Then again Nina, the younger sister, was a notable beauty.

The older sister was an energetic, still-handsome woman; in her day she might have had Nina's looks. But time had used her hard. Her husband worked in Holland and was home only two weeks in the year. She was often unwell, suffering from some nameless ailment. Lhassen hinted darkly that her husband had given her syphilis. 'Those Dutch whores,' he said angrily. But Lew wondered. He knew something of the careful, conscientious Dutch, among whom he imagined even their whores were careful. He judged that venereal blooms flowered closer to home, in the slums of Tangier and Tetouan.

Nina, however, still kept her looks and her health. She had some devilry in her face, a sensuous slither in her step, and she didn't mind being looked at. She was ready to flirt, in a demure way, up to a point. She had a husband and the rules seemed clear to her, though not to Lew and Jeff.

From across the dinner table – no lounging on cushions or on sheepskin rugs on the floor when guests came – Vera studied the sisters, Nina in particular. An oval face with clear, creamy skin darkening at the temples from which she had pulled back her abundant black hair, hair with just the slightest hint of kinkiness. Eyes deceptively dreamy but ready to narrow when she spoke her mind on some unpleasant subject. Those eyes, drifting round the table, glancing off Lew's bold look from time to time. He didn't make much of it, but his lips were slightly parted. She was always well dressed – a pearl-grey djellaba, silver slippers, but careful Western makeup on her face. One night she wore a black and gold caftan, rings on her fingers, gold rings in her ears.

'Nina, how pretty you look tonight,' Lew complimented her, 'though of course you're always a picture for the eye.' It sounded sexy and feline in Spanish, or so Vera thought.

Nina's cheeks dimpled. She performed a neat pirouette, to show Lew all her angles.

'Yes, you may well look,' her blockhead of a husband added sourly. 'It takes a fortune to keep a woman in fashion these days.'

Thereafter, she wore that caftan every night they came.

Lew sat opposite her at the table. He watched her hands, graceful and almost fragile, with pink nails and a tracery of henna on the palms. She took a shank bone from the communal pot, holding it delicately between the fingers of both hands, attacking the meat on the bone with strong white teeth. Her eyes fixed on Lew, then she tore off a strip of flesh. It was as blatant as that.

*

'You were tempted?' Vera asked him. She had undressed to bra and panties and was brushing her hair.

Lew looked at her for a long moment; what he saw would be enough for any man, surely. 'Yes,' he replied slowly, 'I was.'

'What does that say to me?'

'Nothing important, I think.'

She was naked now, and lay on the bed, propping her head up on a couple of pillows. Looking down the length of her body she tried to take stock, being severe and critical. So far as she could see, there was not much wrong with her. The more daring of the glossy magazines might have printed her picture: the new naked *maja*.

'Perhaps I deserve an explanation,' she said.

He nodded, but was slow in finding the words. It was still something of a puzzle to him. When he was ready he still stumbled a little.

'I was looking at fantasy,' he said quietly, 'a life in dreams. Our image of this Eastern world is still stained by the colours of the *Arabian Nights*. To retreat there is to voice our criticism – our revolt from the West we know. When I look at Nina I'm another man, almost a disembodied man. It's a game, maybe even a spiritual game. I don't mean to insult you by that. When I'm with you I'm flesh and blood, bone and muscle, heart beating fast here and now, and what we do is a matter of living and dying. Still, I can't help lapsing. The contemplation of unworldly imaginations is one of the keenest joys of the mind. I can't avoid the history I've been drawn into here.'

She considered that carefully. 'Is that why you're here at all?' she suggested. 'Not for the hash, with its pleasures and profits, good though that may be, but for stranger fruits forgotten or lost in our parts of the world. They say the Garden of Hesperides was to be found in these lands, somewhere below the shoulders of Atlas. Perhaps you are after those golden apples?'

Lew had nothing to say to that.

*

One night, after eating, when Lhassen was drinking again, he found he had fibres of meat between his teeth. He turned to Jeff in a bullying way.

'*Jefe*,' he ordered in Spanish, 'I need my toothpick. In the car, over the radio. Get it for me.'

'A toothpick?' Jeff replied. 'You expect me to go all the way to the car for a damn toothpick?' Then he added, in English, 'Man, you're crazy.'

But over the years Lhassen had learnt the odd word of English.

'I crazy? I crazy?' he shouted, leaping to his feet. 'No, no, Lhassen not crazy. You *bad* crazy.' And he stormed out.

Jeff hurried after him and brought him back. There was too much to lose to leave him wild and spiteful. Now he was in an angry sulk, daring anyone to say a wrong word. Fatma had watched the drinking and the drunkenness in silence, with downcast eyes. She would not shame him. He was her husband and in many ways a good husband, a good provider. She said nothing. She did not have to. The turn of her head said it all, if he cared to look.

But Nina and her sister had no inhibitions. They disliked and feared alcohol, both as Muslim women and as witnesses to the temptation that alcohol had for Muslim men who thought they were emancipated. The sisters spat out Berber dialect at Lhassen, Nina lowering her light and musical voice to something like a growl. Then they became a little shamefaced. They were in the presence of foreigners, and Lhassen was family, after all. Too much time with these Westerners had left him unbalanced.

'It's not Lhassen who speaks,' Nina apologized in Spanish, 'but the wine.'

'So if I don't speak,' Lhassen said in drunken triumph, 'you don't know if I'm drinking.' And he clapped his hand over his mouth.

'Ah,' Nina replied, hardly hiding her contempt, 'but the eyes speak as well as the tongue.'

Jeff and Lew looked at each other. The car was just about ready; they should take off without delay. It was wise, for present safety and future business, to get away from Lhassen.

Tangier/Algeciras

The Peugeot was something of a mess, however you looked at it. But Lew was at the limit of his patience. He bought a pitch-like compound which he spread over the bumps and hollows; then he painted the floor black and replaced the underlay and carpets. It created the illusion of what a car floor should be, but it would hardly bear a close examination. 'To hell with it,' Lew said, tossing the paintbrush into the waste bin after the final touches, 'I'm going.'

On the last evening, all in the Martil household were invited to Nina's house in Tetouan, an invitation imposed on them by custom and which they could not refuse. The small house, off a little plaza with a muddy fountain, was cramped but neat. They sat in the front room with Nina's father, a gentle old man who looked very frail. He had lost a thumb and had several mutilated fingers, but he handled his snuff deftly, smiling into a corner with private memories, not speaking at all. On the other hand the dolt, Nina's husband, grumbled constantly of bad dreams.

In her own house Nina was hardly visible to the men. All the women retired to a back room, from which singing suddenly emerged. The connecting door was ajar, and the three foreigners, moved by the hesitant music, went softly and peeped in. Nina and Fatma were shaking tambourines, Nina's mother and sister were caressing gurgling sounds out of drums like congas, and four bronzed girls from the mountains sat in a row on a couch, like big birds on a fence, singing and clapping a rhythm. Their movements were curious – hands rising from the lap to describe a circle, coming together in front of their noses with a hollow thud. Looked like they were catching flies.

Then they saw the men and the singing collapsed into giggles.

'Go on, go on,' Jeff called out, his face alive with pleasure. But they would not – or rather could not. Every time the instruments started again, the girls tried a few notes and stalled. They were much too shy.

When the gathering broke up Nina gave Lew her soft, warm hand.

'I hope for another evening like this,' she said.

Lew did not know what to reply. He wished her pleasant dreams. What else could he leave her with?

Next afternoon, Lew had the car at the front door of the house, ready to depart for Tangier and the road north. Vera was in the passenger seat, her face a little aloof and pensive. Jeff Gartree, who was flying out the next day, gave Lew a casual hug and a breezy promise to meet again in about ten days. Coming and going were routine for Jeff. Lhassen, now sober and thoughtful, embraced Lew and, to Lew's surprise, so did Fatma.

He thought her embrace was as soft and delicate as the fond, remembered arms of his maternal grandmother.

*

Lew took a double room at the Rif Hotel in Tangier. If there was any luxury to be had, he wanted it. He reckoned also that he had some ground to make up with Vera; let her relax for a short while and see the better side of his soul. He wandered for an hour or so in the streets, taking in the old and the new, thinking how charged and energized one had to be as a modern man in a modern city. He had his hair cut and returned to the hotel to soak in a long, hot bath. In about half an hour Vera entered the bathroom, anxious and wanton in a loose slip, and looked at him in a way that excited him. He felt flesh begin to boast, sprang out of the bath and into a towel, and soon they were heading for the bedroom, breathing hard and hanging on to each other, and at last it seemed to Lew that they were talking a better language.

Later, when Vera was resting, he went down to the bar, which was quiet and nearly empty, as the bars of Moroccan hotels often were. The bartop was made of thick glass placed above a lengthy aquarium tank. Beneath his whisky glass strange fish with frail fan-like tails rose to the surface, extending pouty lips like sucker cups, as if dying for a drink as well. In the corner of the room a crewcut pianist with an exuberant bowtie – he looked American – tiptoed into a medley of sentimental show tunes, like a diver holding his nose and sinking slowly into cloudy water. Lew had another two whiskies and tried not to fret about the morrow and beyond.

The dinner was almost as good as Lew had hoped for. Excellent French cuisine, cooked with skill and panache, the best Burgundy the wine list could offer. Lew would accept nothing less, considering the expense. The waiter had his eye on their table, especially when Lew sent back the cheeseboard for being dull and badly kept. The waiter swept it away at once. He expected a heavy tip, if he could extract it.

Jeff had warned Lew at the start of their association that the rewards of a drug-courier were akin to a hallucination, as quick to vanish as to appear. '*Carpe diem*,' he advised, using the old Latin tag, and certainly he was one to seize the day. Lew was less demanding, less flamboyant than Jeff – a different temperament. But he thought he might learn. If not under sentence, he saw that he was likely to be under the whim of a customs officer, a policeman, a border guard, a nark. If he went down he intended to go with body satisfied but pockets emptied.

As he drifted towards sleep that night, Lhassen's melancholy refrain came back to him. 'Eat, Señor Luis, eat meat.' He intended to eat meat, and the best only.

*

The ferry was due to depart at three in the afternoon. Lew had planned to travel via Portugal, but the ship to Lisbon was out of service for a winter refit. And the Malaga ferry was withdrawn for emergency repairs. That left Algeciras. Lew hated that place, a blighted, four-flusher of a town in itself, but also the point of entry to Europe of most of the Moroccan cannabis, The customs and police there were seasoned watchdogs, with a wary eye open for irregularity. Lew could only hope that with so many rank amateurs to lay hands on they might pass over the better prepared. The traffic was heavy, the work tedious, the humans frail.

In Lew's experience all smugglers felt they were fated to some degree. No one could cover all the eventualities, and in general, as long as the preparation was careful and cautious, a bold front was a strong front. So Lew laid aside his misgivings and bought the ticket to Algeciras. He thought he might like to try a small prayer but could not decide what deity might accept it. Chiefly, he worried about Vera, that she should be caught as an accessory; but then again, she might be a lucky talisman.

They slept late and breakfasted well. Lew criticized the coffee and asked for toast less scorched. Then they dressed carefully, casual but very respectable, Vera in a pretty dress, with a hint of light perfume about her person, Lew solemn in his Basque beret and well-shined shoes.

Lew drove down to the port in good time, easing the car along as if on a Sunday outing. He made made this sea journey several times and was used to the rigmarole of boarding. His immediate problem was where to place the car in the ship so as to be in the best position on unloading. Customs work was intermittent labour between periods of boredom. When a ship came in the officers were sharp enough at first, giving the early cars a searching eye. Then the rush pressed on them and they began to feel harassed by the impatient queue piling up. They had to clear the docks, and maybe vigilance relaxed. But for the last few cars, with the end in sight, they could spare again a little of the care expected of them, and perhaps expend some of that vindictiveness so often bred in such a tedious and interminable job.

To be about a third of the way down the disembarkation line, with a long tail behind, seemed about right to Lew.

But did any of this calculation matter? As the ship departed Lew was walking the rear deck, his mind jumping, with gulls cawing at him, and garbage streaming in the wake. All this finagling, was it just an exercise in fantasy to try to form some basis for hope? It took just one sore official, just one bully with a keen nose, even just one man who liked his work, and then he was sunk.

He went below for a drink and found Vera at the bar, reading a book. As he slumped in a chair she looked up sharply, her expression changing from surprise to concern.

'You'd better ease up,' she said, keeping her voice low. 'You look wretched. Wretchedly guilty or wretchedly afraid, I don't know which.'

'Both, I expect,' he replied mournfully. 'I can't get the jumps out of my heartbeat. I'd better have a double brandy.'

'Careful' she warned. 'Alcohol on the breath is not a good sign.'

'Oh, that's the least of my worries. After a brandy I'll have plenty of time to get comatose with panic.'

He sighed and fetched his brandy, but that didn't hold him down and soon he was out on the deck again, in a stiff wind that he wished would take him anywhere but Algeciras. He began to make a circuit of the deck, ticking off every point he could think of, those things he had done in preparation and those he had skipped from impatience or foolishness, and then to his surprise he found he was walking so fast, bow to stern and back, that he was quite out of breath. He sat on the canvas cover of a liferaft and breathed deeply with his eyes closed, trying to visualize calmly step and counterstep in the contest ahead. When he opened his eyes the port was in sight and a voice came over the loudspeaker, sounding like Donald Duck, advising drivers to go to their cars.

He had been puzzling how best Vera might help him, what stance she should take. As they sat in the car, waiting for the engines to start and the bow doors to open, he went through it with her.

'The idea,' he said, 'is to distract but not to annoy. No leg shows or low cleavage, no flaunting the tits. Just show the natural exasperation of the well-off European tourist frustrated in her rightful and God-given desire to go where the hell she wants at any damn time she chooses. Put bureaucracy in its place, but in the nicest possible way. Pleasant smiles, but a glance at your watch now and again, a bit of byplay with the map, chewing your lip, maybe even a polite question how to get out of town to such and such a *parador* . . . ' Then he saw how she was looking at him.

'Okay,' he apologized, 'I'll shut up. It's my ragged nerves speaking. You'll know how to act.'

He closed his eyes again and breathed slowly, counting up to five on each breath. Seeing how things were, she hoped fervently that they would be waved through without inspection.

When they left the ferry the car was placed just about right. They inched forward and then a customs officer was standing in front of them, pointing to an inspection bay. At this moment, Lew told himself, the drowning man miraculously discovers how to swim.

The inspecting officer was on the passenger's side. He opened the car door and leaned into the aperture, almost stumbling into Vera's lap. She put out a hand, as if to defend herself, and the officer drew back. He ordered them out of the car in a voice curt enough to hide his blushes. They got out promptly, trying to look relaxed and interested. And in fact Vera did seem interested. While Lew went to rest his bottom on the edge of the inspection-bay counter, Vera smiled at the officer and asked sweetly, 'Do you need me to do anything?'

He shook his head with a scowl and went to work. He did everything Lew expected, testing, poking, opening, lifting, tapping, searching in, under and around. But it looked routine, not a serious attempt to tear the car down. The back seat was a jumble of coats, books and maps, hiking boots, food they intended to use later for a picnic. The officer was impatient with all this, thrusting it aside like trash he did not need. Pulling himself out of the car – he was a stout man and slightly out of breath – he indicated brusquely that Lew should open the tailgate of the station wagon.

The rear luggage space had been deliberately kept tidy and clear of junk. Look, nothing to hide! There were three soft cases of clothes, a rucksack, and a battered wooden box the size of a small suitcase. The officer pulled the cases towards him, not bothering to lay them out on the counter, opened each one and ruffled through the contents. He shook the rucksack, untied the flap and pawed inside. Then he pointed to the wooden box. It was a handy old catch-all, something Lew had picked off a rubbish dump, and had no locks, only a simple sliding bolt to fasten it. It never failed to get the attention of the customs. Lew lifted the lid and revealed tools for the car, a can of engine oil, shoe brushes and polish, and a portable typewriter in a padded case. The officer turned away dismissively. He let the tailgate swing down, tapped the metal, peered under the rear wheel arches, and waved them on their way with a backhand motion, wafting a fly away that disturbed him no longer.

They got back in the car slowly, normal folk doing ordinary things. Lew started the engine and had begun to ease away without rush when he heard a thump at the back. He realized that the officer had not clicked the tailgate shut and neither had he. He stopped, got out and walked back, cautioning himself not give way to hysteria.

The customs man balefully watched them go. There's nothing so foolish, his attitude said, as foolish tourists. They only added to the confusion of the world.

STOCKHOLM

Lew thought his nerves might pop at any moment, but in fact the drive north was easy, along the main arteries of Europe, the border crossings busy, bureaucratic and inattentive. On the way, they lodged at night in motorway motels, a quiet couple, arriving late and leaving early, taking keys to any room offered, all as bleak as the interior of soap cartons. Lew paid in cash.

When they reached Stockholm, Lew took to bed for the best part of a week, in a state of collapse or in a euphoria of relief, he was not sure which. Anders looked on benignly. 'Let him rest,' he said to Berta. 'Feed him and then leave him alone. He's done very well but now he's mentally exhausted.'

When he was not dozing Lew puffed up the pillows and reached for an Herodotus in the two-volume Everyman edition, which he had found on Anders's bookshelves. On the journey north, knowing the Swedish national agony over alcohol, he had fortified himself with a bottle of excellent malt whisky and he rewarded himself from time to time with modest sips. He opened the volumes at random – one story was as good as another – and took a look at brave Greeks and despotic Persians, and then at great-hearted Persians and Greeks who were cringing fools. Herodotus was too interested in the variety of human character to read anything universal into his stories. And sometimes Lew was laughing, and sometimes arrested by thoughts of his own he could not quite get a hold of.

Eventually he plunged back to the very beginning of the history, to the Lydian story of Canduales and Gyes, and he saw at once how vanity, stupidity and ambition shaped judgement in council chamber or bedroom, how a woman's naked body came between men, how anger, revenge and violence followed, and then Lew saw he was on the telltale track of the human heart, and that things then were more or less how things are now.

*

Vera looked into the bedroom from time to time during the day, hopeful or puzzled, though she didn't speak much and his answers, though friendly, were brief. He was reluctant to let his eyes go far from the book. At night she slipped into bed with him and sometimes they did and sometimes not, though neither of them seemed sure what led up to it and what didn't. Remembering his earlier days in Canada, with Elaine, he feared he might be wounded in some complex region of the affections, and though he knew friendship and sexual desire well enough he felt himself to be completely adrift when it came to love. About domesticity he was quite certain. He wanted none of it.

At last she said, 'Are you staying there for ever?'

She was trying to keep it light, her eyes looking off through the window, but there was no hiding the slight edge to her voice. She was getting bored – all this inaction, the sad north. She liked and even admired the Swedes, for their intelligence, their egalitarian social conscience, their steady footfall through life. But she found that the habitual temperature of their daily existence seemed to hover around zero. All that gloom and cold wind and mystery. Swedish life, it appeared to her, followed a Bergman film rather too closely. She longed for the south.

'Oh, I feel quite restored now,' he said cheerfully, 'and I'll be up soon. This imitating Oblomov really doesn't suit me. Perhaps it's a local talent for which I haven't the character. I think I have more jump in me than that.'

'So what now?' she said, 'Will you go on with this business?'

She watched him begin to get his thoughts in order. His holiday, if it had been a holiday, was over.

'I've been talking to Anders,' she continued. 'He says you can take your time to decide, if you wish. Commit yourself to nothing immediately. He has an uncle who runs a small country estate, where there's always a need for a handyman – carpenter, tractor driver, stock keeper, hedge layer, ditch digger, painter, thatcher. Versatile labour, which is always hard to find. You could vegetate there for a while, Anders says.'

Lew, once a farmboy, had always been useful with his hands – he knew that. Thatching roofs – he liked the sound of that. A working view of the world from a new angle. Up in the realm of the birds he might see earthly things in their minor, proper place.

He almost considered it seriously.

'No,' he said after a pause, 'I've found my trade, at least for the time being. It's what I've been doing in Morocco. It's hazardous, insecure, no rules, mostly illegal, and perhaps too exciting. But I think I have the knack. It's rare that a person can fall into an occupation so completely. It's something worth discovering.'

Costa del Sol

They went south and felt easier at once. 'How do you explain it?' Vera said, feeling more buoyant by the minute. 'I feel as if I've been given a new pair of lungs, or an extra ration of sunlight. Perhaps it's as simple as that.'

Anders had given them nothing but kindness and consideration. But once Lew had made his delivery what happened concerned him no further. In the Stockholm house he and Vera were without function, tripping over their own lives. In Anders's scheme of things, no matter how kindly Lew was treated he was no more than a mule, and he needed to imitate the narrow purpose of that stubborn, canny animal. Know what he could do, concentrate on that, and let the rest go hang.

They went back to the old village on the Mediterranean coast, to the old familiar territory. Yet somehow it was no longer familiar. The villages of the Spanish coastline were filling up dangerously, filling with foreigners too much like Lew and Vera themselves. Only even more lost. Too much sunburnt flesh, young women in briefs or bikinis, youths in cut-off jeans and flip-flops, sprawled in beach chairs or on café terraces, yawning, idly rearranging their private parts, waiting for the next drink. They were speaking, it sometimes appeared, almost any language but Spanish. Amazed at themselves, that they were there, looking like they owned the place. And perhaps, in a sense, they did.

*

Lew went into the hills, to a quieter territory still hazy with traditions and memories. About fifteen kilometres inland, grinding through the bends of a bad road, he saw on a distant hilltop a village looking as if it deserved a place on a picture postcard. A white church tower with a little domed cap in red tiles, a clock pointing relentlessly at ten to four, huddles of whitewashed houses on steep paths, wrought-iron balconies in need of paint, a profusion of geraniums in clay pots. Behind the village, the foothills ascended green and grey and rugged into the harsh heights, and the big birds wheeled over the hidden *basura* dump. He saw oleanders by a watercourse, and wild asparagus in the banks between the olives, and he caught the scent of thyme and other drifting smells too evanescent to catch.

On his way into the village he passed women working at a concrete trough under a roof open to all the airs. They were hammering sheets against the cement slope in chill mountain water. In the middle of the village was a square, spacious enough even though it had to struggle for level ground against the crowded pitch of the streets all around. It almost had the look of a deserted bullring, without the fury and carnage. A dog and two men possessed this plaza at the moment, the dog comatose in mild sun, the men walking slowly on divergent courses as if unaware of each other.

There was one bar in sight and Lew entered it, a long dim room with a few ill-assorted tables and chairs in plain, hard-bitten wood, and a bare counter at the end of which sat a shiny espresso machine. There were no customers. He ordered a beer and the barman served it with slow care, as if it were of a vintage that required respect, and Lew took it to a corner table to be out of the way. Time passed. The frame of sunlight in the doorway began to slant and lengthen. An elderly man put his head in and looked around. He said nothing, but after a few seconds he gravely touched his hat to Lew and withdrew. Lew felt at peace and utterly at home.

After a second beer, judging that his presence was at least tolerated, Lew spoke to the barman.

'Could it be, in a village as quiet and pleasant as this one, that some houses might be for rent?'

The barman thought about it. A small round man, he stroked his belly, as if that were the seat of knowledge. 'God alone knows for certain,' he said, 'but I think it may be so.'

'It would be a great kindness if you could show me where such a man lives, one who might have a house for rent.'

'Señor, we are on earth to do just such kindness for each other. It is no trouble.'

He came round the counter, took Lew by the arm and led him outside to the fringe of the plaza. He pointed directly across to a house a little larger than the others. 'You see the one with the brown door, and the cat asleep on the doorstep? Ask for Manolo. Say that El Cebollino from the bar sent you. And, señor, be careful of that cat. It's a wild thing, with teeth and claws.'

*

An arrangement was easily made. Manolo rubbed his grey stubbled chin and thought there might be more than one house to let. He gathered a walking stick and an old black hat and offered to show Lew around. They went through the village, visiting a few houses.

'The people here,' said Manolo, explaining the empty houses, 'have left for the city and the coast. They work in construction and in restaurants. One moment they are farmers and the next, without any training, they are builders or cooks. It is a case of necessity. Who needs farmers? And it is better on the whole not to starve.'

Lew chose a narrow house on three floors a couple of streets back from the square. The interior was eccentric, with a dark glory hole of a kitchen on the ground floor and stairs setting off upwards in an unexpected direction. But the upper rooms, though not big, were light and airy with windows on two sides. From the top floor Lew could see not just a patch of the plaza and the immovable hands of the church clock, but also the large country beyond. In one direction the foothills collapsed towards the coast, and in another small *cortijos* with fields and olive groves came up sharp against the cleft of an arroyo with the wild upland beyond.

Lew felt he could draw this habitat around him like a favourite cloak. He had found the base from which he could work.

*

She had a good look at the house, the airy height of it, the arrangement of the rooms, the view from the top. She poked about, looking in places a man might not think of, making judgements that would escape him. The kitchen was a dark disappointment but it was of no consequence to her since she had other plans.

'I like the house,' Vera said, 'but I won't be living there with you.'

He didn't want to say it but he was not unhappy to hear that. He still could not span the gap between the short-term pleasure of her presence and the long-term meaning of being together. The jump from one to the other seemed beyond his skill, a leap over a precipice. She was scared of the precipice too, he could see that. He smiled when he thought about it. In a funny way it brought them closer; the fear of ties became a bond between them.

'There's a small *cortijo* about a kilometre out in the country,' she said. 'I think I'll rent it. It's nothing much, some of it almost a wreck, but it has good points. Off the beaten track but not too remote. No houses near by. A bit of land where one might grow things. Great views and clean air. The structure is sound enough but there's lots of work to be done. I thought that might amuse you, give you something interesting to do in the intervals between the runs for Anders. A project in which you could take satisfaction. I know you could do it.'

Was she just stating a possibility, or pleading with him for it to happen? He was willing. It would keep them within easy reach of each other yet allow unforeseen developments on both sides.

'I thought we could come and go between the two houses as we liked,' she went on whimsically. 'A sort of town-and-country living. Give ourselves airs, perhaps beyond our station. It would be living a kind of dream, at least for the time being.'

For the time being . . . Now she had said it, and it was out in the open between them. That was good enough for both of them.

*

He bought a new car, a Citroën Dyane, one of those strange French flimsies on springs, a vehicle that wallowed over bad surfaces like a liberty ship in a long swell, enough to make the unwary travel-sick. But the simple construction made it easy to modify, and the soft suspension let the wheels patter light-footed over the worst North African tracks and potholes. It was economical, reliable and unobtrusive.

He took the Citroën to a large *taller* sitting like a filthy wart on the main road into the mountains towards Granada. It was a busy, sweaty, commercial place, not known to tourists, where keen mechanics of native talent, born almost with axle grease under the fingernails, did intricate and surprising rescue work on ten-wheel Pegaso trucks. There was no car or truck they could not alter or rebuild.

He was not sure how to approach the matter. Dealing with a garage of this size meant estimates, bills, receipts. Written documentation, a paper trail he would rather avoid. He wanted to reduce it to the simplest transaction, a handshake between two shadows, a transfer of cash from one back pocket to another.

He parked the car up the road, by a bar that dozed behind a dirty bead curtain, and strolled back to the open double-doors of the garage. Inside, mechanics were fighting metal, hammer blows on steel ringing out of a general noise like earthquake. For a while he stood and watched and everyone was too preoccupied to bother him. Then he wandered among the hoists and grease pits and machine tools, eyeing the mechanics as discreetly as possible. After some minutes a curly-haired young bruiser with plentiful white teeth, wearing his overalls with some flair, asked if Lew needed help. The enquiry was friendly, curious but not suspicious. Lew asked for the manager and was directed to a small glassed-in box of an office at the back of the garage. The manager was busy with a customer, so Lew hovered by the door but kept the curly-headed mechanic in view. He saw that the young man was fizzing with high spirits, clapping pals on the back as if he owned the place, joking, grinning, showing those pearly teeth. For him, the job was entertainment and life was just grand.

When the manager was free Lew had some questions ready, those that an ignorant foreigner might make. Were Citroën spares readily available? Was it feasible, or wise, to soup-up the engine? Could the car stand a towing-hitch for a light trailer? The manager was patient and serious but Lew appeared to be in a dither, so no decisions were made. He promised to think about it. He left the garage slowly, still looking around, and walked back to the bar, which was the only place of refreshment within reach and an obvious haunt for thirsty mechanics. It was approaching midday and he expected them to show up soon.

Lew stood at the bar, pacing himself with small glasses of the local white wine, which was rough to drink and disastrous to get tipsy on. To occupy time, he spilt a little on the counter and pushed it around into gargoyle shapes. Then he heard a cheerful voice by his shoulder politely enquiring if Lew had found what he wanted.

'Unfortunately not,' Lew replied, turning to face the young mechanic. 'it's a bit more complicated than I thought and could be quite expensive. You know what big commercial garages are like.' And here he pulled a rueful face, 'But I was wondering,' he went on hesitantly, 'if you or one of your friends in the garage might be in a better position to help me, as it were privately.'

The handsome young man looked at him sharply, instinctively judging Lew's standing and position – his essential loneliness – in the new and shifting relationships of this tourist coast. Then he smiled and touched Lew shyly on the arm.

'Of course, señor,' he said. 'Naturally such a thing is possible. Let me get a *bocadillo* and a beer, then we can sit back there and talk about it.'

Lew bought the drinks, for the mechanic a beer, and then a couple more while he played with the glass of the bad wine. Soon they came to an agreement. The work that Lew wanted done – the mechanic carefully refrained from comment on that – was not so hard, if you had the tools and the ability. The mechanic had both. He had a shack on the edge of town that served as a workshop for the jobs he did in his free time; if he needed specialized equipment he could use the garage on a Sunday, when a certain amount of moonlighting among the mechanics was tolerated.

Lew took a roll of banknotes from an inside pocket of his jacket, shielding the wad from prying eyes. The mechanic looked away, at an advertisement for Larios gin on the far wall. Lew detached some notes and slid them under the table, touching the mechanic's hand. The young man started and may even have blushed, though he was a little too swarthy to tell easily. In general, Lew guessed, he would not be a blusher.

'Something to keep you going,' Lew said in a low voice, 'and to pay for any materials. I'll bring you the car on Monday.'

They smiled at each other, and Lew wondered if he should be afraid of this easy complicity. Of course, there was nothing illegal in modifying a car, as long as safety was not compromised, and what the young man did with his own time was nobody's business. They both intended to avoid the blight of bureaucracy – estimates and bills and taxes and such things. But Lew saw something more in that curly-haired head than financial calculation. The mechanic had an impulse, perhaps irresistible, to cheek the world, to slide by always on the outside, in the scrubland where there were no distinct paths and plenty of cover. It was a world of chances and secret imaginations for those with an itch to play a bravura hand, the cards held tight against the chest.

THE LONG ROAD

Once again, he was driving down from the hills, ticking off points as he went: a suitcase of nondescript clothes, no particular marks or style, nothing to speak of identity or purpose; a sober departure in early morning, the car clean and serviced, papers in order, a story rehearsed and learnt by heart; different crossings worked out at different times, no regularity, no pattern; cash for present purposes but not so much as to appear reckless; names of contacts and arrangements for meetings committed to memory.

After many journeys he had the feel of it. And though in tense moments he still tasted the bile of fear and his scrotum tightened and his hands began to sweat, he knew from experience that, despite these emotional storms, planning and careful preparation weighted the dice in his favour. His was a purpose reduced to a vanishing point, lost in the vast complexity of the world.

This morning, as so often, Lew was driving with the radio turned down low. On an old record Pastora Pavon was painfully wailing a *siguiriya*. He thought of the tragic destiny and fragility of life contained in that *canto hondo*. A soul stripped bare. For a moment, it seemed to mean more – much more – than security, safety and the good pension.

*

The task had become almost routine – almost, but never quite. There was too much hidden danger in it for that, like the pea under the mattress in the fairy tale. But often he had to remind himself to pay attention. There were aspects of the life that were nothing but joy.

He had always looked on himself as a good driver, perhaps in his youth a little too sporting. But the accident in Canada, and the damage to his jaw, had taught him caution and sobriety behind the wheel. He had taken out much of the risk, but the pleasure remained. Now, from Al-Hoceima to Ar-Rachidia, from Taourirt to Kenifra, the freedom of the road was his, all those heaven-ascending, world-bitten roads, going from loneliness to loneliness, or so it seemed to Lew.

He had names, contacts, places to go, nearly always remote places in the Berber Rif or the Middle Atlas. As much as possible he avoided the towns and the middlemen, avoided the entrepreneurs of dreams. Slowly and carefully, over the course of several years, Anders and his couriers had established a network of connection as close to the source as possible among farmers and village elders, among those with tribal authority. Anders always told his men, speaking in the quiet way he had when he was really serious, that they should make no purchase unless the provenance was completely clear. See the crop, look the seller in the eye, squat with him on the ground with a glass of coffee, taste salt and break bread, pass the money into the hands of the community.

Riding the roads, an arm out of the window as if stirring the pure air, Lew saw wherever he went how big and strange and raw this country looked. Taking expansive views expanded him and his understanding. He was alone with the world in a way he had not been before. Able to see more, he felt more. He was a Canadian, used to a gigantic scale in nature, but this land had a spin on it that often bemused him. He was used to wilderness, a profusion of landscape too extensive to tame. But even under the hand of man this Maghreb seemed to Lew to be irredeemably savage, within an inch of some fundamental disorder. And in the distance, on almost every journey that he made, seen from a high pass or through a gap in the forest or slipping off the end of a long hill-flank, there was the full stop of the Atlantic. The Western world had stopped there. In historical times – in the times that mattered most to the West – this land had been man's last handhold. Grip here, or slide into unfathomable depths of ignorance and doubt.

Was that, Lew wondered, the message of the place? Here, on the rim, you proved at last who you are? Others in the past had done it, those Berber tribes from Sahara or High Atlas, the Almoravids and Almohads, who forced an austere Islamic splendour on the North African Maghreb and gave Spain, for all too brief a period, a light and a glory that Western Christendom could never repeat nor ever equal.

The Berbers were reeled back from Spain, of course, by the usual accumulated faults and errors of mankind to which they were as prone as any other people. Yet something important still remained to them in their homeland, if only the look in the eyes of the men in deep country. Not in the eyes of the women, which were still often hidden or averted. That, for Lew, was part of the problem: they gave you nothing, acknowledged nothing, assented to nothing, except to a secret interior life. He had gone a few steps down that well-guarded path. He recalled Fatma in Ketama and Nina in Martil, in astonishment at the presence and the rich resources of femininity behind the veil. But that door ajar on to a brilliant interior closed too soon and no more light emerged.

The look from the men, however, from hooded eyes deep in the shadow thrown by cloak or turban, made Lew uneasy and a little afraid. The look expressed innate animal power, the fury of both the lover and the warrior, the wish to command the world or to withdraw into the contemptuous silence of the saint.

The look had the power to injure, and men knew it. Even to the present time, when a *marabout*, a rebellious warrior-saint of the mountains, was captured it was best that you stabbed him through the back, lest face to face his magic eye bewitched you.

Nor was that the only dangerous look. Perhaps more ominous was the look of complete indifference, the glance that said only too clearly that the person and the piece of the world in view were nothing but a part of the emptiness. That look triumphed over all conquest, all colonialism, all technological change, all modernity. It declared the native unscathed, entrenched in his long story, his family life, his sexuality, his economy of being, his hopes and desires for here and hereafter. Though he had suffered the battering of history and the victory of the West, he did not look on himself as defeated. He was not alienated. His life was reintegrated; it was the others who had foundered. He baffled all science and the power of the victors. For what is victory but the longing to possess, not just the land and the chattels and the economy and the law, but to possess the very being itself? It is what the victor aches for, and to deny him that makes a vanity of triumph. For the winner, disappointed in his victory, there is always an answer. It is the last sign of barbarism, to resist the full submission that the West craves.

Lew was not so sure. He thought he agreed with a contrary opinion that he had read in a French historian of colonialism: far from barbarism, it was the last refuge of human dignity and liberty.

*

He had been driving down from the Jbel bou Iblane shortly before sunset. After several hours on poor roads he was tired. Behind and way below him, edges of the desert were as desolate as a darkening sea. But the airs above the hills were beginning to fidget with the approach of thunder and the leaves on the few trees danced on the boughs.

The road down was twisting like a bad argument and potholes gaped. Lew was driving slowly and carefully, aware of the value of the load he was carrying. Ahead, overlooking a tight bend, a man in dark robes sat on a rock above a small bluff. He was quite still and composed, so that he might have been a part of the landscape, and he had an old, long-barrelled rifle resting against his knee. As the car went by, in low gear on the bend, passing hardly more than a dozen yards from the man, Lew gave him a wave of the hand and a weary grin, fraternal gestures of fellowship between two souls at the end of nowhere. The man on the rock made no movement, his face as utterly blank as the surrounding boulders.

Fifty yards down the road, the car still creaking along slowly, Lew heard the crack of the first shot and the zing somewhere above of the bullet. Lew thought it strange, that a hunter should be after game at this place and hour. Then he heard the second shot and saw the kick of dirt and gravel as the bullet dinged the verge a few feet from the offside front wheel. Lew's foot jabbed the accelerator and the car swayed perilously over the ruts.

There were no more shots, though the car was still in view of the bluff for several more moments. Thinking about it when he was out of range and his heart-rate came down from the stratosphere, Lew reckoned that the shooter had aimed off deliberately. The car had been too close and too easy a target for a rifleman of any experience to miss. The shots had been a warning, but a warning of what? The message had been composed in a script he could not read and a language he didn't understand. As near as he could get to it, he thought it said that he was there under sufferance; but under sufferance of what?

*

He crossed the strip of Mediterranean, that insignificant gap between North Africa and Europe, and the whole feeling was different. He felt emptier, as if something vital had been drained away, something he could not quite measure. Perhaps in compensation for that unspecified disappointment he became brusque and oddly assertive, like a man angry with himself. It gave him an air of impatient confidence; in a way, perhaps, he was pushing upward the probabilities of survival in a chancy undertaking.

At national borders, he hardly paid attention to the guardians of the crossing, staring at some larger future, daring them to make his passage awkward. From time to time they did. They took him in hand, inspected him, patted him down, rumpled his luggage, poked and rapped at parts of the car, but in a cursory way, admitting fatigue and boredom, the investigation being just an apology for their official trade which, they hoped, would not detain him too long from his proper business. He had developed that sort of presence, not because he was arrogant – or not consciously so – but because he was grieving, lamenting pieces of a recent past. To a degree, he was suffering.

He was still cautious – it had become almost second nature – and he varied his routes every time, testing the road grid of Europe as if engaged in some huge game of snakes and ladders. He had learnt that the safest passage was often the most expensive, so he became a careful student of guidebooks put out by motoring organizations like Michelin. Quiet country hotels not too far off the main routes, where waiters seemed to glide on cushioned feet and the desk staff spoke with a hushed awe appropriate for surly gods, suited him well. In towns, he headed for large but old-fashioned hotels, the more stars the better and as stuffy as possible. He found he could put up with a large part of the life of luxury, no trouble at all. He still paid in cash wherever he could, and that was another part of the attraction of old-fashioned hotels. They were the slowest to expect the spreading use of the credit card, a development that worried Lew.

Somewhere along the line he had gained the remote manner of moneyed confidence, scrupulous but cold. 'This room will do well enough,' he would say, '*If* you have nothing better.' Then he would smile briefly.

At dinner, which for him was the peak of each travelling day, he would keep waiter and sommelier in order, refusing to be browbeaten or patronized. 'I hardly think a *Boeuf à la gardiane*,' he would say, frowning and pushing his glasses down a little to study menu and wine list, 'warrants a Saint-Estèphe.'

Or if the waiter's sneer provoked him too much, 'I do not recognize this as a *bouillabaisse*. Maybe the chef would like to reconsider it.'

It was not that he knew so much about food and wine. It was the life he had fallen into, and the protective cover he drew over it.

ROUTE R511

He regarded the Spanish hilltop as home; perhaps the two houses – the village house and the *cortijo* – were both homes. In the intervals between his journeys, sometimes long and sometimes short, he was content and busy enough. For that, he had to thank the native skill of his hands.

In the country, at Vera's *cortijo*, he rolled his sleeves up, cleared old broken stonework, mixed cement, patched and rebuilt. The craft of stonemasonry was new to him but he found he liked it, shaping stones, calculating angles, working out points of stress, filling space evenly and economically. The work was often hard and grimy, lugging cement bags and grappling big stones, and at the day's end his muscles knew that they'd taken on gross, material stuff. Then he didn't need the shower. He stripped off naked and Vera hurled buckets of water over him. It was an intimacy he welcomed, not so much sexual as tender.

Inside the *cortijo*, he saw that the blackened fireplace in the corner of the main room smoked atrociously. It was a peculiar, lumpen structure, rather like a beehive with a hoop cut from the front for the logs. Lew took it apart and refigured it, taking his time, to make a fire draw. He altered the proportions of the flue opening, and on the chimney put a little vane that swayed in the wind. It worked wonders, and in the long cool mountain evenings, in lantern haze and flickering firelight, he and Vera watched the glow of the olive logs, replenishing without hurry their wine glasses from the bottle on the floor between them. In his mind's eye Lew was already considering the old terrace for re-paving, and putting off the thought of what he should do about the leaks in the roof.

*

'Next trip you make,' he heard her saying in her soft mumble, 'I'd like to come with you.'

His hand stopped on the way to the wine bottle. The mood was no longer dreamy; he was paying attention now. She looked up in sudden alarm, sensing his hesitation. 'It's not much to ask,' she added.

They had travelled together, in the line of business, on a few occasions. And though the responsibility for her presence made him more nervous than need be, nothing in particular had gone wrong. But he had no feeling of rightness either, and for Lew that was the problem. Something in Vera's attitude suggested that they might be on an extended holiday. He had an uneasy feeling that she might stop the car, strip to her bikini at any moment, and lie on the beach. What she had in mind was a café or a hotel terrace or a long drink. One pretty place was as good as another, though she hoped she would see the sunset stretched like a curtain of gold over the Kasbah, and the evening would lead to a hot shower and dinner at a clean tablecloth.

She did not appear to see what he was seeing, though he had a hard time telling even himself what it was exactly that he saw. But he knew that he was invigorated, puzzled, set on edge, tested, inspired by the milieu in which he travelled, and he wanted no excursion into the world of the holiday brochure. In some ways, of course, she was an advantage. All the world likes a good-looking woman. She was discreet and quiet and inscrutably calm behind her dark glasses. She had a way of wringing the tension out of what looked like trouble.

'They're just people,' she would say placidly in the face of some potential catastrophe, some human explosion likely to shipwreck them entirely. 'Try to be calm and pleasant.'

They *were* just people, but for the life of him Lew couldn't see what being nice had to do with it. The relation he was trying to establish was too important for just that.

She said she could help with the driving, and it was true that she could take some of the fatigue out of long distances and bad roads. Often, Lew was short of time and needed to press on when he was also short of sleep. But she was an inattentive driver, losing concentration at the wheel, her eyes on the view not the cyclist in front. It was a habit she made generally, to get the ranking of things wrong. More than once Lew had woken from a doze in the passenger seat to find the car lurching over the centre line, squealing on a sharp bend taken too fast, or almost up the backside of a slow moving truck. It offended his sense of competence – like many men he made good driving a mark of virtue – but, far worse, it endangered the cargo they were transporting. It was bad business.

'Hmm,' he had said in reply to her request, wondering if he could get away with just that. There was a cool silence, neither of them anxious to make the next move. Then he sighed. 'It's going to be tough, this time,' he said. 'No fun at all.' He was making his voice as gentle as possible. 'I have to get into a miserable bit of country and get out again fast. There's been trouble down there, local trouble

and trouble with foreigners. I've heard some bad tales from other couriers . . . '
He let his voice trail away, hoping that she would think the worst.

'I'm not afraid,' she said simply, and he knew that was true.

She thought there was some principle at stake here, some urgent matter that covered everything they did, affected their whole relationship. He saw it was wise for him to give way, though he tried a last throw.

'I can't promise any success on this journey,' he said sourly, 'and you might get hurt.'

'I hope you're not too blind to see that I'm hurt already. The point is now, what are you going to do about it?'

*

Lew stood by the side of the road, kicking the dirt, but she was giving him a cool once-over from head to foot. 'Maybe the reason things are going downhill,' she said, 'is because that's the way you expect them to go.'

He scowled, suspecting that she was right.

A tyre had punctured soon after they left the ferry – a jagged scrap of metal among some trash across the road – and he had forgotten for once to check the spare wheel. It was almost flat. They had limped a long way to a garage, and Lew was in a grim mood by the time the problem was fixed. Too late to press on, and on the ugly border of light-industrial sprawl they found sad lodgings in a room with a rusty iron bed and leprous plaster. Up in a corner a spider fondled the desiccated shards of its victim. Waking in the night, Lew heard through the partition wall short cries that might have been pain or pleasure.

Next morning, they had been driving for about an hour, and the day was smiling in a way calculated to salve wounds, when Vera suddenly touched her wrist and found that she had left her watch by the tin basin on the washstand in the room. She insisted that they go back.

'We've lost too much time already,' he grumbled. 'I can buy you another one.'

'I don't want another one,' she replied. 'It's an old watch, not easy to replace. It's beautiful and it has sentimental value. I want to go back.'

'It can't mean *that* much,' he protested.

'Don't be so damn sure. If you knew anything about real feelings you'd go back.'

That sounded ominous, so Lew wrestled the car around with bad grace and drove back rather too fast. In the house, they found the owner beaming with untrustworthy candour, denying that a watch could ever have been there, for was it not he himself who had cleaned and tidied the room no more than an hour before? It was no use arguing, and to call the police was pointless. The watch was gone. They drove on and for all the calm brightness of the day they might as well have been ploughing through snowdrifts in darkness.

Lew felt lost, though he had a place and a name to look for. He had a map and his map-reading was fine. The land looked, in its gross features, as if he were seeing in monochrome a country that only revealed its full features in colour. He was hunting through hills and gaps and passes that seemed to him to be battlements rather than landscape. It occurred to him that he was not so much engaged in trade as in a strange warfare between a solid historical past, and a present of radical, irreconcilable doubts and fears. No wonder the people clammed up. Was he an ally or a fifth-columnist? Was there any way of knowing in truth what *kif* or hash meant to this society? He was not sure if he was helping, but he certainly didn't want to betray these people.

By mid-afternoon Vera had made peace with him. Neither of them cared to prolong the bitterness; the day was too fine for that. The sunroof was open and she had hitched up the long sober skirt that he had advised her to wear in traditional country and was trying to get some suntan on her thighs. He couldn't help sneaking some admiring looks in that direction. The road was looping towards what looked like a small battered fort in a high, dry valley, and there was something about the commanding position that made Lew hopeful. At least they might find a place to eat and to rest.

Just below the fort, stopping by a scruffy teahouse with, outside it, a bench and a couple of busted chairs lying in shadow, Lew saw a youngish man dressed in parts of a Western suit. He had straddled one of the outside chairs, leaning on the backrest, and he was smoking a cigarette. He wore well-pressed trousers and an unbuttoned waistcoat above an open-necked white shirt, and Lew knew then that he had come to the right place.

The man stood up and began without preliminaries. 'So you've come at last,' he said in English with an American accent. 'I was beginning to worry and had almost given up on you.' He shook hands in a distant manner as if conferring some vague honour.

So this, Lew said to himself, is the new man of the Maghreb. He was obviously Moroccan, a Berber most likely, but only partly attached, a citizen of a wider world, travelled, intimate with airline schedules, darting between languages. Buying and selling. He was a type that made Lew uncomfortable – the things the man surely knew, which were very many, were filed in unrecognizable, untraditional pigeonholes, and you never knew what he might pull out and what use he would put it to.

'The lady,' he said, giving Vera an uncompromising stare, 'I think it is best if she stays here. Our friends are shy and perhaps a little wild still. They are not used to foreign women. If she stays in the café here, I'll tell the boss to look after her. She will not be annoyed or disturbed.'

He had said his piece and that was enough. He turned and walked away without looking back. Lew hesitated, started after him, and then stopped. He shrugged, saying apologetically to Vera, 'That's the way it has to be, I can't help it.'

Her face went stiff and she didn't deign to acknowledge his apology. The shutter had come down between them again.

*

Later that evening, when the business was complete, Lew returned from the fort to find Vera eating a kebab and a dish of sliced cucumbers. The meat on the skewer looked greasy and underdone and the edges of the cucumber were shrivelled and puckered like an old mouth. Her glass of mint tea, the last of several, was cold.

'Well?' she said, wiping her fingers on a piece of Arabic newsprint. Her voice was challenging.

'Well enough,' he answered softly. 'The hash is good but the atmosphere was tricky. I'm a little afraid of that man, though he comes recommended, and he was very businesslike in a Western sort of way. Perhaps that's what worried me. I had a moment of palpitations when I went to fetch the money from the car. Then he threw me further off beam by turning on the charm. The packages were all in order and of the correct size, and he got his ruffians to help me stow them. Then the chief ruffian made a little speech which I couldn't understand, even when it was translated to me. Something to do with honour and friendship and straight manly dealing. He was a kind of huge Gog or Magog with a beard, and I trembled lest my face might take on the wrong expression. The whole deal took a few hours, but it seemed like an eternity before I could drive back here, fearful that there might be a gun in the background.'

He rolled his eyes and puffed his cheeks in mock terror. 'So, here I am.'

'Where are we going to stay tonight?' she asked.

'They offered me a room in that old fort. But I said I had a woman with me and the offer was withdrawn. Ask in the village, they said.'

'Let's just leave. It's creepy here, and the food is horrible. We can drive into open country and find a spot to park. The weather is mild enough, and it's not impossible to sleep in the car.'

He looked at her doubtfully, but saw that she'd had enough of nearly everything including, if he didn't watch his step, himself. He put some coins on the table – more than enough–and they left. A few swifts were still sky-plunging, chasing them down the road for the bounty of the insects swirled up in the cars wake. Lew drove for an hour or so, looking for a secluded spot where he could pull off the road. It was difficult to judge in the gathering dark; the headlights flushed over rough banks and uninviting borders. Vera felt the beginnings of stomach pains, the result, she supposed of the vile meat in the kebab. And then it was necessary to stop immediately while she made a run behind a boulder. It was senseless to go on, so Lew slid the car between two southern pines a few yards from the roadside. The car rested at a slight tilt, but it would have to do.

Lew removed the car seats, which in the Citroën was easy, but the space was still cramped and the night surprisingly cool. At another time they would have huddled together for warmth, but Vera thought the state of her stomach might lead to sudden exits into the night, and there was still some frost between them after the events of the day. When they lay down obstinate bits of car body dug into them while they listened to the strange riot of the night, chirring and ringing and rasping, and the crepidation of tiny unknown beasts.

In the morning they were stiff and grouchy, neither of them having slept much. Vera's innards were still disturbed, though the trouble seemed to have slipped from the stomach to the bowel. Lew filled his hash pipe, and after a long thoughtful pause sharing it they both had a better view of the day. Vera took a critical look at herself in the rear-view mirror, brushed her hair vigorously, applied some lipstick and a few dabs of scent. Lew replaced the seats and then inspected the hidden compartments, making sure everything was sealed and secure, He was planning a long run to the boat at Melilla; there would be little chance for further adjustments.

He studied the map. They had drifted into an area of blankness where roads seemed to be an afterthought and one route looked as circuitous as another. He decided to head for R511, a pale, insignificant trace on the map but running fairly straight along a rivercourse for most of its length and then emptying into the main road to Melilla. He knew nothing about the condition of the road, or the traffic, but a straight line surely had advantages over the wild twists of the road rippling out of the hills. But he guessed it would be a long tiring haul needing some patience and charity towards each other.

*

The sun was high, a great bloodshot eye in the heavens, too hot to have the sunroof open; dust blew in the windows, getting under their sunglasses. There were few signs of humans or animals, and another car was a red-letter event. The landscape had turned suddenly inhospitable, turned alien and ugly. The note of the engine at first went unnoticed, then it irritated every atom in the body.

Only in short stretches could Lew put on some speed, and the nagging progress fretted him. He was weary already, from the worry of the journey, from the poor night, and he was yawning by midday. Vera, who had settled into a doze, shot awake twice and pulled them over, muttering about diarrhoea as she headed for wasteland. On the move again, Lew tried the radio but soon snapped it off, unable to bear Arab lamentations. They came too close to his own despondency.

By the middle of the afternoon he knew he was beat. They had stopped yet again for the sake of Vera's bowels and Lew waited for her, leaning on the bonnet and smoking a cigarette. She emerged from bushes looking wan and dragged out, but possibly more alive than he felt. At least she'd got some sleep in the spare seat.

'Do you think you could manage some driving?' he said doubtfully. 'I'm just about out on my feet.'

'I can take over,' she replied. 'I'm awake now and it will give me something to do. Take my mind off the rumblings below.' She felt as if she had been out of control, flying low with the bomb doors open, polluting the country beneath.

Any diversion was welcome.

There were still some twisty miles of the road ahead, and then the flat bottomlands of the river valley would take them north. Lew anticipated a smooth ride and stretched himself luxuriously in the passenger seat. Vera pulled herself up to the steering wheel, adjusted the wing mirror and looked determined.

*

He was dreaming of something delicious which, later, he could not remember at all. He woke with a jerk, already in a state of panic, though he had no idea why. Something large, dark and heavy blasted by much too close with a furious tirade from its horn. It seemed to hit somewhere; there was a noise like ripping canvas along the side of the car, and then the Citroën shimmied, shaking its hips, and began to wobble with a curious rowing motion as the soft suspension induced an oscillation widening towards chaos. Vera gave a cry, almost a moan, and began to saw at the wheel with no effect. The front end was already going its own way. Then something grey and stumpy and four-legged loomed beyond the windscreen; the head was turned towards the car, teeth bared as though offering the grimace that follows a malign joke. The car lifted the donkey and threw it aside and it was past in a flash, and then the car was sliding into a broad, shallow ditch. Friction took speed off the car rapidly and after banging along rough ground for about fifty yards it bumped the offside front wheel against a rock and tipped them forward, not too violently. A long crack ran diagonally across the windscreen but it did not shatter. Then there was a near silence, the only sound the ticking of hot metal and Vera's quiet sobs.

They were shaken and a little bruised but not badly hurt. Lew had an abrasion on his forearm, leaking thin blood, but he felt the claustrophobia of the battered car more than anything else. He thrust his door upwards, clambered out, then reached in and pulled Vera out after him.

'That poor animal,' she said between sobs.

'But what were you doing? You were in the middle of the road when that truck had to squeeze by.'

'I know, I know. I saw the donkey about to cross the road and wanted more than anything to avoid it.'

'But the truck was coming . . .'

'I know, I know,' she almost whispered, and she was crying again.

The truck had gone on, not bothering to stop, and was out of sight and sound. Light was fading, dying into the half-tones of dusk, and at first they missed the donkey. Then they saw it, indistinct, lying beyond the road next to a big shrubby bush. Lew could not recall that he had ever seen a donkey lie down before. Miraculously, it was alive despite the fearful blow, watching them approach with drooping eyes that seemed to hold no memory of recent near-death. When they were almost within reach of it, it struggled up, revealing a long bloody slash down one flank, and limped away, bones cracked or muscles torn. Vera wanted to go after it, offer it some sort of solace, but Lew stopped her.

'Best to leave it alone,' he said, remembering the farm animals of his youth. 'A hurt animal needs to be alone more than anything. There's nothing we can do except terrify it even more. At least it's moving. Instinct will take it home.'

He took her by the arm and led her back to the crashed car, and then she sat on a hillock while he assessed the damage. She did not look at the car, as if they were slightly apart now, not quite in this trouble together.

One of the suspension struts was bent and the wheel had tucked under. He saw that the car would not run, even if they could get it back on to the road. There was torn metal down the offside and across the rear wheel arch, where the projecting bumper of the truck had just caught them, tearing the skin of the car. It was not structural damage, but one of the hidden compartments had been ripped open and a split package of hash had spilled on the ground. Lew looked around guiltily, as though the world was watching. But all around the dusk settled on an empty land. He went and stood over Vera, an unspoken accusation in his stance.

'It won't run,' he said brusquely. 'Things are bent and it will take a garage to straighten them out. Worse, the body's ripped and some of the hash is leaking. It's too far gone to patch here, and I can't afford to let others see it.'

'What will you do?' She didn't much care; she was remembering the donkey heaving over the bonnet and flying away.

'Burn it, I reckon. Torch the car, let it all go up in flames, destroy as much as possible. It won't deceive a close inspection, but out here perhaps it won't come to that. With luck, they'll just think it's a car crash gone up in smoke. And if they have second thoughts we'll be well out of the country.'

She shrugged – it was his decision. She searched in her bag for a cigarette while he went to fix matters.

He took out the toolkit and unscrewed the number plates, stowing them in one of their travel bags – as usual, they were travelling light – which he then placed in the ditch well away from the car. He opened his bag for a tee-shirt, which he ripped into strips and knotted together to make a long cotton wick. He inserted this wick deep into the petrol tank and waited for the cotton cloth to soak up the fuel. While this was happening, he detached the fuel pipe from the carburettor, then turned the ignition key to activate the electric fuel pump. When the petrol spurted through he splashed it around as far as he could reach, over the engine and inside the body. Then he was ready.

He found an old map of Spain in the door pocket, tore it apart and crumpled the paper into balls. With his lighter he set fire to the cloth wick, and then lit the balls of paper which he tossed within the car. He walked away quickly, looking over his shoulder, and stood by Vera. Still seated on the hillock she glanced up, showing little interest, as if at some inferior son et lumière too tedious to contemplate.

Flames advanced hesitantly, spluttering and at one point nearly dying. Then something caught and a rosy glow leapt and spread like an aurora, momentarily as cheerful as a log fire in winter. Lew grabbed Vera's arm, pulling her up and away. There was a boom as vapour in the petrol tank exploded, and then roaring flames climbed into the dusky heavens, making the shadows writhe.

Looking at the conflagration Lew allowed himself a perverse smile. A gigantic offering of cannabis – almost a celebration – flared into the sunset sky.

*

The junction with the main road was no more that two or three miles ahead. They could walk it, if they took it easy, even though each had a bag to carry. She walked in front, not wanting at this stage to be touched. She thought about the donkey, and what kind of pain it had felt, and if that mattered.

'What were you doing?' he said suddenly from behind.

'What do you mean?'

'You were in the middle of the road, right?'

'I told you – the donkey.'

'But the middle of the road, with a truck coming. Surely you saw that?'

'I know,' she said, as if it didn't matter, 'I know.'

Nothing seemed to matter now. Or at least not in any comprehensible order of importance. Why was she thinking of the damned donkey when she could have got them killed?

Trudging on, they said no more. After a while they heard a light noise of traffic, and later saw a few headlights up ahead, passing back and forth on the road to Melilla. They turned on to the big road, put their bags on the ground and waved down the first car.

Costa del Sol

From the cracked paving of the *corjito* Anders was considering the landscape in his fastidious way, as if judging a painter – Claude Lorrain perhaps – whose conception of the view had surprised him. There were points in the composition that appeared anomalous – a quarry, an electricity pylon, a tall smokestack. Almost an idyll, Anders's frown seemed to say, but not quite.

Lew was bringing out drinks on a tray and Vera was sitting in a torn canvas chair, looking from one to the other, hoping they might be able to make sense of her world again. They could begin with the landscape and go on from there.

'Awkward to be up here without a car,' Anders said, measuring in his mind's eye the distance from the coast up into the hills. 'Very few buses, I expect. And a long way to walk.' He laughed briefly, to signal a Swedish joke.

'I'm after another car, a secondhand one,' Lew replied. 'In the meantime, we'll manage.'

We – what was she to make of that?

'I've made some enquiries across the water,' Anders went on. 'From old contacts, of course. All is quiet, so I'm told. Just a burnt-out car by the roadside. Mysterious, maybe, but these things happen. The authorities are showing no interest. Better things to do, thank goodness.'

He took a glass of wine from the tray and gave them both a solemn salute. 'The main things are, you are unhurt, no investigation was made, no one was fined or went to jail, and our line of communication is still intact.'

'But the loss,' Lew asked, 'what about that? How do I make it up to you.'

Vera wanted to say, 'And what about me? Have I no responsibility?' But she kept silent.

'Oh, I see no problem there,' Anders replied. 'You stand the loss of your car and, of course, the loss of the profit you would have made from that run. As to loss of the stock-in-trade, let's just say that it's a hazard of the business that we have learnt to bear. A business write-off.'

He gave a sketchy smile and waved the topic away. 'Besides, we are coming to the end of our operation in North Africa. The field is getting too crowded and the newcomers play it too rough. They are, as you say, not gentlemen. In fact, many of them are riff-raff, too greedy, lacking all discipline, too violent. We all get a bad name and the authorities begin to panic, then they also become violent and crooked. We've had some good times there, but they are almost over now and it's time to get out. I have some other plans.'

He took a long drink and looked at Lew quizzically, like the examiner about to ask the tricky question, the one you had better answer right. 'You don't mind long-distance travel, do you?'

'Travel to where?'

'Well, I was thinking of India and Pakistan.'

*

If he went, she thought that might be the end of it, the page on which she was tentatively writing her life blotched beyond recovery. She was not sure what to make of that. There were other pages open, other stories to compose. Disaster was an episode, not an absolute; it got roiled up with everything else in life, including success, and what emerged eventually was something you often had no reason to expect. It was possible, even, to take some satisfaction in failure, as a test of character, as an incentive to change.

Working these matters over, she thought there could be some interesting possibilities for her either way. But when she tried to address the dilemma from Lew's point of view her mind went blank.

*

He'd bought the cement and the sand and now that the weather was fine he wanted to make a start on the paving. He had staked out a sinuous plan, following the flow of the ground, helping the house blend into the landscape. He did not want this terrace to be a scar upon nature, like so many others he saw in the converted farmhouses of rich foreigners, offences to frighten birds and beasts. And after the terrace there was the roof to fix, though he tried to forget about that.

They were having breakfast in the village house. Anders had gone down the hill last evening, and for most of the night they had been stumbling over the proposition he had left behind. Nothing was certain, though they both knew he was inclining towards Anders's plan. For the moment, however, the intensity of this preoccupation threw Lew in a loop from which he was anxious to escape. Manual work would be a relief, and there was labour he could get under way at the *cortijo*.

Vera was squeezing the last drop of coffee from the breakfast pot. 'Go out there, by all means,' she said indifferently. 'But don't bother to start work.'

'Why is that?' he asked, halfway to the door.

'Well, will you be around to finish it? I'm not keen to live on an abandoned building site.'

'But it's something I've had planned for quite a time,' he protested. 'I'd like to get going on it.'

'Seems to me,' she said in a tight voice, 'that you plan many things important to *you*. I see few things realized, but many unanswered questions and a lot of painful turmoil on the way.'

It needed an answer, he could see that, but he did not have one at the moment. He could only reach for his beret and head for the door.

'Damn you,' she called after him, 'can't you see that your way of doing things has victims? Are you always going to leave the wounded behind?'

She did not know what else to say, since everything was partly her fault. In a rage she hurled her coffee cup into the sink; she found she was snivelling like a child.

WEST TO EAST

Where was he now? The plane had departed from London Heathrow late afternoon – about the rush hour – and to get up into the unburdened air at that time was a relief. The airport had been, as usual, a hell devised by mankind in the name of rush and money. The tourist class in the Delhi-bound plane was packed with Indian nationals shuttling between alternative lives, running away or skipping home, standing in long impatient lines at the check-in desks, tripping over large cardboard boxes secured with twine, nudging forward foot by foot battered cases big enough to contain a small boy. Ladies in beautiful saris were about as much out of place as a Hawaiian beach shirt on a miner fresh out of the pit.

Darkness at 30,000 feet. Lands below mysterious enough at the best of times, desert or mountain, a question mark between East and West. The cabin lights turned low, a few reading lights still on, and a glow down the aisles pointing the way to the toilets. The drone of the engines muted and comforting, people tumbled into sleep, or vacant in space when sleep wouldn't come. Lew was awake, didn't want to sleep, too much stubborn matter in his mind. And below the earth was turning, getting ready another wide swath of difficult land. At the moment, from his window seat, there was nothing to see. The pall of dark night below was just beginning to show a purple tinge in the east where the rising sun was rushing towards them.

Seated next to Lew was a bulky Sikh, dark turban tightly wound, looking like a clinker-built hull upside down. After the take-off the Sikh had put on wire-rimmed glasses and directed them studiously at the London *Times*, the large sheets of newsprint cunningly folded into a manageable handful. When dinner came he picked at the vegetarian offering without enthusiasm; he and Lew exchanged some pleasantries and that was enough. Then the Sikh slept, askew in his seat, mouth a little open and snoring lightly to some quiet interior rhythm.

Looking around, Lew was content. He sighed with satisfaction. He had suspected it before but now he knew it: to travel alone was the only way. He shuddered at the thought of company. Vera or another, friend or partner, it didn't matter. In his line of business he had to admit that colleagues were useful and often necessary, to show the way, to open doors, to brush the path. But he wished to go no further than that. Moments of departure pleased him most, the expectation of what was to come like a white city of dreams. The middle passage was fine, the future still almost inexhaustible. The troubles began on arrival, events crowding in unexpected and so often painful.

Next day, as the plane taxied to the stand at Delhi, and they undid their seatbelts, the Sikh opened the overhead locker and reached down Lew's bag for him.

'End of the line for you?' he asked politely, now that the intimacy of the journey was over and he could be safely rid of Lew.

'No, I meet a colleague here, and then we go on.'

'Not too far, I hope for your sake,' said the Sikh. 'About to the Red Fort and back would be far enough.'

'Oh, why is that?' Lew looked up sharply, hearing something in the Sikh's tone that sounded not from the guidebooks or the business manuals.

'The whole country is cracking up, in my opinion,' he replied sourly. 'It's moved too fast since Partition, an onrush of competing ideals and traditions. And questionable practices. No idea where it's going, just hoping to pluck money from the air. An ant heap, without the organizational ability of ants. I have to do business here but I don't stay a minute longer than I can help. Let me tell you something that may amaze or appal you. You know the town of Slough, in the outer wasteland of London, that joke-town of English comedians? Well, I rush back to my home in Slough. It's paradise, I can tell you, compared to my birthplace in Chandigarh.'

The Sikh moved towards the exit and Lew followed him, seeing that the man was working up an anger that everyone knew to be hopeless. He had not the weapons for this struggle; rage, courage, cunning, intelligence, perseverance were as nothing, all drowned in the bog of the homeland.

Outside the plane, Delhi awaited them, hot, dirty, nearly naked, flaunting some evils of humanity you could hardly imagine.

*

Karl Kruis had tried halfheartedly but couldn't like dark-faced folk, all those people he called 'kaffirs'. His birth, history and education were against him. He was a Boer, a white South African from a dying age. He was not cruel or vicious towards them, but how did liking come into it? Some people had to stand in the mud to support the privilege and well-being of others. He saw nothing particularly wrong with that. It is what had always happened, almost a theorem of life.

And even if it wasn't a theorem, luckily it worked out pretty well for the whites.

*

Lew had a name and a hotel: Karl Kruis and the Good Time Hotel, and he was apprehensive about both. He took a taxi from the airport, a fat old-fashioned vehicle of a type he had not seen in the West for years. The least thing enraged the driver, a squat man who swelled like a toad with venom, driving as if thrusting a broom through debris that wouldn't clear, debris composed of disintegrating traffic and frantic lives. The angrier he became the more random and wild was his onrush, missing humans and hard objects by a hair's breadth.

The hotel was in New Delhi, in Paharganj, a name that the driver ruminated on in horror, so much so that he refused to locate the hotel exactly, dropping Lew off in a main street of many sleazy establishments. To ask directions Lew entered a small shop smelling as peculiar as a bear cave and the courtly shopkeeper, speaking a ravaged version of English, offered to send a boy, for a few small coins, to guide him. The Good Time Hotel was in fact up an alleyway just around the corner, but Lew reckoned that a safe arrival was worth some small change. And the hotel would have been hard to distinguish among the jumble of signs, announcing places of blistered paint and broken shutters and rusty grilles. The Good Time also had a manager with a runny nose and eyes that believed nothing. It was a cheap place, carelessly run, none too clean but uninquisitive, a staging post for backpackers and hippies. Lew saw at once why it had been chosen.

The taxi ride had taken a long time, and though in general Lew did not mind the heat, he found that the misery and frayed nerves of the journey had worked him into a troubled sweat by the time he arrived and shook the cool hand of Karl Kruis.

Lew had never met Kruis, who had the reputation of an experienced courier on the East-West route. It was said that he knew the way the game was played and dealt his hand as well as anyone. Looking at him for the first time Lew was not so sure he could believe it. The bold, bulging eyes suggested a lack of imagination, that Kruis might miss the fine cracks in the fabric or not estimate the depths of the pitfalls. But there he was, a survivor, and his bland stare spoke of confidence and even cunning. Lew imagined him touching his nose with his forefinger and winking, claiming to have the day by the balls.

Later, when Lew had washed and cleaned up, they sat on two hard shabby chairs in the little lobby of the hotel, and Lew allowed the bodily discomfort to relieve him of some of his mental anxiety. They were alone as evening quickly descended on a space already gloomy, deliberately wrapped in shadows against the heat. Lew had no wish to go out yet; he thought he needed some rest and some deep breaths before he risked the Delhi streets.

Conversation was cautious. Forced together by Anders's plans, they were still stumbling over each other's feet. 'The secret of this continent,' Karl said after one of the long pauses, uncapping a silver flask and handing it to Lew for a tot of whisky, 'is to believe nothing before you see it, trust no one, test everything.' It sounded like a meagre, uninspiring programme. 'And always try to get a good night's sleep,' he added, taking back the flask, 'or you'll find that there are enough provocations to drive you to permanent insomnia.'

They retreated upstairs and Karl softly closed the door to his room in Lew's face. That appeared to be about as friendly as he got; but Lew didn't mind. He was looking for an efficient partner, not a pal.

Next day, Lew took it easy, resting and reading. Karl was out in the town, making plans, and Lew didn't miss him. He felt that his new companion might be a useful guide in practical matters but no fountain of wisdom. In the intervals between reading Lew took a stroll in the streets, curious but not anxious to be immediately engaged. He feared that it might be dangerous for him to become committed in India either for good or bad. In a land so vast and various it might take a geological age to reach sound conclusions. His task was to get in and out safely, leaving the least shadow on the ground and the waters unruffled.

In the street, at one of the many food-stalls, Lew bought a helping of rice and some spicy vegetables and a couple of chapatis – he didn't like the look of the meat – and returned to his room in the hotel. After the unsettling turbulence of the streets, the privacy of his room was comforting. The food was good and he enjoyed it, and he had enough sense to avoid the tap water in favour of Pepsi. Then he began to read again into the early night. After a time he was nodding, and then his head jerked up in some alarm, not quite remembering what it was that lay on the other side of the dingy wall. He closed his eyes again and drifted, despite the heat, into an early sleep.

KASHMIR

A day later, Lew was up in the air again, with Karl Kruis, flying towards Srinagar in Kashmir.

The flight had begun peacefully over the baked plains of the Punjab, but as the weather started to swirl off the foothills of the mountains the plane – not one of the giant airliners – began to buck and shake so that Lew wondered if he were going to be sick. Karl, sitting next to Lew, was looking comfortable and complacent – the world traveller at ease – and was rooting in his mouth with a toothpick. It was a vulgarity that gave Lew further unease and he closed his eyes, only opening them again when he heard Karl talking between the bumps of the flight. He was explaining the world as he saw it.

'I didn't do much when I was a kid,' he was saying, 'except play sport. Oh, I was an average scholar and got by okay in that respect, without trying too hard. But I was a damn good cricketer, and I put all my effort into that.'

He paused as the plane tried to drop from under them and waited for Lew to choke back the blockage in his throat.

'But then in South Africa,' he continued, 'I'd gone about as far as I could at my level and reckoned my game needed the wider experience you could get in England. We were popular there, in club cricket, more talented and less idle than the locals, and if you were good enough you could survive the season on expenses, handouts and sleeping on a friend's floor. The wives of the club cricketers liked us too. Many were bored housewives and didn't mind the occasional thrash around with an energetic, suntanned hunk of southern manhood. Besides, among us ex-colonials almost every young fellow wished to spend some time in England, if not in Europe, to sort those places out.'

Lew reflected that he, a Canadian, was a colonial also, at least if looked at through the wrong end of the telescope. Yet he had never discovered in himself any nostalgia for England, nor a particular desire to be there. But then he knew almost nothing about cricket; it appeared to him to be an irrational, slow, difficult pastime, as much about hierarchy and social ritual as about sport.

'It was a good time,' Karl was smiling at his memories, 'and I thought I would stay as long as I could. But there's a problem in England, if you come from South Africa. You miss the sun, even in the summer, and I'd rather not talk about the winter. Word got around that the place to be in the winter was the south of Spain. Life there was said to be easy, cheap and warm. I had a bit of money tucked away, so I went.'

He stopped as the plane eased out of its groans and in a while the seatbelt light went out. He shifted in his seat, giving his bottom a new purchase, and seemed for a moment to have lost his place in the story.

'So how did you get into our trade?' Lew prompted him, still anxious to get his mind off the sickbag in the seat pocket ahead of him.

'Spain suited me fine,' Karl went on, 'and I bummed around. I'm a handy guy, ready to have a go at most things, and I soon fell into various jobs among the expats. I'd meant to return to England for the next cricket season, but there I was after six months, serving bar at a lively spot in Torremolinos, enough cash to be going on with, and making out with a bouncy German girl. I saw no reason to leave – I was like a pig in muck. I reckoned I had plenty of years left to face up to responsibility. For the present, I lay on the beach, drank a beer or two, put in my hours at the bar, then met the girlfriend, smoked some grass ... well, you get the picture.

'And then this guy, this Swede called Anders, comes into the bar from time to time, in the dead hours when no one much is around, so we get talking. We share a little hash, which is first-rate, then he sells me some at a good price, and soon he's sounding me out with a certain proposition. I guess he summed me up pretty quick – footloose and happy-go-lucky, no ties, no burdens, no local history, ready to travel and able to look after myself. Suddenly I'm in business.'

Just like that? The way it was told, Lew wondered at the lack of reflection. A cricketer one minute, a drug-courier the next. Perhaps it was a key to the character. 'And then?' Lew said.

'To North Africa, back and forth, for a couple of years. Without languages, I was the low man on the team, limited to driving. Others prepared the delivery car; I collected it and took it away. I didn't even know where the stuff was hidden. And that was an advantage at the borders. It stopped me having kittens when the investigators got warm. I had enough sense to keep rigidly to instructions. No deviation, no foolishness. In fact, to be a young South African rambling around Europe was not a bad cover. I think Anders saw that at once. Policemen and officials used to smile at my hearty colonial innocence – my stupidity – banging around Europe and North Africa with a sunny disposition and hardly a word beyond English, scratching my head at difficulties. I got help from people who might well have locked me up.'

'As easy as that?' Lew said with some irony. 'No dark moments?'

That stopped Karl for a minute and his face lost its look of self-satisfaction. He seemed adrift for a while, puzzled by his own response.

'Well, there was something,' he began again slowly. 'In North Africa – all those black and brown faces. I was in their country, of course, trading with them on level terms, so they demanded respect. That I understood. But I felt naked there, almost at their mercy, and I just wasn't comfortable. Were they sneering at me, in their funny language? I saw something in their eyes that seemed to make me less than what I had been. I wasn't used to that and didn't like it.'

He sighed, wondering how the world had come to that, and then went on. 'I told Anders my troubles and immediately he suggested a change of scene. What did I think about India? I gave it some thought and was surprised to realize that I didn't mind. In South Africa, Indians were no mystery to me. I reckoned I had that relationship worked out. And a whole lot of Indians speak English, more or less. Going to India seemed in many ways like a homecoming. There was an expectation, among Indians, about the white man, arising out of a long history of empire. I think they know in their hearts what's what.'

'Like good dogs, you mean?' Lew said. 'Well-trained, obedient, wagging happy tails?' Karl looked shocked. He could barely understand such a remark.

'No, you misunderstand. We're not talking morality here, nor human rights, nor social justice. I'm sketching a situation, an existing state of affairs. I accepted the land as it lay and took whatever advantage that gave me. I'm here for only one purpose, not for the love of the place. Look here, why do you think we're going to Kashmir? Obviously, there's plenty of cannabis there. The farmers are anxious to sell and the middlemen don't mind helping them. Makes money for everyone, including us. But the place is in some chaos, under permanent expectation of war. Soldiers are forever prowling around, stirring up resentments and hatred. That's what 'peacekeepers' do. Authority has a narrow limit. Daily, life requires some reinvention, and law – martial law, really – is something you step around if you can. Yet at the same time the region relies so heavily on tourism that the military dare not stop the flow. Control it if you can, but what are you going to do with many thousand holidaymakers and foreigners, young folk mainly, restlessly coming and going all the time? That makes fertile ground for us. We blend easily into the mix and everyone is quite pleased to see us. Even the military tolerate us, so long as we're discreet. The military brass have sterner things to do – shoot Pakistanis and insurgents. Cannabis is only a minor nuisance. And the poor ordinary soldiers have no prejudice at all against hash or grass. If you're freezing your butt off on a mountaintop, watching for shadows along the Line of Control, a little *charas* helps pass the time nicely.'

*

Srinagar, city of lakes and gardens, haven of peace, favourite retreat of the Mughal emperors, looked to Lew like the crap-end of the military lines in a cantonment. Soldiers everywhere, bored and uncomprehending, pushing people around because that's what soldiers do when in doubt. Officers in four-wheel drives splashed through dirty puddles, spraying a kind of contempt, marking a distance from the local population. Checks and searches, men with guns stifling their yawns behind barricades of sandbags. Big trucks in olive drab trying to navigate lanes designed for mules and tongas. And as if it didn't notice the River Jhelum still rushed through the city, at this stage in its development still a sparkling Himalayan stream dashing beneath its handsome bridges. It put matters in some perspective.

But out towards Dal Lake, where Lew and Karl went looking for lodgings, something of the old serenity returned. Fanciful houseboats, looking too fine and select for ordinary living, added mystery to quiet waters. To launch out towards them, even over a short distance of lake, seemed like the abandonment of a bad world for a richer history. Beyond the lake, the hills of Pir Panjal spread an unflawed covering of dark woods towards the grimy lap of the city. And to the north, the snowy folds of the Himalayan peaks pulled a sky of mists and clouds towards them.

They sat in a teahouse low down by the lake, where it was hard to tell what was land or water or sky. They were drinking the green *kahwa* tea.

'See what I mean about Kashmir?' Karl said, beaming like a TV ad for toothpaste.

Lew sipped his tea. He didn't quite see what Karl meant, but he hoped he was getting there.

*

Azhar, the Kashmiri called 'AM' by his Western friends and contacts, as if he were the host of an early-morning talk show, had a nervous disposition. He regarded it as his warning system, attuned to the minute ground shifts that might lead at any moment to fracture and sudden catastrophe. He needed to watch those signs – he more than most – for he was a middleman in the hash trade, the linkman between the heartbreaking insecurity of the farmers and the shifty dreams of the West. It was a trade built on the fault lines of contrary human desire, and a missed step could lead to a fall without recovery. He ascribed his modest success to his nerves, and listened to what they told him. And now he was worried.

He had a favoured customer – a South African – awaiting him with a bundle of cash and an impatient courier in tow. How was he to satisfy them? He had the hash ready for delivery. But not only did he have to sidestep the rigid lines thrown out by military practice – in itself a problem he could get round with no difficulty – but he was also becoming aware of a turf war developing among his own kind in his own territory. Some rough and dangerous men were making threats. Azhar was a peaceful man and frightened of violence. It was this that made him a popular man with the Western dealers.

*

They had expected the exchange to take place somewhere in crowded Srinagar. The monsoon was over, the weather was at its best. The trekkers, the holidaymakers, those in flight from the stress-torn plains were making the most of the good times. There was, Lew thought, enough natural hustle to hide under.

At breakfast on the second day in town Lew found Karl in a solemn mood. Lines were crawling across his forehead, as if his thoughts were having trouble getting up there.

'A message from AM,' Karl said, hardly waiting for Lew to pour his tea. 'Change of plan. We're to take the bus to Gulmarg and AM will meet us there. Do the business there. I detect some extra caution, a slight panic maybe.'

'Trouble?' Lew enquired. 'Perhaps we should draw back a bit, wait a few days. Scout the land.'

'There's no time to spare,' Karl complained. 'Once the deal is set up each extra moment adds to the risk. In and out quickly, that's a golden rule. I know enough about AM to have confidence in his judgement – up to a point. Besides, at this state of play he calls the shots. We can deal, or we can cut and run. Damned if I'm going to run.'

His voice rose a little, showing an unexpected excitement. But long ago Lew had been forced to see that, in their business, to embrace danger was part of the fun. They thought they were free agents, with choices lined up like taxicabs, but in fact most of them were fatalists. Fortuna was their goddess, the highly respected deity Machiavelli called the Bitch Goddess. It was a test of their prowess and virtue to take the given circumstance and run with it, dodging and weaving as the obstacles arose.

'So we go?' Lew asked.

'We do,' Karl replied without hesitation.

The instructions were simple. Each of them was to carry a large rucksack, of a familiar sort, in a dark colour. The make was not important. Fill the rucksacks with picnic things, maps, papers, it didn't matter so long as they looked full. Wear hiking boots, clothes for trekking, maybe take a sturdy alpenstock. Catch the early morning bus to Gulmarg, with return tickets. At Gulmarg, stroll to the upland meadow where the day-trippers and the walkers gathered, and then consult maps as if a long hike to Ladakh or the monasteries of Lahaul might be irresistible. In time someone would pick them up and lead them to the next step.

And bring the money, in dollars, in the denominations specified, laid in the bottom of the rucksacks under the picnic.

The bus looked likely to be full to overflowing. They jostled aboard with the crowd, elbows working but amid smiles and apologies in the local way. Lew settled towards the back, rubbed up against a tiny toothless greybeard with two anxious chickens locked up in a basket. In the press of people Lew saw several young Westerners, some with rucksacks, and he felt inconspicuous enough. The bus ground its gears, swaying away on tired springs, sounding none too healthy. But the sun was up and still rising over a mountain world composed of blue and ice. The air smelt as fresh as a baby's skin.

The bus ground along for about two hours and after a while Lew began to think that the bus ride alone might be worth the whole Indian journey and all its consequences. He did not know a better way to see the world, or a better world to see. The mood was calm and contemplative, brisk airs from the half-open windows distributing dust and the smell of evergreens. Passengers were chewing betel, smoking pungent cigarettes or *bidis*. Lew was content and then so relaxed that he fell into a doze. He woke in Gulmarg, finding himself keeled over against the uncomplaining little greybeard with his head almost on the basket of chickens.

They walked away from the bus, following the drift of the day-trippers, to the wide spaces of the big upland field. Gulmarg offered little beyond its scenery but that scenery was worth the journey. There were signs of an infant ski development – some of the necessary infrastructure was in place – though the ski season was still some months off. An old church of the Raj was locked and abandoned on a grassy rise in the meadow, evidence of the changing gods in this ancient home of many gods. The mighty bulk of the Snow View Hotel, now mightily neglected, seemed to be listing towards a slow oblivion.

They waited, doing not very much. A pleasant stroll of an hour or so showed them all they needed to know, and let others see them.

At last, a slight and hesitant native figure approached them.

'Good afternoon, sahib,' he said quietly, addressing himself to Karl. 'I am thinking that you are ready for walking and then picnic. Mr Azhar, he send me to bring you.'

He turned and walked away slowly, leaving them to follow or not. He led them to a crumbling wall on the edge of a meadow, and from behind the wall AM popped out, a small genie looking scared.

'Ah, Mr Kruis,' AM said, pronouncing the name as 'Cross', 'I'm happy to see you. I'm sorry that I leave you so long but there were some precautions. You have what I ask? Good. You have a picnic also? Good. I think we eat here, very pleasant view. Take our time, no hurry, just sightseeing. Plenty time before bus to Srinagar.'

They shrugged out of their rucksacks and AM's young assistant began to unpack them, laying out a cloth and placing on it samosas and bhajis, fruit, a large thermos of tea and some plastic cups. Then AM slipped behind the wall and reappeared furtively with two other rucksacks very similar to those that had held the picnic. He placed the new rucksacks tight against the wall and sat with his assistant close in front of them so that they were hidden from all but the most searching view.

'When you go,' AM explained, 'you take the new bags and leave your picnic ones behind. So you leave the money and take the *charas*.'

'Hold on a minute,' Karl replied. 'First, we all make some tests, is that not so?'

'Of course, it is naturally so,' AM agreed, glancing around nervously. Not so far away people were coming and going, family parties and groups of men wandering about, lazy and cheerful. Some youths making a ruckus and a few solitary figures looking momentarily stuck or lost; you could read into that whatever you wanted.

'Then have your friend peep in our bags,' Karl continued. 'He'll find the cash at the bottom, as you ordered it. But look cautiously, as if you can't find some of the picnic.'

The young man poked about in the rucksacks, nose close to the opening, bringing nothing to the surface. He slid slim packets between his fingers, making a rough count, and then he nodded to AM.

'And now,' Karl said genially, 'your turn.'

AM took a small packet wrapped in foil from a deep pocket and dropped it on the cloth in front of Karl. Lew took out an ordinary briar pipe. Karl unwrapped a brown lump and started to work on it with his fingers. It was rather oily and sticky and smelt potent, a gateway to unaccountable worlds. Lew filled the pipe and lit up. They smoked in turns, looking far away at the mountains. In a little while they leaned back on an elbow and smiled.

'So, you see?' AM said, also smiling. 'That is what you have.'

Karl was not quite finished yet. The pipe had made him playful. 'How do we know it's all of that quality?' he asked, putting on a severe voice.

'Mr Kruis, please, you know me. I do not cheat you. We work together before and I hope we work again. Azhar is honest man.'

And that was true, as far as any Westerner knew. So Karl laughed and shook AM's damp hand. No tricks, no sweat.

*

They had more than an hour to fill before the bus left, so they settled on the grass in the lee of the wall, sipping tea from the thermos, entering into the idle spirit of the day. After the pipe, Lew and Karl were content, but Lew began to notice that AM was uneasy. Perhaps his usual caution. He looked around constantly, trying to keep a smile on his face. Some men in Kashmiri dress, with round flat caps and baggy smocks, were loitering near by. It was not certain that they were doing anything, but had they been there rather too long?

'What's going on?' Lew said suddenly.

AM jumped a little and tried a wan grin. 'I think it is not so much. Well, nothing to worry you. Those men,' and here he gestured slightly with his head, 'those men do not like me. They want to steal my business. That is why we come to Gulmarg. They do not expect me to leave Srinagar. But I am wrong; they watch me better than I think.'

He shrugged in resignation, acknowledging that there was no way to defeat the world. 'But I do not think they annoy you,' he tried to reassure them. 'It is too dangerous for them to make bad trouble with foreigners, and anyway it is my business that they want.'

That was enough to make Karl frown. He was not intimidated, never had been afraid of darkies. He turned and scowled at the men until a couple noticed him. Grasping his stout walking stick he made as if to get up, and then the group dissolved, slipping out of sight, uncertain how to read the ferocity of the red Western face. AM let his breath out in a rush and this time he smiled with real relief.

'Ha, they run away,' he growled softly, like a dog that had scared them off. 'So we go quickly and disappear – poof! like that – before they come back. We take the bags you bring for the picnic and you take the others. Then, goodbye! One minute we are all here, and afterward . . . nothing!'

In a few seconds they were up and away, each one clutching a rucksack. Karl and Lew went fast down the hill but something, some small alarm, made Lew stop and turn back. He saw from a distance that the unfriendly group had re-formed and closed around AM and his helper. A tall man with a dark beard was poking AM in the chest, then one of the others reached from behind and tried to rip the rucksack from AM's shoulders. AM began to shout but the tall man took something hard and shiny from under his tunic and slapped AM a blow on the side of his head. Something dark and wet spread over the light brown cheek, and Lew registered that the shiny object was a large pistol. As AM fell to the ground Lew saw that the money was lost, and that a certain part of the power had changed hands in the Kashmir valley. Nervous Azhar, timid, cautious but brave enough at the last, was out of business.

Though he was too far away to do any good, Lew made as if to run back. He felt a firm hand on his arm and strong fingers pressing into his flesh.

'Don't get involved,' Karl warned brusquely. 'It's not our quarrel. If we get mixed up in this we will compromise ourselves. It's not for us to carve up the territories here. Bad luck on AM, but if and when we return there will still be someone to deal with. Takes a little time to work it out, that's all.'

East to West

Were they already compromised, whether they knew it or not? They wanted to get away, as fast as possible, and if they could have made the bus fly from Gulmarg they would have done so. But it took its usual two aching hours, stumbling and rocking through a landscape fit for a CinemaScope western they no longer noticed.

In Srinagar, back in the hotel, they locked the door of Lew's room and dumped the contents of the rucksacks on the bed. The packets were well-prepared, flat, thin and flexible, triple-wrapped first in aluminium foil and then sealed in clear plastic. They counted the packets and then Karl, choosing a few at random, weighed some on a small, hand-held balance. He smiled and gave a thumbs-up. Lew took a packet and held it to his nose. The smell through the wrapping was very slight, like a faint sweet fug in an unaired room. You had to sniff for it and it certainly didn't knock you over. AM, Lew thought, was indeed a fair and competent man, though it was useless to mourn him. Sentiment was a luxury Lew could keep for his memoirs.

'Okay,' Karl said, 'this is how we'll handle it. There's a lot of stuff here, too much responsibility for one person under pressure. Too much value tied up in one place. We'll split the load, then each of us will go on his own way, using whatever route he cares to choose. Gives us a better chance of getting at least half the consignment away safely. So it's best we keep our own secrets; what we don't know we can't tell.'

They divided the packets into two piles, one of which Karl stuffed back into his rucksack. He unlocked the door, put his head into the corridor, and withdrew it again.

'A small drink before we split?' he said, pulling out his silver flask. His face had settled back into the expression of bland confidence, and he was working his shoulders as if for a new spell of crafty bowling on the cricket field.

'Bottoms up,' he toasted Lew cheerfully, passing the flask over, and that seemed to sum up the position at which they had arrived.

He licked a drop of whisky from his lips, shook hands swiftly, picked up the rucksack and went out. Lew held the door open and watched him go, sliding down the corridor close to the wall, like a heavy predator on a nocturnal prowl.

He did not look back, and that was the last Lew saw of him.

*

He remembered an old Latin tag from the dim distant days of his education. It said 'Hasten slowly,' and he took it as a warning. If you wished to run safely, mind where you put your feet. For a quick getaway, he knew that the airport was the obvious place to start; so he chose the long, circuitous alternative of the bus route, aiming to hide his purpose under the familiar discomfort of the poor and the thrifty.

Next morning at eight he boarded the bus to Delhi, for the long-distance journey of twenty-four weary hours, without a rest period on the way.

He was dressed for the trip in the tough casual wear he had worn at Gulmarg. But he was carrying the courier's large suitcase, a strong, light case in some kind of plastic laminate, with a false bottom carefully fitted and disguised for transporting hashish. The case was new and shiny; it closed with a combination lock and was further secured with a tight webbing strap. It looked a little peculiar among the battered and time-worn bags and boxes of the other travellers. Lew was anxious to divorce himself from the suitcase as soon as possible, and he breathed more easily as he saw it disappear into the baggage hold of the bus. He could forget it until Delhi.

In the bus he tried to avoid seats where the sun would be fierce. He chose the western, more shaded side and dropped into an aisle seat halfway back, next to a balding man wearing a dhoti, open sandals and what looked like a worn Harris tweed jacket. A soldierly row of pens peeped over the rim of his breast pocket. The man glanced up with the briefest of smiles then looked out of the window to where the scrum of departure was about ready to release the bus on its way. Lew preferred a polite silence, so he also sketched a smile for his neighbour and settled quietly into his seat.

As the engine started and throbbed, and the heat began to rise, Lew took in his fellow passengers. He thought it possible that nothing drew out the contours of a strange place, or the social constitution of strange people, better than a long bus ride. As the landscape outside goes through the full magic of its transformations, so the confined interior of the bus outlines, in a vital but difficult shorthand, the how and the why of ordinary lives. This was a journey Lew was determined to observe keenly, though perhaps he would not enjoy it.

But for the moment he felt safe, as if he had outflanked demons, and that thought sustained him for the first part of the ride. At first, the way was slow and tortuous, a farewell to the mountains that filled the imagination but impeded swift progress. Through the clefts and valleys of the great empty ranges the bus crept along almost apologetically, as if afraid to disturb country that man had never been quite able to grip firmly. Beyond Jammu, the road untwisted itself, crossed over from Kashmir into India proper and began the long tedious stretch through dust and flies on the brick-hard plains to Delhi.

By late afternoon he felt groggy, and then a little nauseous. A combination of heat and indifferent roads; perhaps a sickness that comes from apprehension also. He closed his eyes in the dusk as the headlights of traffic came on and began to wink against the window glass. After a while he was starting to feel better when he felt a hand on his shoulder and a voice said something quiet next to his ear. He turned his head and the voice said something more, and this time Lew knew for certain that he did not, and never could, understand. The man in the seat behind was speaking to him in some Indian tongue. Lew shook his head ruefully; he would answer if he could, if only he were more capable.

'The man ask,' said the balding man in the next seat, speaking for the first time, 'if you are not feeling well. You look to him not so good.'

'No, I'm all right now,' Lew replied, half-turned between the seats and nodding to the man behind. 'I've had a little rest and I'm feeling much better.'

'It is no use talking directly to him,' his neighbour said, like the teacher giving the lesson. 'He is speaking Hindi. He speaks no English, but I will explain for you.'

He spoke a few words rapidly and the man behind patted Lew twice on the shoulder with a plump, soft hand and leaned back, satisfied, in his seat.

The incident seemed to pull aside whatever veil of restraint there had been between Lew and his neighbour. 'I am wondering, sir,' the balding man asked, as if the question had been bubbling within him for a long time, 'why you are making yourself uncomfortable on this long bus journey? We are only poor Indian people here.'

'I'm not so rich myself,' Lew replied defensively.

'Forgive me, are you hippy?'

Was he? The question made Lew smile. 'Not exactly,' he said. 'Perhaps I don't have any deep purpose, just trying to extend my experience of life. An adventure, you might say.'

A modest lie, which was not entirely untrue.

'Well, you are welcome, of course. We Indians are very hospitable. I hope you find secret things you look for. But sometimes I wish that you foreign people, in general, come here less often. For us, it is very upsetting, you know. We are shamed because we think you judge us, when so many things are awful in our society. And you are shamed because you know so little and understand less about our land and people. I do not wish to be rude, sir, but I think maybe bus should be a private place, where Indians can be Indians without inspection. The man behind speaks to you kindly, he is solicitous for your health, but you can say nothing to him. You see? Is that correct and polite?'

Lew turned and said nothing, not because he was angry but because he had nothing to say. He did not even know if the Indian was right. And then it didn't matter. The question was too large for solution here and now, involving as it did the interpenetration and whirlwind of the modern world. The best he could do at the moment was to sleep on the problem. He hunched himself in his seat, as close as he could get to comfort, and eventually the rumble and throb of the bus rocked him to sleep.

When he awoke they were fighting the early traffic in the sad and ugly approach to Delhi.

*

He was out at the airport by midday, after another vicious tangle with the city traffic. He had no flight booked but intended to take the fastest route out. India made him jumpy, with his large, smart suitcase.

His first task was to change his clothes, and then re-pack the case. He entered a men's toilet, with few people about, and decided to change dress right there, in front of the mirror, observers be damned. He pushed the suitcase under the basin and carefully extracted the clothes he needed. He discarded his mountainwear, put on a white shirt with a plain green tie, and then a lightweight summer suit that he had ordered from a Malaga tailor. It was perhaps a little too sharp, nipped at the waist in the manner of Spanish dandies, but Lew had a trim figure and the clothes looked well on him. A pair of handmade Spanish boots completed the impression of elegance.

From the big case he took a leather briefcase, fit for a person who was every inch a businessman, and he was about to redistribute the cargo and re-pack the case when he noticed an Indian cleaner with a whisk broom looking at him intently. Perhaps the cleaner was a Dalit – an Untouchable – who would be neither seen nor heard, but Lew was taking no chance. He gathered all his belongings awkwardly and withdrew to a cubicle. He locked the door, laid the case on the throne, and made sure that everything was stowed, the cargo securely hidden in the false bottom and the clothes looking innocent on top. He changed his glasses for a pair with heavy dark rims and emerged from the cubicle in a new persona, respectable, weighty, assured, with an expensive suitcase worthy of the man.

To his annoyance, among several airlines he could find no convenient flight. He wanted to get to Stockholm but, booking at the last moment, he found flights not available or fully occupied. The best he could do after a lengthy search, if he did not wish to stay another night in Delhi, was an evening flight to Rome. Arrival in Rome was badly timed, causing the delay of another night before the connecting flight to Stockholm. He thought he could bear a half-day and a night in Rome. Better, and safer, than Delhi. He paid cash, saw his suitcase checked in, and collapsed into the restaurant in the departure area.

*

Waiting for his suitcase by the baggage carousel Lew was surprised where he had got to. At Fiumicino Airport he was a long way from Delhi and not so close to Stockholm. Then he considered that it was no bad fate to be in Rome for the first time, dipping briefly into the spring from which so much that was important to the West had flowed.

He had experienced his usual tight moment at passport control. But he relied on flying under Canadian colours, his passport the most innocuous of flags, though the man at the desk had hesitated when he saw the various entry and exit stamps, for North Africa and India. He looked at Lew quizzically, his hand slowly tapping the passport. He said something in Italian, then switched to a rudimentary English.

'You stay in Rome?'

'No, not really. Just in transit. I am here for one night only.'

Still the man hesitated. 'You have business, sir?'

'Yes, I buy spices and herbs from different countries. Eastern lands mainly. For the European market.'

The man relaxed, stamped the passport and slid it back to Lew. '*Benvenuto*,' he said, suddenly affable. 'Enjoy our city.'

In the baggage hall Lew plucked his case from the carousel and headed for the customs channels. He was thinking he that he would treat himself to a taxi in the centre of Rome, then he came abruptly to the tail end of a long line. He stood and waited, sensing a nervous expectation in the air. Men and women stood around the customs post looking too casual. At the exit two armed policemen or paramilitaries looked tough and ready. Ready for what?

'They're looking at everything,' complained the young man in front of Lew, an American, knowledgeable as usual.

'Oh?' Lew replied, feeling a sudden sweat.

'Searching for the bad guys,' the American went on cheerfully, 'the ones bringing in guns and explosives. You've heard of the Red Brigades?'

'Yes, but . . . '

'Where have you been hiding? Aldo Moro? The big politico they murdered in May? Well, after that you expect a clampdown, don't you?'

He smiled benignly at Lew's troubled face, as if such excitement were a guaranteed part of any trip abroad.

Lew had, he supposed, registered the work of the Red Brigades and the death of Moro. But he'd had other things on his mind. He could not run now, there was nowhere to go. He followed the line slowly towards the officials.

*

The customs man indicated that Lew should lay his suitcase on the counter and unlock it. He was very methodical. First he took Lew's briefcase and went through it quickly, expecting nothing there. The he patted Lew down, a tap on his pockets, under the arms, round his belt and down his legs. Though this was the routine, Lew thought it shamed him, actions by a stranger that only intimates might do. Then the man reached for his suitcase. He went carefully now, working slowly with experienced hands. And then his face changed to something dark and spiteful.

He closed the lid and gestured, and someone Lew guessed must be a plainclothes cop detached himself from the wall and touched Lew's arm, pointing to a door off to one side. They moved towards it, and the customs man followed carrying the suitcase. In the corridor beyond, the cop motioned for Lew to stop, took his passport, gave it to the customs man who entered a room and closed the door. The cop, who clearly spoke no English, grinned at Lew in a friendly way, as if they both knew this game.

In about ten minutes the door opened and Lew was summoned. In the room were three men: the customs man standing humbly to the rear, a grey-haired man pulling on a pipe, and a middle-aged man in a smart uniform who appeared to be in charge. He looked calm, even slightly amused. Before him, on a table, was Lew's suitcase, open and ransacked, and around the case were neat piles of wrapped cannabis.

The smart officer looked at Lew and then at the hash. Fastidiously, he pushed some of the blocks around with a pencil, not getting too close to them, still standing stiff and upright, perhaps for the sake of his creases.

'Well, what do you think?' he said to Lew in smooth, barely accented English. He waved at the piles on the table in an offhand way.

Lew shrugged. The less said the better; it was pointless to deny the obvious.

'Nothing to say?' the officer asked again, this time with an edge to his voice. 'We look for urban terrorists, we find a drug smuggler. Not such a big fish. But we have room for all types in our prisons.'

He waited, to see if Lew might be stung into words by this open contempt.

'Well?' he said again.

The act was over and the officer came round the table and took Lew by the elbow. 'Come along,' he said simply. 'I don't think we need handcuffs.'

STOCKHOLM

'A mistake,' he said. 'Lew was not paying sufficient attention. And it is always the unexpected details that matter.'

Anders was drinking gin, failing to notice in his agitation that he didn't really like it.

'But what do we know?' Berta asked. She was watching the weather-map on the TV with the sound turned off. Rain was coming their way.

'Very little. The Italian authorities got in touch with Vera. Informed her of the arrest but damn all else. She telephoned me.'

Berta switched the TV off. The mood was gloomy and oppressive enough without bad weather. 'So what happens now?' she said, still staring at the empty screen. She was unwilling to challenge Anders, to look him in the eye.

Anders frowned, more at the gin, which he had suddenly noticed, than at the question.

'We get him out, of course.' It was a flat statement, not open to doubt. 'First, we take the ordinary legal route. We have some experience of the law in Italy. Justice there – if I can call it that – is slow and tortuous and tricky and ready to be influenced by certain acts. Certain interventions, perhaps I may call them. This Red Brigades panic complicates things, but maybe in our favour. If you are after terrorists and brigands and murderers, who cares too much about low-grade foreign drug mules? So you fine them, give them a suspended sentence, tell them to get the hell out and never return.'

Berta went back and forth with this, not wholly satisfied. 'And if that doesn't work?'

'Well, we approach the law in a different way and try to bend it a little. Certain payments will have to be made, bearing on well-known human weakness. I think in this respect Italy is as weak as any place in Europe. It may be expensive, I know, but we will afford it. We have a duty to our colleagues. We cannot ask them to do what they do without protecting them as far as we can. There is no argument on that.'

'And Vera?' said Berta, taking the feminist, the human view.

'It is best if she keeps out of the way. We will be gentle, but he's in jail, not her. She must not go there. Emotions muddy the mind, make bad judgement.'

There was a long pause while Anders put the questions and the problems into boxes in his mind and ranged them in order.

'But we need someone in Rome,' he decided, 'to keep watch and to start making moves.'

He smiled shyly at Berta, giving her news that might be good or bad.

'Berta, you have been to Italy on holiday several times. You speak quite good Italian. So go there now, and try to have a not-so-bad time. Think of it as a holiday, more or less.'

QUEEN OF HEAVEN

At first sight it looked to him like a giant starfish. From what he could see it did not look oppressive, or not exactly. Stiff and formal perhaps, stranded, as if it had a purpose no one could quite remember or believe in any longer.

One came upon it immediately after the bridge, with a rabble of embankment traffic brushing by on the east side, just beyond the sullen surging waters of the Tiber. The river took the dross from the city, as it had done since the day of the city's founding more than two thousand five hundred years ago. Trastevere, the raffish suburb, surrounded the dark perimeter of the buildings with a bracelet of lights. Above the lines of blind windows two squat octagonal towers with conical roofs gave the severe and almost chaste architecture the look of a large Roman basilica.

For nearly five hundred years it had been a place of detention; at first for the shoeless Carmelite nuns secured at God's pleasure in the convent of Santa Maria Regina Coeli; and then, when that building was razed and a new project for the reform of man begun, a prison built on the same ground that was now not only holy but also enlightened and dedicated to an ideal of the Risorgimento, the transformation of criminals into citizens of the New Italy, but still under the patronage of the most merciful of ladies, Mary, Queen of Heaven. As if she, perhaps alone in the history of the world, was up to such a task.

The cell door swung shut and what Lew had known as the world was temporarily dismissed. What he had taken to be reality packed up and removed itself, and he wondered, suddenly tense with grief, how he would ever get it back. The spyhole in the door kept an unblinking eye on him. There was nowhere to go beyond that stare, except to sink into nonentity. Become a cipher rather than a man. Then he began to take stock and some of the misery squeezed out of him. It was not so easy, after all, to defeat the familiarity of the world. He saw that this place was not a house of the dead but was nervously alive, even though it was afflicted.

When his heart had stopped thumping he began to notice in his surroundings the continuation of the ordinary. The creep of small indistinct sounds, like an equatorial tin roof ticking in the declining sun; evanescent smells of kitchen and sour bodies; weak daylight chivvying dust in sombre corners. Lew saw that in fact nothing deep or essential to mankind was banished except a certain freedom of movement. And what, in essence, did that accomplish? He thought of Gramsci, for a while in this very prison, still steadily composing letters of beautiful clarity, a sickly hunchback who was strong enough to support all the weight they threw upon his poor shoulders.

So the worst of it was that Lew had been forced to come to rest. He was not particularly sorry to discover this. He realized that his years of incessant travel, playing hide and seek with authorities who certainly didn't intend to be playful, had left him wrung out and bone-weary. For the moment, he did not mind waiting. Everyone around him seemed to be waiting too, people not supposed to be there except that there was nowhere else to store them. They were on remand, awaiting investigation or trial, awaiting distribution or release. This place was not the end, not the doorway to despair, though it might lead to that.

He expected to be lonely, among strangers clammed up by suspicion or ignorance. He did not know their language, though Spanish went a little way in Italy. But he thought he could handle his lot. The years of self-sufficiency had inured him to his own company, and he liked it. Always, when the passage was dark and insecure, he preferred to have his own hand on the tiller.

*

Though he could not avoid other prisoners, at first he wanted nothing to do with them. His immediate impression was of various kinds of damage. He caught a mute appeal in the eyes that he could not meet, a whine in the voice that he didn't wish to hear.

He was placed in a wing that appeared to be given over to the casuals of minor crime, chiefly foreigners up to their necks in miscalculation – illegal immigrants of several colours from poor countries, pimps, panders, black-marketeers, street thieves and hustlers, motoring offenders, and several types of serious nuisance. And then there were the foreigners caught up in soft drugs – users, dealers, pedlars, couriers – the enthusiasts of grass or hashish. These hash-heads were a buoyant, disrespectful crowd still touched by the ideals of anarchy and fellowship. Prison here was not so bad – better, in fact, than some other places they had been in.

They were bolshy and stubborn and refused to be downtrodden, and Lew began to take heart from their innate resistance. He began to share their cynical optimism, their conviction that an Italian prison was altogether too frail a place to contain their contemptuous good spirits. There was always a path through, round or under. In the nature of things, the open sky was part of their inheritance.

Rome

Avvocato Faldini smelt of tobacco and hair oil and Berta regretted the very expensive perfume she had used to go with her prettiest dress and careful makeup. She feared such subtlety might be wasted. He came round the desk, a little sprig of a man in tight trousers, bouncing like a corps de ballet, neat as a new-made bed, and it was obvious that he needed no hints of perfume to spur on his appetite. He had a natural hunger for tall Scandinavian blondes with exuberant figures; in his dreams he had undressed and fondled them as much as he pleased. Now, he covered her hand with both of his and gave her a soulful look.

'Signorina Moberg . . . '

He paused, unsure what language to use. On the phone, her Italian had been about as good as his English, which he suspected she spoke fluently. Courtesy and the wish to secure a client might have indicated English. But they were in Italy, after all. More to the point, he regarded Italian as the foremost language for insinuation and sexual skirmishing, and he looked forward to that advantage.

'Signorina Moberg,' he continued in Italian, speaking slowly and trying to look tragic, 'this news you bring me about your friend Signor Holle is very disquieting. Serious, I would say. But we will see. We say, in the law, that there is no condition beyond hope.'

Berta Moberg cast her eyes down sadly, playing her part. She knew the games of lawyers, and waited for the mental wrestling to begin.

He ushered her to a low easy chair to one side, where her long legs would be in view, and got back behind the fortress of his desk. He was breathing a little heavily. He put on his glasses and pulled a nice clean notepad to him.

'Now, signorina,' he said, sneaking a sideways look at the legs, 'tell me the story of your unlucky friend.' It seemed to her that he laid too much emphasis on the word *story*.

Somewhere beyond the window she heard a sudden squawk and clatter of squabbling birds, momentarily overriding the gladiatorial combat of Roman traffic, and she wondered if that jabbering made any more sense than the story Anders and Lew had concocted. But it was just plausible enough to be possible in a disordered world, and she guessed that should be enough for a lawyer like Faldini. He came to them well recommended.

She gave him a wry, sad smile and brazenly launched into her tale. She went through the details almost with disbelief in her voice – in other circumstances she might have laughed. It was a tale of misadventure and muddle and double-dealing. 'Keep it vague and complicated,' Anders had said, and she tried her best to know very little.

Lew Holle was a journalist – so her version went – a respected and quite well-known journalist setting out to do a series of articles on cannabis production in India and the routes and connections to Europe. He was an experienced reporter but this assignment was rather out of his line; in the sub-continent he was too innocent and too trusting. He did not know enough about land or people to put the story together. He had trouble with contacts, misalliances, deceptions. Fraud even, she dared say. At some point his suitcase went missing and was never found. His helpers were distraught and contrite – more sorry than seemed necessary. They insisted on replacing everything, clothes, a few books, washing things, and the suitcase itself. Lew was surprised but not suspicious. Such was the generosity of the Indian nature. The new clothes were of decent quality, and the case, though a little heavy, was brand new and sturdy enough for the roughest travel.

All this happened towards the end of his assignment. He thought he had enough material for an article of sorts, and he mailed his notes home for safety. He was anxious to get away as soon as possible. In his hurry he had booked a passage via Rome, which was the earliest flight available. And here he was, an unwitting courier with an incriminating suitcase, caught in Rome by a web spun by the Red Brigades.

'If he'd known what he was carrying,' she concluded with as much indignation she could muster, 'surely a man of his worldly experience would have avoided Rome and all its troubles?'

Through all of this the *avvocato* had the politeness to keep a straight face. He took notes with a soft pencil and even the motion of his hand seemed sceptical. When he looked up she glanced at him shyly, dimpling her cheeks. She could see he liked that. He swung round to face her in his swivel executive chair, looking magisterial.

'An unhappy story, signorina,' he pronounced, 'and one with many difficulties.

Our courts are busy, the timetable crowded, they do not want cases that are troublesome, time-consuming and unclear. And relatively inconsequential, I may say, beginning in a far jurisdiction. And this is so particularly now, when internal concerns, perhaps of a revolutionary nature – I am referring to the actions of the Red Brigades – have us all in their grip. Some leniency might well be shown to a respectable foreigner who is the victim of an unfortunate trick. But of course we will need some evidence to substantiate his story. Dispositions, affidavits, documents, witnesses if possible. It will not be cheap.'

The question of money was now out in the open, but he took off his glasses and gave her a stern look, as if to let her know that she was not deceiving him. Suddenly, he was all business.

'So I will take your instructions,' he said briskly, 'and if you will kindly give me a cheque to cover the cost of enquiries and as an advance towards fees I will get to work immediately. It does us no good to leave a talented foreigner in the Queen of Heaven.'

She saw it now, the steel beneath the smirk, and she knew she had better not take him for granted. Then his face softened again, showing her the twinkle of the charmer. He rose from the desk and came round to her with both arms outstretched and practically lifted her out of her low chair.

'Dear lady,' he sighed, 'I will not bother you with all the legal technicalities.' He held her at arm's length, like Fred Astaire about to set Ginger Rogers off in a whirl. 'But rest assured that everything will be done promptly. Leave your telephone number and address in Rome with my secretary, and I will be constantly in touch. My secretary will also inform you what you should pay for the moment. Just leave a cheque or cash with her.'

As he lingered over her handshake she feared he might kiss her hand, or even lick it.

'The bastard,' she thought. 'He can hardly wait to get into my pants.' But in the present predicament a bastard was what they needed, not a saint.

She turned for the door and swayed out of the room with her most seductive walk. Let him see that, to keep his enthusiasm up.

QUEEN OF HEAVEN

Days were long; fears soon gave way to boredom. Hour by hour, slats of light from the window moved with painful slowness across the wall. Nothing was more wearisome than counting these hours. Life was not physically hard, just empty. The remand prisoners could get their hands on many of the small daily comforts, and that too was a trouble, reminding them of the world they were missing. And that world was almost within reach, seen obscurely through the dirty pane of captivity.

There was a warder they knew as Beppo. By arrangement, he was willing to undertake missions and contacts beyond the walls on behalf of the foreigners. Something changed hands, but he was a nice man, instinctively kind, with the thoughtfulness of a well-trained Italian waiter, and he seemed to regard his little tasks almost as charity rather than petty business. Wine, soft drinks, cold foods, fruit, cigarettes and tobacco, books and magazines, writing materials were all easily procured. Hard liquor might be possible, and marijuana at times, though it was expensive. Beppo was as busy as a packhorse.

'Thanks Beppo,' they would say, uncorking a new bottle. 'Have a glass of wine with us.'

'D'you know, signor, I believe I will,' he would reply solemnly. 'You are very kind.'

Letters came and went without restriction, or so it seemed. Nor did Lew notice any censorship. Perhaps officials glanced into envelopes and scanned the text, or zeroed in on certain suspects, but it would be difficult and tedious to have linguists available to cover all the different languages within the prison.

Lew wrote to Vera, though he was unsure what to say and his words sounded to him stilted or false. Her replies were affectionate though cloudy, as if she were heading already for another trail. He didn't know if he was disappointed, neither did he know what he wanted her to say. She was often absent from his reveries now. Sometimes Nina from Morocco, with henna on her hands and in the sweet flow of her long black and gold caftan, fleetingly took her place; and sometimes the space was just empty. He wrote to Anders and that was easier because he needed to send covert messages and it might be dangerous to give moves away. It was a discipline that challenged him, tested his powers as a writer, and he enjoyed it. Anders, who didn't quite trust himself writing in English, replied with abrupt hints and clues buried in news about the weather.

He received more letters than most. He read more books too, and spoke less, and appeared preoccupied and thoughtful. To the others, it was a little suspicious. It was soon rumoured that he had plans. Some would admire him for that and some would be jealous. In the yard a red-headed Austrian with a red bandanna shuffled up to him. His name was Peter and he was one of the nosey ones, and for this reason his feet had been trampled by boots, a punishment for some nameless sin. He walked with difficulty, but he still stirred the pot, sniffing business more safely left alone. He was the sort of buddy Lew did not need, but he was as intelligent as he was nosey and sometimes solid nuggets of value slipped from his loose mouth. Also, he was willing to share a joint now and again.

He offered one to Lew now and they smoked it like Red Injuns, squatting on their haunches in a corner in the lee of a drainpipe.

'Man, I hear you gotta lawyer?' Peter's English had a wildness about it, sometimes TV-hippy talk from the sixties and sometimes the odd cadences of a foreign language imperfectly learnt at school.

'Oh yes?' Lew was giving nothing away, though the offer of the joint required something in return.

'Well, you seen that lawyer fellow? Ask him how to get you outta here?'

'Don't we all want to get out of here? But I don't think I've anything to report to you.'

'Hey, take it easy. I don't go spoil your plans, even though I like it that you are here. Some of the guys around here are dumber than animals.'

'Well, that's a recommendation!' Lew replied sharply.

'That's okay. Anyway, how come you get caught?'

'And what's that to you?'

'Oh, man, I ain't boasting but I moved some hash in my time too. Believe me, I know how it goes. What I hear about you, it seemed like a very dumb move from a smart guy.'

And since that was possibly the truth Lew said nothing, just took a couple of quiet draws on the joint. The cause of his downfall. But when he looked back on his actions in India he found it hard to know whether they were the result of carelessness, foolishness, or some deeper desperation.

'Lemme give you a theory,' Peter said after the last pull on the joint, looking at Lew keenly and seeing the doubt in his face. 'You wanna hear it?'

Why not? It was not as if Lew had intellectual treats lined up all day. Peter grinned and went on.

'I think we people – you and me – get into this business because we enjoy life and like to smoke and like to pass it around so that other folk can enjoy life too. So we're passing the stuff here and there and suddenly it's a business, or an occupation at least, and we are making some money also. Yes? It is illegal of course but we do not have too much respect for the rogues that govern us and we do not think it is immoral or anti-social. On the contrary, we think it is a small communion and good for us all, being together and generally happy.'

He paused, to see how it was going, and when Lew said nothing he continued.

'But it *is* illegal and I think that becomes some part of the attraction. In a very careful and over-regulated world – don't go there, don't do this, line up here, forget that – we like the idea of risk, though maybe not the risks themselves when they come, which luckily we cannot judge at the beginning. I think we are kinda dedicated to trying things that will inevitably lead to failure – a sort of fatalism – because the official forces of the world are so much stronger than we are and sooner or later they will catch us. We will make a mistake, do something stupid, or be betrayed. We *know* that. All the time, we are ready to be caught. What we do is a preparation for arrest. So we are not really surprised when we end up here, in prison, but we find that because of our history we have the resolution and endurance not to be so upset. It is not so much bother, and we can come out without too many wounds.'

Wounds? If not those, Lew guessed he had a few bruises. To what degree were they self-inflicted? And was the rest of what the Austrian had to say anywhere near the truth? He wanted to think about his own case without the distraction of this ferret-like face peering at him from beneath the red bandanna.

He got up abruptly and began to wander, hands in pockets, back and forth between the limits of the walls. The degrees of his freedom. He walked almost blindly, right across the middle of the yard, as if he didn't know that careful men should keep within the shadow of the walls, drifting under a bright patch of Roman sky.

*

It was not the money, or at least not mainly the money. In his years of enterprise he had made plenty, and spent plenty – the best hotels, the best food and drink, first-class travel, efficient cars that made the best of long roads. But all that had been just dressing, the clothing of the trade. Business expenses, you might say. The man beneath the clothing lived very simply. In the intervals between runs he was a modest citizen of a poor Spanish hill village, a man who liked to do useful things with his hands – carpentry, weaving, a bit of uncomplicated building. An enthusiast for books, and for strenuous hikes across rough country. He was a collector of observations, guesses, human twists. A scribbler too, on the occasions when he dared to be. In the local bar he drank without complaint wine not much better than paint stripper, ate mountain chicken as tough and lean as mountain foresters.

He had saved little, not caring to save, knowing from his trade the mutability of life. He was content to let one day slide into the next along whatever fissures and crooked channels it might find. And now the few savings he had were leaking, sinking, along with Anders's money, into the swamp where Avvocato Faldini made his sinuous and hidden movements. He felt no sense of ownership over this vanishing money. It was a wave that swept over him, driving him forward or thrusting him under, according to flow and ebb. A power beyond him. When it passed he would be as naked as he had ever been.

By the light of the Western world he had failed. But he didn't think that was the whole story, or even the right story. The imperative of capital accumulation was not a dogma for sane men. He had observed that, at least, seeing it figured in the smoke and haze of the hashish. Humans came together chiefly for warmth and conviviality, not to rip the throat out of their fellows. To learn this, in this way, was an unusual lesson from a bizarre world, a world of clandestine exchanges taking place in a hidden annexe to mainstream society. But in this despised and illegal space Lew had seen something essential occur, what the Austrian, Peter, had called 'a small communion and good for all of us, being together and generally happy.'

He had plunged into this world as much out of instinct as out of judgement. Perhaps as an alibi to account for a withdrawal from a dominant ideology. He had been afraid of the ugly bared teeth of economic determinism, exuding the sour breath of an ever-increasing GDP. And he was still afraid. He planned to produce nothing much other than ideas and fellowship. To work for nothing but wages was not *the* mode of being, as compulsive and avid as the West supposed, but only an insufficient procedure that left room for other ideals springing out of the peculiar, the singular, human condition. He could never feel committed to a narrow reading of our nature. He wanted days for pause, for rest and long dreams, for festivals and celebrations, for wandering and exploration, for meditation and thought, for attempts to accomplish small things for no other reason than the love of doing it. We were richer, if only we could see it, than money could ever make us. This was not an original or a new conclusion, but it was painful how the West conspired to bury it.

After about fifteen minutes of pacing he stopped and laughed. He may even have blushed at his own muddled innocence. He looked at the perimeter walls and the towers and the gaunt slabs of the buildings and the bars on the windows, and he thought of the cramp that all of this had put upon the soul. It was a shoddy expedient, meanly and incompetently run, and society had every reason to feel ashamed of it. In a larger signification it meant very little. He was irritated to be there and anxious to leave, but not very penitent. But it certainly wasn't the place where life was lived to its fullest, the life he had hoped to find before this interlude. He could see that he had gone wrong somewhere. The end he had in view might have been an ideal, but the means to reach it were misplaced. The path had deceived him.

He had failed, he didn't mind acknowledging that now. He was not so old. He thought he might have the courage to begin again.

*

Peter was really pleased. He had put on his most festive bandanna, lurid and blotchy, and he hopped along behind – his bruised feet were still hurting – as Lew was taken to the administrative block for release.

'So he done it?' he said happily. 'That snake in an office. How did he do it, get you out?'

At this point Lew was not too sure. Anders and Berta had sown the seed, the good manure of money had enriched the ground, the lawyer Faldini was an expert husbandman. But there was nothing in all this that the prison needed to know. Lew gave Peter a puzzled look, as if the whole matter was a mystery and an embarrassment.

When he saw that Lew was not going to reply Peter sighed.

'Man, I sure need a friend like that lawyer,' he lamented. 'Was it money that did it? I guess so. Together of course with cunning, connections and know-how. All damned expensive. They say the poor will inherit the earth but it doesn't say how long you have to wait.'

Then he was cheerful again, remembering that he had something for Lew.

'I got this little present for you,' he said, with a hand on Lew's shoulder, holding him back for the last moments together. 'It's a gift from one of our predecessors here in the Queen of Heaven. Antonio Gramsci. They dumped him here for a while, and then in other prisons, and the important thoughts still kept coming to him. I suppose you call it philosophy. Mentally, he was some tough little guy. Anyway, he soon got prison into perspective, and this is what he said – for the likes of us and for others too, if they cared to listen. It's a quote and here's how it goes: "I'm a pessimist because of the intellect, but an optimist because of the will. I have never entertained any illusions and I have never suffered disappointments. I have always taken care to arm myself with an unlimited patience, not passive, inert, but animated by perseverance."'

He took his hand off Lew's shoulder and spread his arms wide, like a priestly benediction.

'Check it out,' he said finally. 'Letter from prison to his brother Carlo, nineteenth December nineteen twenty-nine. You'd think it might have sunk in by now.'

Then Lew turned away and was led through the locked door on the other side of which all the renewed questions of freedom lay waiting. Here he was, far from home in time and place. A change was imminent, he couldn't avoid that, and he tried to get in order what he should abandon and what he should take away.

HOMELAND

NOVA SCOTIA, 1980

He took a flight as soon as he heard the news, but in his haste missed connections, landed at Gander and had to take the boat across Cabot Strait. His father died the day before he arrived in Halifax. He spoke to people he barely remembered, and some who had hardly heard of him, and he knew then that his late arrival was not important. His father, in the last month of his life, had been in no condition to recognize anyone. He saw the body in the coffin and would not have recognized him either, save for the hands.

Looking down into the box, Lew tried to see beyond the wasted figure, primped up according to the ghastly practice of morticians, but nothing much came back. A few images to shuffle from childhood and the farm, but no solid words for memory to hang on to.

The funeral was mercifully brief. Since the grave was full of water they could not put the body in the ground. 'It would break my heart,' the undertaker confided to Lew, 'to put him down in that.' The corpse was returned to storage until the weather relented.

And suddenly the event was over. A few elderly figures in raincoats shaking a wet film off umbrellas drifted out into the clammy air. Lew was in misery, whether from the death or the funeral or the day he did not know, but he thought that some gesture, some salute from him was needed. He went to buy a bottle of brandy – his father had enjoyed a drop or two of brandy on most winter nights – and he was emerging with the bottle in a brown paper bag when he heard his name called.

The accent was local, thick and hearty, and Lew put a name to the voice before he could place the face. Then it all came back, and he was shaking the callused hand with its iron grip of a man he remembered as Dan, a hillbilly with whom he had been at high school and who now introduced himself as the gravedigger. Dan had noted Lew at the funeral and came looking for him.

There was a moment of pleasurable recognition, then a minute of embarrassment. To cover his awkwardness Dan plunged into professional matters, the condition of the grave and the difficulty of burial at this time of year. As the words flowed, pithy and blunt, Dan began to wax enthusiastic about the mysteries of his trade, going into details about the digging and the spade, the length of the handle and the shape of the blade, the peculiarities of the ground at each season, the fear of collapse and the necessity at times to shore up the sides of the digging. That brought him on to the subject of carpentry, a field in which he confessed notable failings. 'I couldn't make a wood plug for a pig's ass,' he said sorrowfully, as if it mattered, 'without splitting the pig.'

Lew was entranced. He forgot his misery and wanted to hear more of this strange trade. He took Dan by the elbow and they sneaked into an alleyway, to liberate the brandy from its paper bag. They were careful, for drinking in public in that town made you liable to arrest. With a salute to the dead, and as an encouragement to the living, the bottle went hand to hand. Dan was obviously used to such open-air festivity, and perhaps occasions such as this had helped shape the local drinking habits. In three swigs he had lowered the level in the bottle to half full, and only then did he remark on the taste.

'Damn it,' he said, slapping his stomach, 'does a power of good to a man's innards on a day like this.'

So this was home, in a sense, where Lew had spent his best formative years. What he saw puzzled him. He had been away a long time.

*

He remembered the night before he left, that night in London, when he had taken Vera to dinner in Soho. He had not yet told her that he was going away. The restaurant had charming pretensions and good French cooking. Good food he expected, and he was at ease with charm and pretensions. He had eaten in three-star restaurants up and down Europe. He was relaxed and felt good and expected to tip well, and the staff soon saw it.

The meal was pleasant, the wine excellent, the mood between them comfortable though perhaps a little constrained, as if they were both wary of surprises. After the cheese he ordered coffees and a cigar (that was a surprise to her and perhaps to him, for he had only formed this desire, unusual to him, on the spur of the moment). When he had the cigar glowing well he gave her a sideways look and cleared his throat.

'My father's dying,' he said, 'may even be dead by now. I have to go back to Canada. I've booked a flight for tomorrow.'

She stopped stirring her coffee. 'When will you be coming back?' she asked.

'I don't know that I will.' He seemed reluctant to say it. 'It's a long way to go and even further to return. When I think of this move, it has the look of finality about it. I'm played out here in Europe, after what's happened in Rome with one thing and another. You know very well what I mean. The reasons for my being here seem to have dissolved and flowed away.'

'What about us?' she asked, her voice flat, suggesting nothing.

'Yes, us . . . Would you come to Canada with me, or maybe follow later?'

'With what in mind?'

He drew on his cigar, gaining time. 'I don't really know. I can offer no more than what we already have here.'

'Is that enough?' She gave him a sad smile. 'No, I don't think so. If I go thousands of miles, to a land so big I can hardly imagine it, I want something more than an intermittent view of you disappearing into the distance, as you have done in Europe. I want a promise from you, though I know in my heart you can't really give it, no matter what you might say now. And also I want something for myself, to catch and to keep and to develop on my own terms. And you don't even come into that bit of it.'

They were not arguing. Neither had a point to win or lose, so he had no more to say. He sighed and shrugged, and then there was one of those long silences so familiar to both of them, she inscrutable behind her dark lenses and he giving the eye to the plaster mouldings on the ceiling.

But there was still one thing on his mind and after a while he let it out.

'Are you coming back with me tonight?'

'Well, ye-e-s-s . . .' A tentative pause, and then, 'Maybe no.'

She looked distressed, listlessly fingering her coffee cup, unwilling to hurt him. She tried to explain.

'There's more to fucking than humping and rubbing and licking and so on. One looks for more than that, for some hope for the future, for some suggestion of stability, if not of permanence. When the importance goes, most of the fun goes too. At least for me. It becomes dreary and sad and rather hard work. I think we should not put ourselves under that burden.'

'Okay,' he said, suddenly cheerful, relieved in all parts of him except the genitals. 'So what do you say now to some Calvados?'

She laughed and nodded, and when she took off her dark glasses to give them a polish, a gesture perhaps of resolution and right decision, he noted a tear in the corner of her eye. But by the time the waiter brought the drinks her dark lenses were back on and she was grinning.

They had a Calvados, and a couple more each, and at a late hour left the restaurant arm in arm. They walked towards the Underground on a damp windy night, under a sickly London winter sky. In the Tube station they had to split hurriedly for the last trains. They gave each other a long hug and a short kiss and went their ways without looking back.

*

On the journey from London his plans had come adrift at Gander – the reason for his late arrival. He'd had enough of flying – the cramp and discomfort, the stale recirculated air, the food you wouldn't feed a dog, the rictus of bored desperation on the face of the stewardess – so for the final hop of the journey he decided to take the boat from Cape Ray, in Newfoundland, to Nova Scotia.

Gander was a shock. Twenty years away and Canada had slipped from his mind. Newfoundland was perhaps not quite Canada, but close enough. Gander had been planned as a convenience for planes, not humans. A vast runway in a forest, a scar on the earth as brutal and dramatic as a head shorn for brain surgery. And now, since the big jets with longer range overflew the airport, Gander had the woebegone look of last year's enterprise, fast becoming irrelevant. There was still some solicitude for planes – there had to be, to keep them safe – but very little for travellers. Lew tried all around the airport to buy a postcard but none was available. Sold out, like the place itself.

And then, when he got on the ferry, he discovered a new affection for planes. The boat was due to leave at night, but the gale kept it pinned to the pier. Next day, about noon, the captain tried again, engines labouring at full power, but the ferry could make no headway. Frightened passengers, secured behind bulkheads and locked doors, watched storm water lash the windows and flay the decks. Lew thought briefly of what it might mean to drown, the peace of the seabed. Then in late afternoon the boat clawed into the stream, tossing tumultuously, and Lew, with many others, was sick before they had cleared the harbour limits. A shallow swell of seawater and vomit pitched restlessly about the toilet floor. The cold was intense, the wind bellowing at every crack and opening of the superstructure. It made his damaged jaw ache to the roots of his teeth. He lay down, wedged into a booth fitted with damp plastic upholstery, wrapped his head in his arms and tried to outlast the storm.

In Halifax, he drew the final curtain on the life of his father, and what was there left? The family farm was sold long ago, the family scattered. Those who had been close to him were in Saskatchewan and Alberta. Gone west. Nova Scotia was an old, hard-bitten community, full of ancient virtues and worthwhile traditions, but not for him. The first decision he came to, hunching his shoulders in raw streets, was that he could never make it year by year through the winter climate. Southern Europe and North Africa had ruined him for this weather.

His roots were here. Landscape and history had made him. But that development had come to an end, and he knew it. Coming from Europe, a Europe that had also come to an end, he threw no shadow for the moment. He wished to re-form himself, and he saw clearly that this was not the place to start. He bought a train ticket and headed west.

GOING WEST

Now that he was on his way he wanted to hurry. He had no specific plan but a vague purpose pointed him towards the west. He stopped for a week in Toronto, briefly delayed by sentiment and curiosity, and he was surprised to find that the new was no worse than the old. The city was stretching upwards, and perhaps that was no bad thing in Canada, where a high viewpoint might help to clarify the immensity of the land and lead to sober judgements, seeing the scale of all the things needing to be done. But he knew he was not one of those to do it. He was out of sympathy with the world of big talk and soaring glass towers.

For a week he wandered the streets of his past and found no encouragement for him there. The city offered nothing he wanted, and he left.

He had been told in Halifax that a favourite uncle now lived near Regina, and his sister's family in a small town just outside Calgary. He thought family feeling demanded something of him, so he went to Regina, then southwest to farmland with the features blotted out by winter. His uncle was pleased to see him, but Lew could see his visit was no more than a minor wonder, a little circus come to town. His uncle was getting old, should have retired, but farmers never retire, the land wouldn't let them. Or was it the government, granting such a poor pension?

'Hey, boy,' his uncle greeted him, folding Lew into his thin, wiry arms, 'where you come from? You been away?'

'Well, just for twenty years, here and there.'

'Twenty years! How about that? Somehow I didn't notice.'

He grabbed Lew's bag and limped on to the porch on arthritic legs.

'Damn this climate,' he said, 'gets a man all seized up.' He rested a moment, leaning on the railing. 'Went away myself,' he went on, 'during the war. Abroad. Not a good time, not good places. Glad to come back. I expect you'll be glad too.'

Then he put a faded blue eye on his nephew. 'But you'll stay for Christmas, I hope. Just us regular folk, nothing special, the usual grub. You're family, after all.'

The usual grub was something Lew had missed for many years: turkey with stuffing, strips of bacon under the wings, roast potatoes and parsnips;

homemade apple pie with thick cream; a big wheel of farmhouse cheddar with a hard rind; and later muffins and Christmas cake, and shots of Canadian rye whiskey to get on top of the indigestion. And then some more of the same, for Christmas feeling.

He ate, and rested for a couple of days, and then he was on his way out. The affection for him in his uncle's house was real and generous, but what was the point of staying? Lew could say nothing of his life; he might just as well have tried to speak in Russian or Chinese. And in any case the old man was smiling but not listening. A farmer's ear was usually directed elsewhere, cocked for catastrophe.

*

Calgary was another city growing taller, with a waistline expanding too. This time, Lew did not like it. It seemed to have come from nowhere, a burst of cancer cells, an artifice of excessive new money. Oil money, which always had a stink about it.

In the little town close by, getting bigger by the day, Lew could see from his sister's house the skyscraping tops of the city. He could not understand why, on the edge of a prairie as wide as the ocean, the buildings needed to huddle and rise so aggressively, cheek by jowl. A chinook wind started blowing just after Christmas and the weather in Alberta was suspiciously mild, almost ten degrees warmer than Florida where the citrus crop was shrivelled on the trees. After a few warm days the construction workers were already out on the house foundations laid before winter. In this economy there was never a moment to lose. Carpenters had a house framed in two days and soon a new family was looking at bare plaster within and raw sidings without, people partway on the road to an elusive dream. And for those too impatient to wait even that long there was an instant nirvana, a mobile home that was anything but mobile, a trailer set on hardcore, 72 feet of fitted furniture, fitted carpets and fitted ideals.

'It's the North American way,' his sister said. 'The future comes in a handy package, with discounts and special offers. Just pay up and take delivery.'

She had learnt the consolation of humour the hard way, which was also a North American way. Her husband had exchanged alcoholism for holy-roller Pentecostal Christianity, and she did not know which had been the more difficult to bear. At some stage he had dropped away, almost unnoticed, the jetsam from her life of mistakes and good hopes. She had always worked hard; for her there was no other possibility. She recounted for Lew some of her experiences, in particular from the time when she was an occupational therapist at a large mental hospital near Montreal.

'I formed the opinion,' she told him, between a laugh and a grimace, 'that R. D. Laing was fundamentally right. The people on the inside needed refuge, but most of all refuge from the weird inhumanity of the keepers and guardians. I saw more heartfelt tears and affection among the inmates than I ever saw kindness among the keepers. When I left *I* cried, because to go away was to abandon them. They cried too, as they knew what was happening; they were sane enough for that. Oh, we were like incompetent dancers who didn't know the steps, stumbling about with arms around each other, hanging on for dear life.'

Hanging on for dear life. Perhaps that was a clue.

THE ISLAND

The weatherman on TV spoke of unseasonal weather – exceptional warmth in Alberta, torrential rain in British Columbia. Lew stayed where he was, in Alberta, keeping an eye on the skies. But he quickly grew tired of bland streets with no history, no style and no sidewalks, tired of taking the car even to the corner drugstore, tired of office workers in cowboy boots and ten-gallon Stetsons. Even life in a raincoat under a West Coast downpour seemed better than that. He took the last step through the Rockies to the end of the line.

He had a name and an address on Vancouver Island. No matter what composition he tried to make between his life now and his life then, the past was not wiped out. It reached out and touched him, often when least expected. Janie Haydon was a friend from his old Toronto days. He had hardly thought of her in a dozen years, yet those brief moments of recollection were warmly attended with happy memories. Her husband had been a philosopher at the university, professionally a strict positivist but with an odd leaning towards entrepreneurial business. His last scheme, so Lew had heard, had been to rent out baby buggies to tourist families on the beaches and promenades of Mediterranean resorts. Before he could put the plan together – if in fact he ever seriously meant it – Janie was an ex-wife, while he died of a heart attack in the back of a Toronto taxi.

After the divorce Janie went west to work for the Canadian Broadcasting Company in Vancouver. She had some success with CBC, producing and preparing scripts for radio, and after another casualty in love she had the temerity to think that she might make it as a writer, particularly as she now had friends and connections within broadcasting. Wishing once again to make some distance from a disaster of the heart, she rented a substantial log cabin on the banks of the Cowichan River on Vancouver Island. There, she uncovered her typewriter and gazed with excitement and apprehension at an empty page. She was going to write stories, maybe even a novel. But she was a little hurt by the past and a little afraid of the future; she was also a little lonely in this remote cabin. Hearing from acquaintances in Toronto that her old friend Lew Holle had passed through and was footloose in the West, she tracked him down and invited him to visit. The cabin was big enough for the two of them.

Lew phoned her from Vancouver, took the ferry to Nanaimo, and a bus to

Duncan. Janie met him there in a borrowed car. He recognized her at once, a lady with some added years, some new grey hairs, her slim figure a little thicker, but the same sprightly manner. She hugged him and then held him at arm's length.

'Yes,' she said approvingly, 'you've changed. For the better, I would say. You left as a callow young man with a dissatisfied face and unlikely expectations. I don't know what you've done in the last years but you seem to have rounded out nicely. Grown into your skin at last, I suspect. That Basque beret gives you away, worn with confidence, and it suits you.'

Setting out in the car she began to explain her situation. Her log cabin was about fifteen miles upriver, on a rural property of a few acres, with an old farmhouse and the cabin and a few outbuildings, and the waters of the Cowichan gambolling past.

'Secluded and peaceful,' she said, 'altogether a mouth-watering piece of real estate.' Then she added, 'But I guess it could get a bit boring. No doubt I'll find out – I've not been there that long.'

Lew was looking at the countryside. Winter snow had yet to arrive, but the recent rains had left a bedraggled landscape, the wet earth deeply rutted, pools in the ditches, conifers drooping like soggy cavalry moustaches. It was overwhelmingly green, almost oppressive, but a different green from that he had known in Nova Scotia, with far fewer broadleaf trees. He hoped the sun would come out soon.

'My landlord lives in the old farmhouse,' Janie continued. 'He's a retired trolley-bus driver from Vancouver, a stringy old soul with a turkey neck. One of those cautious types who chews the inside of his cheek and doesn't seem to like what he tastes. His wife is shy, and they are both friendly enough. My car collapsed and I don't have one at the moment. Don't really need one. Where am I going, having just come here? I need concentration and steady work, not gadding about. And a friend lends me her car when I occasionally need one, as of now. It helps that the landlord drives into town twice a week in his smart new pickup. Either I go with him or he does my shopping for me. He quite likes doing it. His life is not overburdened with activity.'

Lew found it comfortable sitting next to her, comfortable drifting along quiet roads tunnelled through the woods, comfortable thinking about nothing more than the moment. At a clear bend in the road he thought he saw a bald eagle.

*

Two days later the sun did shine and by midday it was warm enough to sit out in the front of the cabin. Lew had his bottom on a canvas chair and his feet on an upturned bucket when Janie emerged with a tall glass of vodka and orange and a proposition from Bradley, her landlord.

On the land, besides the house and the cabin, there were other outbuildings in various states of disrepair. Most peculiar was a structure, more folly than habitation, that appeared to have started as storeroom or small cabin and then had been elongated into a sort of watchtower. In the event it served no firm purpose and had been abandoned into the keeping of the big mower and the garden tools.

'I've been talking to Bradley,' she said when Lew had his nose in the vodka. She was unsure how he would take what she had to say. 'He was curious about you, naturally. Who were you, and what were your intentions? I didn't want to say much, but I told him you were a handy fellow, a carpenter and suchlike, and had done a lot of casual labour. You'd also been a reporter in the past. As to your intentions, that I didn't know. You'd just come back from a long time abroad. You had to find your feet again.'

'No harm so far,' Lew replied cautiously. He wondered what was coming next. At the moment, his intentions didn't figure at all in the mental notes he kept to remind him that he was still alive and functioning.

'Well, Bradley says he's been meaning to renovate that old tower but hadn't got round to it. How would you like to tackle it? Done well, it would make a neat little dwelling. And when it's done you might like to rent it. In the meantime you can stay in my cabin. He'll adjust the rent so we both pay something. And he'll pay you for the work you do on the tower. I don't want to press you but the plan suits me pretty well. I pay a little less rent and I get to keep you for company. Makes a change from Bradley's memories of fighting the downtown traffic in Vancouver.'

Lew went to look at the building, and after studying it and taking some measurements he warmed to the project. He needed some income and was prepared to do many things for it, even if a job was only temporary. He liked carpentry and it tickled him to have the design all to himself. He was in a most pleasant spot and Janie's company was just fine. It was as nice a piece of good fortune as he could wish for.

He negotiated with Bradley and the old man snuffled and hemmed and hawed. He looked shifty but was just indecisive, worried by matters of money. Finally, they made an agreement. Lew would pay seventy-five dollars a month in rent, and Bradley would pay him eight bucks an hour to work on the tower, all materials provided. Lew began work the next day, going at his own pace. Within two weeks he had accumulated enough money for two months' rent, and the outlines of the basic structure were in place.

So far, the task needed little expense other than Lew's wages, and a good part of that came back to Bradley in rent. Then things began to go wrong. Lew arrived at the stage when he needed materials. Bradley was paying and soon he was chewing his cheek and looking hurt. Good, seasoned timber was expensive. What was wrong with ordinary tongue-and-groove, or plastic sidings? Steel fittings would do as well as brass or copper. Why have skylights in the roof? The windows would give enough light. Wooden worktops in the kitchen were hardly necessary. The store had standard stuff in laminate or metal. Ceramic or terracotta tiles in the bathroom? Really, plastic would do just as well.

Slowly, Lew retreated step by step from his ideal, which even he recognized as rather flighty. At last, it came down to plasterboard and imitation panelling printed to look like inferior pine; formica surfaces and plastic tiles, bought in job lots; a tarpaper roof without skylights, and without the cedar shakes to cap a house of the woods.

What Lew wanted, what the woods wanted, what nature would gracefully accept, all meant nothing when plans came up against Bradley's impoverished imagination and his material fears. Lew was relearning how narrow the focus was in the normal world of contract. A raw sufficiency was good enough. Bradley had a thirst for a bargain.

Lew put up with it for four months, for the sake of his pocket, for Janie's sake. Then, with the project nearly finished, some ultimate petty meanness made him snap.

'He's just a rusty old fart,' he growled to Janie that evening, pouring another shot from the vodka bottle. 'He's a bigot, a hypocrite, a penny-pincher, a jerry-rigger. That man has no grace, manners or taste. To hell with his damn watchtower.'

Grace? Janie sat up at that and glanced at Lew strangely. It put him in a new light, that he should look for such a quality in the ordinary business dealings of humanity.

Next morning, Lew returned his tools, settled outstanding sums, and gave notice of departure. It gave him pleasure to tell the old skinflint that he quit. Bradley went red and gobbled a bit; he didn't know whether to be offended or pleased.

*

It had been in both their minds, Lew thought, that he and Janie might become lovers. But friendship saved them. It was too valuable an attachment for both to risk on the possibility – perhaps the likelihood – of emotional shipwreck. In the recent past both had been somewhat battered. Now, for the moment, they were too sober and experienced for the ravenous appetite of love. He liked Janie better than he would ever love her.

So his departure had less importance than he might have feared. Friendship endured without physical proximity.

But he would miss her. Renovating the tower he had worked when and how he liked. Bradley was easy with that; if Lew put in no hours he got no pay. On fine days Lew often took a walk in the woods, or did some chores around the cabin – bucking alder branches into logs with the chainsaw, or splitting logs into firewood with the axe. To do that was a memory, almost a reflex, of his youth on the farm in Nova Scotia, and he took an obscure pride in the continuation of a talent long unused. He began to think he was a Canadian once more. And when the weather was foul – there was no shortage of drizzly days – he took to his room in the cabin, with a book and a pot of coffee, and didn't stir until his stomach rumbled.

On these idle days he could hardly avoid the presence of Janie. At breakfast, he would see her preoccupied, a frown gathering, and silence descending. About nine-thirty she firmly closed the door of her room, and then Lew could hear the signs of the beginning struggle. A splutter of fast typing, then pauses and sudden rushes leading to longer and longer pauses. Footsteps sometimes, and the occasional expletive through the door. Then her door swinging open abruptly and hurried steps to the kitchen and in a while the kettle hissing and bubbling. He knew enough to keep out of the way. At these times she needed no sympathy, no comfort, no criticism. The task she had undertaken, she was in it alone.

Then, at the sundown hour, harried or glowing according to the effort of the day, she stopped dragging the train of her thought over heavy country and joined Lew on the grass outside or on the stoop or by the stove in the big room. Then they might talk and set the world right. Sometimes she lamented the problems of her work, but more usually not.

Seeing and hearing her reminded Lew of where he thought he had been going when he left the newspaper twenty years before. Now, he felt at one with her in spirit, although he did not tell her. He said nothing because she made him feel slack and slightly guilty; she raised up for him the spectre of his own failing.

In these circumstances he considered it was no bad thing for him to leave. Carpentry was an excellent trade, and he enjoyed it. But he was not *that* good, only an amateur having fun. In a lean world of an economy that owed favours to no one it was a reliable standby. A stiffer task awaited him, and by staying here perhaps he was denying himself some pain important to his soul. He would miss Janie, sure, but he packed his bag and went.

Sunshine Coast

The side road was newly graded, still dirt but looking as if tarmac might follow soon. It went from the coast road to the inlet on the land side of the peninsula, a country track, wandering a little through deep, second-growth forest, past the occasional cabin or timber house half sunk under the dark green of the woods. Sometimes a house was far back and completely hidden; only the thin rutted line of a meandering driveway, branching through the roadside scrub, indicated the presence of a home. Sometimes a rough board with a faded name or number was nailed to a tree by the roadside. Once or twice he saw the familiar small kennel on the top of a post, so often placed at the border of property in rural North America for receiving mail and newspapers. The little doors of the kennels hung crooked and open, as if tiny animals within had fled.

The place Lew was seeking had a faint number, hardly noticeable, on a board fixed high up in an old fir. The number meant almost nothing, and no one remembered it, for all mail was delivered into the nests of metal boxes stacked like drawers at the exit from than main coast road. Those in search of the house had instructions: about a mile in towards the inlet, an opening on the right, just after the small switchback in the road, the double doors of a big wooden workshop visible shortly after the turning. In the event, it was not hard to find.

Lew was hot as he turned off the dirt road. He had left his luggage at the motel in town, thumbed a ride for about twelve miles on the only road going north until he spotted the small sawmill by the roadside. Then he walked in towards the inlet, slowly gathering the silence about him and savouring once again the unmistakable tang of the Western woods. He made the turning and the temperature dropped pleasantly. High branches touched each other across the narrow track. The workshop loomed suddenly, surprisingly large, elbowing room for itself amid the strict confines of the trees. He skirted a ragged open field full of unwanted weeds, past a disused water tower shedding its cedar shakes, then round in a half circle to the eccentric wooden house of first thoughts, half thoughts and afterthoughts fronting on to the far side of the field. A large dog stirred itself, barked in a deep gloomy way and ambled towards him, followed soon after by a lean man a little over average height, dressed only in a timeworn and disgraceful pair of workman's overalls. He had prematurely grey hair, and crinkly eyes that were shy and friendly at the same time. Lew had arrived.

He had always thought it was something he would never do: pick up a name recommended to him, and impose himself upon this stranger in some far-off place. He thought he was too private and reticent for that; nor would he wish to force this indignity upon another person. One might have to leave home for ever, to guard against such intrusive presumption. But he had been given the name of Terry Carroll by a mutual friend in London, a friend in whom Lew had confidence. In London, Terry's name had often been mentioned, generally celebrating mild oddities, a direction askew from the main line, a quiet but singular way of doing things. Lew remembered how his friend had pictured Terry – quoting the description of the Greek poet Cavafy – as a man 'standing at a slight angle to the universe'. Terry was tucked up in the woods of Western Canada, secure behind the vast green rampart of the trees, emerging to have a look at society when he wished, but generally on his own terms. He could do for himself everything that a simple life demanded. On the whole, he preferred to stay where he was, watch the robins and the hummingbirds, listen to the harsh call of the ravens, or puzzle out a way to keep the bears out of the chicken run.

Listening to these tales of the West, Lew had felt that there was something in Terry's life and circumstances that might have instructions for his own future. A place and a method to start again. So when the London friend had offered to write to Terry to warn him that Lew might be coming his way, Lew had put aside his distaste and agreed.

Now they stood under the cedar trees, with the big dopey dog sniffing Lew's boots. Lew gave his own name and the name of the mutual friend in London, and they shook hands awkwardly. Two strangers, they could not help but be a bit embarrassed.

'I was wondering if you'd come,' Terry said. 'I heard news from London that you'd left for Canada quite some time ago.'

'Well, I've been rolling this way but there seemed to be some blocks on the road. And then suddenly time had passed.'

They grinned. To both of them it sounded like an adequate explanation.

'Come on in. Don't mind the dog, he's harmless. We'll have coffee and then I'll show you around.'

Terry led the way, as if for an old friend. Lew had navigated this far and there was no further to go.'

*

For the moment he could not escape from carpentry.

At first, Terry offered him temporary use of the loft above the workshop. 'You'll need somewhere to stay,' he said, as if Lew's place in the community was signed and sealed, 'until you get going.' Lew bunked down in the large roomy space, with creaking boards and a froth of cobwebs in the corners and the shrivelled bodies of dead flies, but with a big dormer window at the level of the treetops and a suffused tawny light from the coloured glass of the bull's-eye window in the gable end. He fetched his case from the motel in town, and once he had his clothes hung on a line between the beams, and a lamp set up by the bed, and cushions against the wall at the head of the mattress, and a book handy, he could not think what more he needed for the time being.

He did not have to be in any hurry. He was not after material things. A faith in the future had grown on him as stealthily as a new beard.

In this tranquil state he had two placid weeks. Nothing was forced on him, he just mooched around with Terry observing the lay of the land, the bias of local life. He saw that what people did here – how they lived – did not follow the recommendations from schools and colleges and the masters of business. There was a lot of time in the day, people did what they felt they could do without much interference. They were not unhappy.

The late summer was hot, sometimes too sultry in Terry's crowded house to make cooking comfortable. Rose, Terry's partner, prepared some cold food on these days and they ate on the deck under the spreading grapevine. On this evening there were bagels and cold salmon and a green salad, placed on an old upended cable reel that served as a table. Fresh juice but no alcohol; Terry could take it or leave it, Rose definitely left it. Lew was still a little cautious in her presence. She was a small, compact woman with a beaky nose, Mediterranean complexion, long brown hair. At first glance her spine seemed excessively rigid. Her look was steady and stern, ready to confront the lies and evasions of menfolk. Then she smiled and everything changed, and Lew could guess what Terry had first seen in her.

'I heard some news from up the road today,' she said. Plugged into the network of women she had her own sources of information. 'Alicia's caretaker has just quit and she badly needs another. She's off to the States as soon as possible but doesn't want to go before she finds a replacement.'

She put her steady eye on Lew. 'I thought it was the kind of job that would suit Lew.'

The word *job* raised some alarms. But Lew reflected that he might be something of a cuckoo in this nest where he was; Rose might want her territory fully restored to her. Men, when their games and toys were out and scattered, forgot how intrusive they could be. So he listened quietly while Rose explained. Alicia Lamarr was an American, aged about fifty-five, with a cabin and forty acres of BC forest that she had owned for many years. Since her husband had died, and having grown-up children below the border, she now spent little time in the northern woods, but wanted to keep the property in good order. She was quite well off, but knew the meaning of money. The land was potentially valuable.

Next day, Lew went to meet her, retracing a path halfway to the coast road and then branching a quarter mile into the woods. She was a good-looking lady with white hair, a full figure and plenty of Yankee get-up-and-go. Lew liked her at once, though for peace of tenure he thought he would want her to get up and go as much as possible. That, too, seemed to be her aim. After a brief discussion they quickly reached agreement. He would look after the property, staying temporarily in her cabin while he built his own. She would pay for the building materials and also pay a monthly wage, small but adequate for simple living, to do all the many tasks required of a caretaker.

'What I need,' she said briskly, 'is someone with initiative and sense. Anticipate what needs to be done and get it in hand without having to be told. I haven't time for all that. You'll be on your own and I'll expect you to be responsible and careful.'

Lew gave her a long look, as if she could save her breath. Then she laughed and shook his hand.

Within a few days Lew had taken over the spread: a cabin, woodshed and outhouse; five rabbits, a platoon of ducks, a black dog and a timid cat; a small vegetable garden; forty acres of tangled forest. Despite Alicia's ownership, it was his domain.

*

So it was back to carpentry. His first task was to get out of her cabin, gloomy, dank and badly positioned, and to construct something more to his liking. Terry Carroll designed a new cabin, drawing it out on a coffee shop napkin, a simple floor plan based on two standard sheets of plywood, with a light frame of cedar poles, to which was attached cedar lap siding, inside and out.

'You'll be needing some help, I expect,' Terry said. He was the expert, an accomplished and imaginative housebuilder.

'No way!' Lew replied indignantly. 'This job is all mine. Every measurement, every sawcut, every driven nail. The only help I need from you is the temporary loan of some tools.'

This was an initiation he imposed upon himself, a trial of his competence to be himself in a changed life. Help was fine; but it weakened you if you called for it when you didn't really need it.

In early autumn he began to clear the site, a rocky hump on a slight slope in a break of the trees, overlooking the cleared land around Alicia's cabin. The site let in air and light, though the view from the floor, apart from the cabin below, was still nothing but forest. He thought that might be enough to look at for one lifetime. In two weeks he had the little building up and weathertight; in another two weeks he had it at the point where it was habitable. There was still much to do – finishing and trim and shelves and worktops, and some furniture to be bought – but essentially it was complete. It was small, merely eight foot by twelve, but Lew was not a big man and he liked the tidy use of space. He had once visited Thoreau's little hut at Walden, which was just about the same size. At the end of the cabin Lew had a fixed table with benches, and above that a sleeping platform across the gable end. The walls were eight foot to the eaves and another six foot of clear space to the roof ridge. His windows were large frames culled from the town dump with old panes still in place, the wavy and irregular window glass fracturing the light into distorted patterns.

He liked the intimacy of his four close walls, everything to hand and hardly more than an arm's length away. In his loft bed he found he slept soundly and dreamed well. At a later time he might extend the cabin. It would be easily done. But for the moment he wanted no more.

*

He was up on the ridge of the roof fixing the last of the cedar shakes. From that elevation the view was expanded, more comprehensive. In the distance, a faint line of high mountains under a haze of weather; sharp bones of the coastal range nearby; a tantalizing glimpse of sea where the portals of the woods opened briefly. And forest everywhere, thick and thin, scarred more or less by tracks and clearance.

Looking around, he was suddenly surprised by the relative absence of the works of man. It was a portrait of the land as he wished it to be. He looked forward to the return of each season, familiar but still strange, known but not completely read. No doubt man had work to do, but it was labour of care, conservation and quiet development, not spoliation. There was a balance, and he thought the struggle to maintain it was a duty, and worthwhile.

Box 29, RR3

Lew had an address now, which he took as a sign that he belonged. It was only a box number on a rural road, but he liked the impersonal, inscrutable nature of the label. He felt he could be easily reached but not easily found. He was not hiding, but that was the way it worked in these woods, a way that had Lew's approval. Those he wished to see, or those who had a kindly interest in him, knew where he was by word of mouth. Others had to start from outside a zone of privacy, violate that circle, and it was not certain that they would get much help.

He usually rose early, a fact that surprised him as it had not been his habit before. He made a small pot of coffee, and that for him was an invitation to the day. Soon he was outside, methodically going about his chores whatever the weather, feeding the animals, checking Alicia's cabin, making the vegetable garden tidy. It was not a heavy labour. From time to time there were branches and scrub and deadwood to clear, and fallen trees to be removed. The early light in the forest was pale and elusive, the long shadows of the trees stretching westward as if on some mission of longing. The silence, after the dying away of the dawn chorus, seemed fragile and taut with expectation.

These mornings were his own, when it soon became known that he did not welcome visits. Visitors with an idle purpose were received with irritation and scowls. After a late lunch he liked a little nap, with his portable radio turned low, a murmur of music, classical or folk or jazz, blues for preference but not be-bop. He liked many types of music and had stopped worrying that he did not know very much about any of them.

In late afternoon the mood changed. From his swivel chair behind the big south-facing window he watched occasional visitors stump up the slope to his cabin, their forms shifted slightly by the distorting window glass. Visitors – at least certain ones – were welcome now. It was a time for conviviality.

Lew had the cribbage board out, and a little hash or grass on hand, and the beer bottles cooling in a bucket of water. He was thinking of brewing his own beer.

*

He bought a secondhand typewriter at the Sally Ann in town, an Underwood

Standard, a clumsy office machine perhaps as old as he was. It worked well enough, in a heavy-handed way. He liked its loud, old-fashioned clatter. It reminded him of the urgent noise in the newsroom in the days when he was a reporter, and he wondered what tales and secrets, what accumulated memories its keys had impressed on paper in its long life. Did he have anything worth adding to that unknown account?

He was pitched into it now, alone with his typewriter and his memories.

After two weeks, and then four, he was still there, maddened by white paper. Most afternoons, Terry Carroll stopped by for a herbal tea and a chance to take the day apart, in what had become something of a ritual. Day by day the uncovered typewriter stood between them on the table, its unmoving silence a testament to something Terry did not understand. He had little conception of the nature of literary labour. He read science fiction chiefly, and yachting magazines.

'I thought you were writing a story,' he said innocently, unaware how galling that was. 'What kind of a story?'

'Some sort of message from my own experience,' Lew replied evenly, indulging the practical man. 'But I seem to find very little other than random episodes that I can't make add up.'

Terry was interested in that. He saw the importance of continuity, of flow, of adding up and rounding out.

'There are plenty of stories around here,' he said, trying to be helpful. 'Perhaps you should do one of those, at least to begin with.'

Lew gave him a look, suggesting he might not know what he was talking about, but Terry had already noticed an error in his own thinking.

'On second thoughts that might not be a good idea,' he went on doubtfully. 'People here – friends I know – have plenty to tell, and they'll talk quickly enough if they like you. Their lives are not secret, just private. They might not want the stories spread around. Most have had troubles with society, fallen through the cracks, and this place has become a kind of refuge for many of them. They're at ease here and don't want to be disturbed. There are some stories that don't want to be broadcast.'

He considered what he had been saying, his face taking on the solemn look that he wore when the world surprised him.

'Oh, I could name you names,' he reflected, remembering the rogues and the heroic ones alike. 'But you'll meet them all in time, if you stay here. We have Vietnam veterans, and draft dodgers, and dropouts, and hippies, and remittance men, and disappointed people from Europe, and illegal immigrants, and bikers, and dope farmers, and fascist gun-toters, and petty criminals on the lam. Isolationists and activists too, and some who might save the world, if they had time on a wet weekend.'

His voice, which began affectionate and then crept sour, ended in a scornful coda. 'But with a lot of them I wouldn't trust their account any better than a TV ad. Out here in the boondocks, with time on their hands, they choose a new personality each day.'

*

Since he could not write, Lew tried to think. What was the nature of his own memories? Diligently he consulted old notebooks and diaries and came up against unexpected obstacles. He had a tale to tell, that he was sure of, one in tune with the times. When he came to consider his memories, helped along by many years of notes, he found that the narrative course of events was reasonably clear. The sequence was firm enough, going step by step. The trouble was that he often saw a discord between the narrative of memory and the pictorial images apparently fixed randomly in his mind, those icons that he took – rightly or wrongly – to reveal the inner meaning of a life.

He remembered strange illuminations. A horse drawing a cart, down on its front knees after slipping on the ice, quivering yet unable to move, its teeth horribly bared. A man swimming on his back, alone in an Ontario lake, howling at the sky. Two small Berber boys trying to race two reluctant sheep, their little fists deep in the wool and their heels going like jockeys'. A man of the Middle Atlas using a broad, polished knife blade as a mirror to reset his turban. A couple of foreigners on a remote Spanish hillside, copulating on the sandy bed of a dried watercourse, gasping and moaning with the anguish of Furies. A car on its side in a shallow ditch observed by a silent man sitting on a boulder, calmly smoking a cigarette. An inmate at the Queen of Heaven trying to mend his shoes with sticky chewing gum. What weight should he give memories such as these, and taken together where did they point?

The doubt worried him, and at night, after the beer bottles and the roaches in the ashtray had been cleared away, and the stove banked for the night, he lay in his high bunk under the roof and let his mind float around the question. In this state he was to a degree detached from himself, and he asked himself for an unbiased opinion. He decided he could call up with a fair amount of clarity a narrative sequence, the tell-tale from A to B and what happened next; this memory was adaptable and functional, aware of the shifting nature of real events, prepared to suggest alternatives. Then there was an aesthetic memory, partial and fragmented, but fixed and ineluctable, teaching obscure lessons but once drawn, pictured for ever.

He did not know how to reconcile the two sources of memory. All he saw at the moment was that he had his own either/or. The task was too much for him. As he lay in his high bed his eyes always closed before any solution came to mind.

Sunshine Coast

Slowly, Lew began to meet them, those Terry had mentioned, the backwoodsmen – and women – of the day, though very few of them were woodsmen in any true sense of the word. He met them in the hotel coffee-shop down by the water, and sometimes the very same ones in the evening in the hotel pub, with the jukebox thumping and the pool-balls clicking on the table over by the toilet. He met them in the post office and at the laundromat and in the liquor store; at the hardware store or at the lumberyard; at the Italian grocery in town, the one place where he could get decent coffee. He met them at the Sally Ann or at the hospital charity shop, picking through baseball caps and fedoras, or when he was looking for footwear to replace his beautiful but worn-out Spanish boots.

Most of them were cautious, and so was Lew. But he had been accepted by Terry, which gave him a kind of passport, and he began to receive in the street a 'Hiya' or a 'How ya doin'?' from strangers. In the pub he bought his share, and more, of drinks, and then he sat back and listened, as had always been his habit. Terry was right. The locals had no trouble talking, under the right conditions. The haze in the big beer hall seemed to Lew like an excessive vapour given off by unlikely stories. He polished his specs – cleared his vision – with appreciation. At a certain stage, at certain tables, hidden by the din and bustle, a little grass was likely to go round, and here it was obvious that Lew knew one leaf from another.

Little by little a few of them began to appear at his cabin door, when the hour of relaxation struck. At first, there was likely to be some simple purpose behind the visit. A chainsaw was damaged, could Lew make a temporary loan? Would he lend a hand to move a boat? Someone had come to borrow a book. A new house in the woods was being framed and could do with some help. He was glad to help.

Then some began to stay for a while, the ones who clicked with Lew. Talk began to go beyond the practical or the trivial. There was a suspicion that his worldwide experience might give Lew unusual authority. A philosopher of the woods. Suddenly people barely known erupted with tales of bruised, frustrated, incomplete lives emerging from various abysses. He wondered at his role; was he a listener or a confessor?

'I had to take a look at myself,' said Frank Belman, one whom Lew knew from the coffee shop. 'It disgusted me what I saw, someone all bogged down with debt and trinkets and impossible relationships. And an ambition to be a rich big shot, one of those you instinctively despise when you meet them.'

He started to sink into these gloomy thoughts and Lew helped him out with another beer.

'So,' he said tactfully, 'how did you get out of that one?'

'Took me some time and some bad behaviour. Drinking and hell-raising and all that. The wife vamoosed and the kid scurried along behind her. Then I thought, hell, I'm a mechanic and there's not much I can't do with my hands. With that going for me it doesn't take much to pay the rent, put food on the table. How much can one man eat? So I drifted up here and rented a little place on the edge of town, where places were cheap because of the stink from the pulp mill. Then I began to hustle around, doing casual jobs here and there. Made out pretty easy, took time off when I wanted. Found myself, you might say. Chances come up when you least expect them, and you can grab them or not. After a time, an oyster lease became a possibility and I grabbed it. I'm there now. Not the easiest life, being beholden to nature, but it certainly has its rewards.'

His voice was happy now, and he relapsed into silence.

Lew saw small destinies, each one intimately worked. The woods became a curtain, to withdraw behind and pull apart when you wanted. Being essentially alone you often needed help. And then the idea of mutual aid suddenly struck home. So you helped willingly, and others did likewise. It made a community though they didn't call it that. The convention was that each was a loner; you shut the door and then nobody had rights over you. Not rights, but if you were asked nicely you would usually comply.

*

'What's he aiming to do here?' Frank Belman was asking Terry. They had finished their morning coffee and were down on the wharf inspecting a boat Frank was half interested in buying. He wanted Terry's opinion, of the boat and other things. Terry was idly kicking just above the waterline. The boat was a wreck and worth nothing more than a kicking.

'Just living, I guess,' Terry said, turning his attention to the question of Lew. A new resident aroused curiosity. 'Does he have to be up to something?'

'Well, Canada's a free country and I suppose he's a Canadian, if a Bluenose from Halifax can be properly called that. But he's not the usual type we get out here. I hear he's been up and down Europe for a good many years, doing all those smart cultural things. Seen a lot of places, a lot of life. I'd have thought we're a bit primitive out here for a person like him.'

'Might do us good to hear a voice from the world,' Terry suggested. 'What have we got to talk about other than fishing and logging and boats and the lousy beer the Alberta nazis serve in the hotel pub? Oh, and who's sleeping with whom. Even when we listen to the radio it's only to find a bargain on *Swap Shop*. I reckon a voice from the big world could help us.'

'Yeh?' Frank said, unconvinced.

'He's an ex-newspaperman,' Terry added. 'He's got a lot of thoughts in his head, a lot of experience. I think he means to get certain things down on paper. Write a book, maybe.'

'Hell,' Frank said, aghast. 'I hope he leaves us out of it.'

*

When the chances come by, grab them. That was what Frank had said and Lew saw the sense of it. He had found that he needed a little more income than Alicia's wage provided. For one thing, he needed to buy and run a car. He wanted a vehicle to carry materials and for his own transport. Buses were non-existent. So when opportunities came by he did grab them. And sometimes it seemed like work and sometimes not.

He saw out his first winter in the West with a pleasure he had not expected. The cold was nothing like the cold he had dreaded in the East. Or on the prairies.

He had hemlock logs crackling in the stove. The temperature in his small cabin was always warm enough to sit in a tee-shirt. It reminded him of life in North Africa.

Throughout the winter visitors came – those whom Lew accepted – drawn by the cosiness and the exotic presence of the world traveller. Lew was generous with the beer and he discovered that he liked to cook. He had only a two-burner stove running on bottled gas, or a stewpot simmering slowly on the cabin's woodburner, but he made forays into the cookbooks of France and Spain. From his European years he recalled what cooking should be and what eating might be, and the favoured visitors were invited to stay and try it. Not many refused.

And amid the eating and the drinking he had adventures to relate, stories of people and places from the wilder shores of the world's commerce, those tales anyway that Lew was prepared to release. The habit of caution that he had painfully learnt made him keep part of that world to himself, though what his listeners heard was strange enough. To start out from rural Canada and reach where Lew had been seemed, in the cabin with the stove glowing and the fronds of the trees combing the fine rain and the darkening of winter light, to contain a hint of magic.

'What do you think?' Frank asked Terry, after one of Lew's long excursions into trials and danger. Frank was a little stunned, and while Lew was outside in the woods relieving himself Frank thought he would test opinion. 'Can all that be true?'

'I don't really know,' Terry replied, 'but it makes a very good adventure and I for one enjoyed it. Some time ago Lew told me of an old poet who spoke of a 'willing suspension of disbelief'. Really, that's not so difficult, if the story is good. I can do that. But it depends on the story.'

Thinking about that, Frank nodded and reached absently for another of Lew's beers.

*

The consumption of beer, beer made by the big breweries, was high, more perhaps than Lew could afford with ease. Nor did he like very much the chief brands of Canadian beer. American was worse. He had drunk beer in Germany and Belgium and England, and he knew what beer could be. He thought he could make his own beer, better and cheaper than the stuff he bought.

When he came to try, it surprised and pleased him how easy it was, with care and dedication and a bit of hard work. By the spring he had production going well. He had sixty litres in various stages of fermentation, and another thirty already bottled and waiting out on his porch. The best was a smooth brown ale with more than 7 per cent alcohol. He resolved to go carefully on that one.

Sunday morning was his brewing day, and it was unwise to interrupt him. His visitors soon knew that the product was good enough to wait for. It was just about as enjoyable as his cooking, his company and his stories.

So by chance he found that he had discovered a new enterprise. His beer was in such demand that he could use it to trade. He would not sell it, for that risked a dangerous clash with the excisemen. The sale of alcohol was a provincial monopoly and too profitable to forgo. But he could use it for barter. He discovered with amusement, entirely in the spirit of the woods, that he was receding in economic time, back to an era of primitive exchange, when beer was as valuable a currency as copper, nickel or silver coins.

*

He realized, after the long and drifting days of the summer that followed, that he had been settled for a year and nothing had gone wrong. In fact, he seemed to be happy, in a way that he had not known before.

'Man,' said one of the stubborn old hippies from the far side of the inlet, after a big joint had been going the rounds in Lew's cabin, 'looks like you're in the groove here, like Miles Davis leaning into that horn.'

Lew was smoking much less now, a few tokes for enjoyment of an evening, no longer needing cannabis to take the dangerous edge off a life of uncertainty. Did he lack ambition? He could not sort out exactly what his ambition had been. His life, for the last twenty years or so, had been a trek through obscure country, the effort dictated by the terrain. Now the path was easier, the beds softer. He no longer witnessed the harsh splendour, the brilliant light and the violent springs of action that had so fascinated him – and frightened him too – in the world of North Africa and the East. He was getting soft. Or was it just advancing age? He feared, not too seriously, that he was also lazy.

There was an easy cure for laziness. All he had to do was to get out in the woods. Rolf DeVere, a high-wire amoralist, whose life was an unsteady balance between grotesque stunts, laughter and instant arrest, proposed to Lew a minor venture in the forest, a small nefarious enterprise in cutting and selling firewood. On Crown land or on logging company land, Rolf was not quite sure which.

'Illegal, of course?' Lew asked.

'To hell with all that,' Rolf waved the thought away. 'I wouldn't know whose permission to ask. Look at is this way. We're just giving the forest a clean-up, getting rid of deadwood, and the trees brought down by storms, and the timber that needs trimming to let the light in. We'll be busting a gut to tidy up their forest. And it's our damn forest too – we the people – so why not put all that junk wood to good use? It's stuff the logging companies care nothing about. Not enough profit in it. Likely as not eventually they would just bulldoze it all into a pile and burn it.'

For 200 dollars they bought a 3/4–ton GMC truck, a twenty-year-old snorting dinosaur of ferocious power and torque, with a rusty cargo bed full of rips and holes. But it was well able to carry a full cord of green fir or alder. For a month they ran the truck on a temporary demonstration licence, swallowed up by the woods before anybody could notice.

Over the ruts and gullies into the forest, down tracks so overgrown they were barely visible, the old truck bounced and swayed like a double bed in a brothel. The steering wheel leaping in his hand, Rolf could not contain his delight, riding his own rodeo. 'Woo-hoo, damn me, nearly lost it there,' he would shout with glee. He said he was 'wired' and nothing could stop him. 'I've got too damn much energy,' he confided to Lew. 'Haven't been laid in a month.'

Tumbling out of the truck he had the chainsaw fired up in a trice and wood flying. Rolf felled and bucked, Lew split and stacked. Big logs nearly took their feet away, and small trees fell like wheat stalks. Lew had to look sharp, ready to leap to safety as Rolf wielded the chainsaw like a samurai sword. There were no let-ups, no breaks for refreshments. 'In and out quickly,' Rolf cautioned, 'same as jackrabbits.'

In two ten-day spells they had their patch cleared and the wood corded. Then they were out and legal again, grinning like successful beachcombers. They sold the truck for the same amount that they had paid for it, and Lew was sad to see it go. It was an ornery brute with an unreliable temper, but it had great presence and character.

It was all too much fun, and he suffered for it. For some time afterwards Lew hobbled with muscular pains, and his back hurt. He had splinters and he had taken the skin off the knuckles of one hand. At moments he had come close to serious injury, from chainsaw or from the kick of falling timber. It had hardly been necessary for the sake of a few extra dollars. To some degree, he thought he understood Rolf. He craved danger, if not the accomplishment of the impossible. Feeling best at home on the tightrope, he wanted the sway of the rope and the abyss beneath him to keep himself alive and productive. But behind his cheerful daring and the invitation to calamity lay an anger at and contempt for a society that had reduced conventional life to something so petty, so timid, so lacking in spirit, yet at the same time so restrictive, so authoritarian, so intimidating.

But what did the venture mean to Lew? A little bravado, a little risk, a small profit. Though he had been carried along on the wild roller-coaster of Rolf's dangerous enthusiasm, he did not need that rush of adrenalin. He had enjoyed himself, though there's a point where enjoyment ends and indulgence begins.

THE CABIN

He enclosed his porch, extending his kitchen, and built a steeple over it with a weathervane on top – a fish – and put a plastic cold-water tank in the steeple, fed by a pump and a long line from the spring. Then, under the floor of the new kitchen, he began to dig a cellar, a simple cube with sides of about five feet.

The work was much harder than he had anticipated, a tough dig through a tangle of tree roots and rocks and wet earth And then the raw sides needed shoring against collapse. But he wanted storage space with a cool constant temperature since he had discovered in himself a feeling and an enthusiasm for fermentation of all kinds. Not only were there beer bottles waiting to go on the shelves of his new cellar, but also an expanding line of wine bottles was ready to join them.

Apple, blackberry, raspberry, rhubarb – he tried many ingredients with varying success. He designed and built a fruit-press which everyone agreed was a handsome piece of work. He painted it red. He began to get a taste for the jargon, too, speaking airily of nose and palate, long on the tongue, short in the mouth, with hints of tobacco or leather. No one was sure if he meant to be ironical.

And then he thought he might even go further. After his many trials he had about fifteen gallons of fermented liquor that would never grow into decent wine, and Frank Belman suggested they might turn it into spirits. He knew of an abandoned chicken shed with a small still installed; a few friendly words in the right quarter would get them the use of it.

The shed stank of poultry, and the ancient gas stove for the still was encrusted with mash that had boiled over. Lew tied a cloth over his lower face to keep out dust and smell, and he and Frank worked fast in conditions that would have distressed a navvy, distilling their own versions of vodka, Calvados, and a fine brandy made from a dandelion sherry that wouldn't clear.

Lew had not expected to like the work, wanting only the results, but he found it perversely satisfying, like a kind of black sorcery. Frank was the supervisor; he had distilled liquor before and knew what to look for, including the danger signs. They watched the spirits slowly dribble out, crystal clear.

'Keep it coming,' Frank urged, sweating profusely in the close, stinking space.

'The trick is to take a sip and spit it on the stove. If it flares up it's still producing.'

They took frequent sips, and after a while they were both listing sideways. The spirit, emerging at about 70 per cent alcohol, scalded the back of the throat. There was only time to run the liquor through once and then they gathered their quart jugs and stumbled into the twilight.

'So, a fully fledged bootlegger now?' Frank said with mock solemnity, looking at the booty in the jugs.

No, Lew knew he was not that. Nothing alcoholic was for sale, though some might be bartered and other bottles might be given as gifts. In fact, everything he did in the line of alcohol was a gift to his own pleasure and to his present circumstances, a step into the fellowship of the place.

He stood a little unsteady in the cool evening, his beret flecked with chicken shit, his glasses gleaming like pebbles in swift shallow water. 'A grand day,' he said in a thick voice. 'At least, what I remember of it.'

*

At first, the typewriter stood on the end of the table against the wall, with a blank sheet of paper rolled into it. Then the blank paper went, and then the typewriter was removed to the top of a low cupboard that sat under a window. Visitors looked at the place where the typewriter had been but said nothing; to raise the subject would be embarrassing. The machine now rested under a patchwork cover, as if needing warmth for a long retirement. Fea, the cat, sprawled on it, basking in the sunny window.

From time to time he had taken it down to write a letter but found the keys beginning to stick from disuse and the spacing jumping about in a cranky way. So when a friend asked to borrow it, to fix it and then to use it, Lew let it go with hardly a thought. He had lost the taste for letter-writing.

Vera Gwinn wrote a few times over a long period, but he found her letters short, stiff, flat and after a while so far from the point of things that they were almost incomprehensible. He didn't know any more what they were writing about. He stopped writing back. The written word was valuable; it should not be squandered. To the few with whom he still corresponded he began to send recorded cassettes, words loosely hurled on to tape in his radio-recorder. He regarded the spoken word as something different, something hastily summoned that vanished into thin air as soon as you had finished with it. Oral communication was loose and free. The written word nailed you down, crucified you.

*

Very few women came to the cabin when the cribbage board and the drinks were laid out, but women – the wives and girlfriends of the back roads – liked him. He had seen life on other continents and had plenty to say on many topics, those that had nothing to do with fishing, logging and boats. He kept detached from local scandal, though the bed-hopping and the feuds and the naughtiness amused him. He kept a genial eye on the variability of human imperfections but usually he did not judge. His moral feelings were tempered by his friendships, except in the scary cases of wrongdoing, and then he did not forgive. He would have nothing to do with such people, turning on his heel when he met them in the street.

Women seemed to appreciate this discrimination, this forgiveness for small faults and condemnation for larger sins. They liked also his easy domesticity. He was a tidy man in a neat cabin where everything had its place. At first, his small space had looked rather cold and bleak, embellished by a few books only. Women looked it over and shivered a little.

'You need something more,' quiet Adele commented, the girlfriend of the dope-grower from two roads back.

'A woman's touch?'

'No, I wouldn't call it that. I'd call it human comfort.'

She was an expert seamstress and offered to make him curtains and cushions and covers in bold designs and colours. He began to like the new look of his home, and he hunted about in charity shops to discover old illustrations – etchings and daguerreotypes – that were quirky, funny or tender, which he re-framed himself. His cabin seemed to bloom now.

He liked cooking and that interested the women too. They were curious to see what he could do. He found himself in friendly competition, comparing and exchanging recipes. He collaborated with others for the communal feasts that enlivened the year, particularly the autumn and winter seasons. Eating was a business into which everyone put effort and enjoyment. A communal feast – out in a clearing, if possible, with a big blazing bonfire – might have three rabbit dishes, two of goat, some more of chicken, a dozen plates of different seafood, fruit puddings from as many fruit trees and berry bushes as hands could reach. Everything was gathered locally and cooked in half a dozen nearby kitchens.

'A man must be a damn fool to starve out here,' Lew said once to Terry as they gathered free oysters from the inlet beach. 'There are oysters here, and clams along there by the sandy spit, and a fishing line from the jetty will come up with something sooner or later. Trees and bushes are creaking with fruit. All you've got to do is get there before the bears and the birds. The woods, at the right time of year, are thick with all sorts of mushrooms. And no sane person should live out here without poultry, rabbits or goats.' He patted his tummy comfortably, thinking of the cooking pot.

So women regarded him as a friend and an ally, one they could turn to for advice and sympathy. He was not dangerous. He befriended them and liked to see them, but he made no moves on them. No sexual games. For the moment he was out of that competition, resting on another plane. Sometimes they speculated whether he was disappointed or tired, or just sated.

*

In the summer, there was the Gentleman's Club – no ladies allowed – at Hal Winter's house on the low cliff edge, drink and food and grass until the midnight hour, men – some as old as grandfathers – growing quietly infantile, and some, undone by gravity or the fall of their trousers, collapsed on the evening lawn while the islands in the strait slipped into dusk like basking whales, and the declining sun backlit the peaks in Strathcona Provincial Park, and the weary log-booms drifted south as implacably as planetary motion.

Then came the feast of the autumn equinox round a great fire of brushwood, with pots of cabbage rolls, oysters marinated and baked, fifty bottles of Lew's beer and more than a dozen of his various wines.

In December, at the solstice, was the festive joint birthday for Lew and for Terry – they shared the same day – candlelight in glowing rooms under funereal trees, punch and spirits to hold off the damp and help the feet wing home. And finally it was Christmas, perhaps in the house of Adele the home-maker, no turkey but three large rabbits cooked in three different ways by three cooks.

And so it went on, in annual rituals. Some years he overdid it. One New Year he was stomping to old tunes from a fiddle and squeezebox combo, a mickey of whiskey in his back pocket, until the mood overflowed and he stumbled into drunkenness. With glazed eyes he dimly saw a local fisherman as big as Paul Bunyan throw one of the Alberta nazis from the deck of the beer hall into the harbour shallows below. It seemed a fitting image on which to end a year, and then he was well out of things and ready to be carried home.

He woke late morning and lay in his high bed on the flat of his back, looking up through the skylight at snowflakes the size of goose feathers. All day they drifted down, and through the next day as well, and he with a terrific hangover, which wasn't too unpleasant as long as he did not move a muscle. He stayed in bed.

Thus the New Year began with a foot of fresh snow, on the ground and shrouding the trees, and his mind as cold and vacant as the white field, knowing where he was but still not quite why, and unsure how he should go on.

*

Alicia Lamarr, the landlady, visited her property less and less. Her family and friends were in the US. It was tedious to make the journey north very often, and not much fun any more when she arrived. Lew was a responsible caretaker and always had the upkeep well in hand. Why was she needed? She did not like to spend money unless strictly necessary.

But she could not forget certain seasons when she loved the place, seasons that had drawn her when she first came, and the best of these was spring. She still liked to be there for the start of the growing season, preparing the earth for the yearly work of nature, clearing and digging and sowing, and feeling the virtuous fatigue that came after. In late afternoon she liked to lie in a long chair on the little verandah of her own cabin, mild warmth on her face as the setting sun fell behind the circling ramparts of the woods – *her* woods.

She was there that spring, looking eager and fit and ready to work. Days were warm and still, flashes of birds' wings flickered through the lower branches, a flick of colour unanticipated and then gone. By mid-morning Alicia was out in the vegetable garden with her spade. In his cabin, Lew watched her from his big window. He had been reading but now he was watching, wondering if he should lend a hand. He was not fond of digging. Also, when Alicia was around he did not like to interfere; it was a matter of tact to allow her to take charge.

She worked steadily, with a practised hand, turning over rows of sod. In the mild heat she began to sweat and after a while she was too hot. She wiped her brow and took off her loose baggy tee-shirt, and Lew saw that she had nothing on underneath. For years, up in the woods, she had been among original hippies, and semi-nakedness, even full nakedness, was no big deal. A worn but handsome face, a sturdy body, full breasts falling somewhat but still suggestive of womanly feeling and sexual power, white hair tied back in a ponytail.

He thought that she knew he was watching but it made no difference to her.

He saw with detachment the gambols of her flesh, nipples hard and proud in the fresh air, and nothing stirred in him. No flag was hoisted. He wondered a little at that, half expecting that he might be moved to desire or excitement. He saw a woman of a certain age working vigorously and steadily. He thought it odd that she was stripped to the waist. She needed something to absorb the sweat. Why did she not put her tee-shirt back on?

*

'I hoped they might get it together,' Rose said to Terry Carroll. Among other talents she had the instincts of a matchmaker. 'She's older than he is but not by much. Two free people, still full of life, thrown together by the land and what it means to both of them. Why not?'

Terry was doubtful. 'I don't think he likes to feel that he's being forced into something,' he replied.

'Well, he seems to like women, judging by the number he has buzzing around, helping him with this and that. Perhaps most are too young for him, but Alicia? He's not homosexual, for goodness sakes. And I never heard him say anything against sex. In fact, when he speaks of Hal Winter down the coast, recently a widower and older than Lew, and still as frisky as a schoolboy, Lew's full of admiration.'

'That's different. What he's looking at is the whole character of Hal, his zest for life. All his appetites roaring away. Lew goes about things differently. He likes to keep a distance, observing what's going on. He appreciates what he sees but it doesn't mean that he's going to do the same himself.'

'What's the point of looking when you can pluck and taste it, if you like?' If you could have it, and it was good, and it hurt no one else, Rose saw no reason to step back. The world was awash with the tears caused by indecision and hopeless moral scruples.

Terry felt an obscure wish to defend his friend but he did not know how. He never had understood properly the how and the why of Lew Holle.

Sunshine Coast

In his early years on the coast he had thought that money might be his problem. In time, he saw that this was not the case, no more than it had been in Spain and North Africa. Canada, of course, was not Africa. There were unavoidable expenses in an advanced economy that did not apply in the Maghreb. But he found that life granted him a sufficiency, if only he would take it. That also had happened when he lived in the south of Spain, and he was surprised to see how simple it was wherever you were, if you could deploy a few talents, to avoid the competitive agony forced on the world by the fashionable economic determinism of our time.

'Consider the lilies of the field,' he often reminded himself. He was not a religious man – far from it – but a good text was still a good text. Consider, indeed!

He took on jobs for others only out of friendship or when he had a sudden need for cash. And sometimes out of boredom. Looking to replace an ancient VW Beetle that had become more rust than metal, he offered to build a shower-house for Alicia, something that had been needed for years to make her primitive and gloomy cabin more habitable. After some dithering – she did not like to spend money – she agreed. Terry designed it, a small elegant pavilion for washing and laundry, and Lew took on the construction, working obsessively alone, as he liked to do. He was not afraid to share the profits of the labour; so long as he had enough to replace the VW he did not care how much he was paid. It was the labour itself that he wanted to gather in, the test of his hand, to see if he could express the delicate lines of Terry's little plan.

Together they looked at it when Lew had finished. The new wood looked raw and bright, though the building sat well within its surroundings. Terry shook his head.

'Not quite as I imagined it,' he said with a frown,

'Well, I had to make some changes. She baulked at certain features of your design. Too damn fancy. She meant to say that it cost a bit more money than she thought necessary. So I made changes, and that took time and new materials, which cost more money. Some people find it hard to calculate their own best interest.'

'I suppose I should be used to it by now,' Terry said mournfully. 'Nothing comes off the drawing-board as it was intended to be.' In his youth Terry had worked in the large office of a famous West Coast architect, and the intellectual and artistic wounds he had received there had helped to drive him into the woods.

'It's about time you learnt,' Lew replied. 'When you enter the world of commerce you are inevitably in a world of compromise, and compromise is nearly always in favour of money.'

'Still,' Terry said, going round the corner to get a new angle on his design, 'there's something nice about this little building. The scale is right and it fits in well. It's definitely not bad.'

And Lew accepted that as a compliment to himself as well.

Sometimes, when he needed cash, Lew worked in the woods, though he came to dislike it more and more. He was mortified that man could do so much damage with such an easy conscience. What the logging companies created seemed to him like one version of Hell. The howl of chainsaws, the painful shock and bump of big trees falling, the demented roar of the skidders, like the death throes of dinosaurs, churning the world into a wilderness of mud and sawdust, the overpowering stench of diesel, the violent lurch of the huge logging trucks stumbling out of the chaos.

In the evening, angry and sore at heart, he often made his way to Hal Winter's house, to sit on the deck above the sea, to take some deep breaths and try to recover. The breeze off the strait was in his face and the faraway island mountains turned purple under the dusty cream of their peaks. Yet even here the insults to the land pursued him, the log-booms and the giant barges threading the nearby islands, each boom or barge containing a mountainside of trees.

'Give them time enough,' Lew grumbled to Hal, shooting off baleful looks, 'and the companies will have the whole world clearcut, from the Amazon jungle to the forests of Siberia. What they are doing here is just a beginning.'

'You're wrong there,' Hal replied. 'This is not just a beginning. They're well on the way to finishing the job here.'

Lew thought of photos he had seen of Picardy and Flanders at the end of the Great War, the land swept by the Angel of Death, stricken, cratered, ruined, empty, silent. Not so very different from the Western forest when the loggers withdrew.

In Hal Winter's life, from early years on through working in the forestry industry and then to an early retirement taken in disgust, he had seen the destruction happen. It put money in the pocket of a large locality, yet most who gained from it were secretly ashamed. Hal knew no way to stop it; but he favoured and supported an individual campaign of guerrilla resistance. A million bee stings might stop an elephant. That could be fun too, from the point of view of the bees.

Lew began to think of the forest around him as an innocent that needed defending. Its life, in the large scheme of the world, was as important as the lives of the humans who came within its ambit.

*

He laid aside his memories and addressed the present. In the early morning, fortified by a pot of coffee, he sat before his south-facing window, leaning back on the springs of an old office chair, taking account of his world. Each day he entered in a large spiral notebook what he saw and felt and dreamt in this small domain. Rigorously, he recorded the passage of the weather, the temperature, the movement of clouds, the arrival of sun or rain or snow. He counted the bald eagles lofting above the clearing and the ravens jesting with the wind. He noted the rumours from the woods, the stealthy comings and goings. To the north of his territory a wolf was seen on the shoreline; a cougar took and mauled a medium-sized dog; a bear harassed a young family of Americans incautious enough to try to live in a tepee while their house was being built. The animal had slashed a cut through the tepee wall from top to bottom and made off with a large Styrofoam box of food, without menacing or touching anything else. Almost as if it had lifted its hat and wiped its feet before leaving.

Frequently, he saw black bears in the woods, and they were more shy than he was. But he was wary when they came too close to the cabin, being fearful in particular for his goats, whose lives he also chronicled. Someone had given him an ancient revolver – a Webley, he thought, a lost piece from the World War – and with this he fired blanks at inquisitive bears. It made a lot of noise. The goats became used to it and it seemed to him that their bleating when they heard the shot was their way of laughing.

From being a place of danger the forest became his protective barrier, the ring encircling and securing his privacy. And it revealed to him its secrets. For him alone, or so it seemed, the chanterelles appeared, granting him in a good season more than twenty pounds of delicacies. In an almost hidden clearing the forest kept for him the few cannabis plants that met his modest needs these days. He shared his crop with the large banana slugs. There was enough for both of them.

He finished his notes and closed the book and sat quietly with the last dregs of the coffee. The day beyond the cabin awaited him, yet there was no hurry. He watched his goats go up the hill to browse, jumping through ferns and salal like deer, the same humping of the back as they lept into the welcoming shadow of the trees. In spirit he too was disappearing with them, into the childhood past of Nova Scotia, his blood running home with the autumnal days.

THE TOWNSITE

'I saw Lew this morning, down by the hospital.' Terry Carroll was telling Rose how his day had gone. 'I collected the sack of chicken feed, then I came back through town and stopped for a coffee at the Marine Café. I saw Lew's pickup parked further down the street.'

Rose waited. She knew Terry's habits. To him, in the reversal of ordinary practice, a day in town was something of a holiday. He had a favourite spot in the Marine Café from where he could observe the steam rising from the infernal maze of the mill, the impatient traffic scurrying towards the ferry terminal. Doctors took a break from the hospital, stretching in the air, having a quick cigarette, looking tired. Terry was happily divorced from all that, drinking muddy coffee in a leisurely way, digesting the gossip with a slightly stale Danish pastry.

'I was waiting for Lew to appear,' Terry went on. 'I wanted to tell him what Jem from the meat market had just told me, a story about the bikers out in the strait. Well, it's no secret that the bikers grow a lot of marijuana, and everyone knows that it's best to leave the bikers alone. But it seems the Mounties decided to make a point. Maybe they thought they weren't respected enough. Wanted to impose their authority, get those wild beasts safely on the leash. So they flew a helicopter over to spray the crop with killer chemicals. It was not well received. The story goes that the bikers sent a message to headquarters: "You send that big bird over here again and we'll blast the motherfucker out of the sky." Word is that they have the means to do it, too – an old bazooka or some such weapon brought up from the States. Vietnam War surplus. Jem is anxious to see the next move in what might be a tricky game for the cops.'

Terry relished these stories. Not that he wished harm to either bikers or cops, but he liked authority to get a jolt now and again, to remind it that neither law nor licence went according to the logic of computer models.

'So what about Lew?' Rose knew how to be patient.

'Yes, I was getting to that. I waited quite a long time and then I saw Lew come out of the door of the dental clinic. I was just going out front to call him when I saw that perhaps it was not a good time. He was walking fast to his pickup, looking preoccupied and tense. His beret was pulled down on his brow – usually a bad sign – and he was rubbing his jaw. Couldn't leave it alone. I think he saw my truck and would have found me if he wanted. So I let him go and he drove off very briskly, which is not like Lew at all.'

'What do you make of that?' Rose asked, and Terry pulled a long face and shrugged.

The history of Lew's old accident, the crash in the Ontario winter in which he had been badly jammed up in a suit of fancy-dress armour, was well-known to his friends – a good story, both sad and ridiculous. But the present state of his injuries was never mentioned. Lew distrusted doctors, for their airs and arrogance. 'When I lived in the south of Spain,' he used to say, 'I read in an old nineteenth-century guidebook that if you went to a Spanish doctor in those days you might as well get yourself measured for a coffin at the same time. I reckon it's not so very different with the doctors we have here.'

The tribulations of the body were intimate and private, and you lived with them as best you could. Old scars and afflictions might be material for a story, but about present ills Lew preferred silence. He was stern about that.

The Cabin

He was putting things in order, but he was also reordering them, which was strange.

'I don't know how it is,' Frank Belman commented to Terry, 'but Lew seems to be taking over our lives. I hear stories from Lew about me that I don't recognize at all. Pretty good stories too, some of them. He gives me a whole other existence that I certainly didn't know about. I don't know whether to be pleased or pissed off. It's quite nice to be talked about as if you are interesting, but then again there's the truth . . . '

'A while ago,' Terry said, 'he was telling us about some events that happened to him and I suddenly thought, Hold on, that's something that happened to *me*! I remember that I had told him about it. Now, in some peculiar way I had been transposed into *him*. It's hard to know how that kind of imagination works.'

'I don't think there's any malice in it, or any deliberate lies,' Frank added dubiously.

'I don't think so either,' Terry agreed, 'but I'd like to think that I had control of my own life history. Perhaps it's living here in the woods. A kind of gothic existence that doesn't touch the real world at too many places. Too many devils and spirits have been chasing us in the past, and now we're not sure where we begin and end.'

*

Sometimes, when the rain came slinging down and the wind blew furious, he worried about two tall skinny Douglas firs bucking and shaking within reach of the cabin. If they should shear and snap in the gale? But usually it was the big alders that went suddenly. He decided that he could trust the firs; he felt safe within the cabin.

He looked at the rain beyond the window and put another log on the stove. He had a crock of Boston baked beans simmering, cooked with a bottle of his own best ale, and the aroma alone was something to live off. He was about to begin the weekly brew, which he did every Sunday morning. At the same time he baked bread, enough for himself and a little extra to give away. Like an Italian without daily pasta, he suffered without good bread, and he could no longer eat the pale bleached pulp that came from the commercial bakeries.

These mornings had become his favourite times. He worked slowly, taking care but not putting in much physical effort, feeling buoyant on the rich smells of the cabin. He worked with the radio on, listening to the Sunday morning news round-up from the CBC, better than any newspaper (and he judged that as an ex-reporter). When the initial labour was done he had time to sit back with a glass of Wild Turkey bourbon in his hand.

In a while he took out the loaves and nibbled a bit of the crust. He could hardly think of a greater pleasure. He didn't know how he came by it, but he thought he must have an affinity for yeast.

More and more it appeared to Lew that the immediate moment was enough. Everything he wanted and needed fell within a small compass. He did not need to go far outside for life. What he required came to him and he received it on his own terms. He no longer had to explain.

The past looked to him like a mystery that it was pointless to try to investigate. He could make of it whatever he wished, as occasion arose. And the future was hardly relevant; it would chase you down, no matter how wise or cunning were your steps.

Whatever sense there was in his life was self-created, self-assessed and did not need words. Writing was superfluous, and it seemed to him that eventually even casual talking might go that way.

Sunshine Coast

He was out on the water in Frank's boat, fishing among the islands. That at least was the excuse, and they had a line over the stern which they tugged on now and again. The day was too fine and calm for strenuous activity. Frank had put up a headsail, just to be moving and to keep them off the rocks. Lew had bought a picnic – some salami and half a loaf of his bread, and apples to follow – and he was judiciously opening a couple of his own beers. They were idle but alert to shifts of mood, going where time and nature took them.

'I brought a book along,' Lew was saying lazily, 'partly because there's a description here that might amuse you. You want to hear it?'

'Sure, fire ahead,' Frank replied, dabbling a hand in the water, which was about as much effort as he wished to make. He didn't mind listening to Lew.

Lew shuffled through the pages and marked a passage with his finger. 'The description of the character goes as follows,' and then he began to read. '"A chronic indolence alternating with spurts of highly intelligent activity, gnawing self-doubt soothed by intimate self-appreciation, a craving for complete solitude coupled with the inability to tolerate it for long." That's Edith Wharton speaking, and she's speaking about *me*. I admit it. It is me.'

Frank laughed. 'Ah yes, that sure is. That sounds right, okay.' And then he added playfully, 'But I don't know about those spurts of highly intelligent activity.'

'Well, Jesus Christ, there I am pilloried – yes, pilloried – and you're not going to allow me a spurt of highly intelligent activity.'

THE TOWNSITE

From the front it was difficult to figure out what this place might be. Something, Lew decided, between the office of a moderately successful lawyer and a shop for goods too discreet to be put in the window.

He pushed open the door which appeared to ooze back on some pneumatic device, closing off the interior hush from the town noises outside. In the room, soft lighting peeped from around the cornice, fat chairs in dark leather squatted before a big old-fashioned desk with a leather top. A bell rang faintly in a back room and after a pause an unnaturally pale man in a sharp blue suit padded in. He carried a folder bound in leather which he placed reverently on the desk. On the front of the folder Lew noticed a small gilt crest. The man gave Lew a soft hand to shake, ushered him to one of the leather chairs and settled himself stiffly behind the desk. Looked to Lew rather like the start of an interview for sainthood.

The pale man opened the folder and began to turn embossed and glossy pages, caressing them with very white fingertips, and talking in a low monotone.

'How wise you are, sir,' he said, 'to make all these arrangements well before the unfortunate event. Of course, I can see that this is merely prudent forethought, but nonetheless many people, out of fear or foolishness perhaps, put off this moment for too long. And then where are you? You are very well advised, sir, to act now. Very well advised.' He paused, nodding sagely and giving Lew a solemn look of approval.

'Now, sir, if you please, I would like you to look at our various arrangements, one of which I'm sure will please you.'

He slowly turned pages, and after each turn reversed the folder on the desk so Lew could look at it. He saw rococo nightmares in bizarre shapes and shades, such scenes and expectations as made the classical view of Hades seem sparse, clean and healthy. When the last page was turned and the folder closed Lew spoke abruptly.

'The cheapest will do very well. I want the minimum fuss and nothing but an efficient disposal. To me, it will mean absolutely nothing.'

The pale man was disconcerted, seeing some extra profit drain away, but put a game face on it. 'Of course, sir, it's entirely your choice. Whatever you want will be carried out discreetly, tactfully and with dignity. If you wish, I shall draw up the papers now, and then you'll have nothing further to worry about.'

He took out a gold-coloured fountain pen and pulled some forms towards him. For five minutes he was busy and then, with a little cough, showed Lew an amount in dollars at the bottom of the page. Lew looked at it impassively, and though the amount very nearly cleared out his bank account, he signed a cheque without hesitation. In another minute he had signed the contract, handed over the cheque, was on his feet and eager to go. He tucked the contract in his back pocket, his contract for some future appointment with MacDaniel & Son, Funeral Directors.

The pale man hurried round the desk and barely had time to catch the door for Lew, holding it open against the pneumatic closing device.

Trans-Canada

He woke in the night and as soon as he realized where he was he felt as secure as a babe rocking in a cradle. When he woke again, still at some dark hour, the train was stationary. He lifted the blind, saw nothing and lay back unconcerned. There was some commotion along the track, some shunting, then a whistle sounded at the rear end, and the train started to move, this time backwards. It did not matter to him, since it was such a beautiful thing to be sleepy, snug and wrapped up tight in a moving vehicle. In the morning he was up soon after daylight and saw that they were in Chilliwack, hardly out of Vancouver, though they had travelled right through the night. A porter told him that there had been a rockfall on the line ahead, forcing the train to retreat.

Lew was on his way to Halifax. The family – what remained of it – had re-settled in the region of lost family land in Nova Scotia, which Lew had not visited in seventeen years, since his father's funeral. His nephew had offered free flights; he was a well-driller in oilfields, a world traveller, and he had a caseful of frequent-flyer points. But Lew would not go by plane. On this journey he wanted an attachment to earth, to feed on and be nourished by all nature. For 800 dollars out of his own pocket he booked a lower Pullman berth on the train, Vancouver to Halifax, first class. For him, at this particular time, the journey was more than a mere transit from one coast to another, from ocean to ocean.

There was something sentimental in his plan, but he knew that it was more than that. A basic instinct, long in abeyance, pulled him on. It was the nomad in him, the wish to be moving, even though reasons were unclear and destination cloudy. This, he understood now, had been a mainspring of his wandering life. Even his years of residence on the West Coast had a temporary feel to them. He was a cabin-dweller, outside the settled ring of society. Nothing accumulated, nothing indispensable. On any morning he might have dropped the latch behind him and disappeared. He stayed poised, ready for flight.

He had persuaded himself in his younger years that he had some stronger purpose, some desire for explanation and rationalization, but the revolving world had only brought him full-circle to his first steps. He saw that he had just been travelling through shifting contours, bending to place and time, moving between human activity and the beneficence of the land, between what mankind could impose by will and what the limit of the land and nature would permit. The search for this equilibrium dictated the pleasures and vicissitudes of the nomad life, including those of Lew's own story. It was an insignificant story that he would no longer write, for he saw now that the nomad makes almost nothing happen; his foot barely dents the ground, and his passing only brushes the land, leaving history hardly disturbed.

In the morning, the train switched across the river and followed the Fraser along the old Canadian National track. Lew had been through the Fraser gorge three times but never on this line. He sat by the window and nothing would have torn him away, just feasting his eyes on the view, couldn't get enough of it. All that sensation, a turmoil in the mind, stability hanging on by a fingernail. Where did everything go, disappearing into a black incomprehension, as puzzling as the raging water?

But his body was saying, Enjoy it, enjoy it. He felt as a dog must feel, riding through unknown country with its head out of the car window and its nose in the air. Assailed by smells and images too rich to ignore but sampled and gone. An ecstasy for the dog, and now also for Lew, gulping at every angle of the view.

Through Hell's Gate the water roiled, as demented as a dervish, a dirty, dirty yellow warning of danger as powerfully as the yellow sign on wagons of nuclear waste. Millions of tons of clay, rock and earth hurled downwards in the stream towards the alluvial plain. Then the train laboured into high wilderness, tugged by three locomotives with half a mile of snaking carriages behind, past little forlorn towns like the first tentative flecks of paint on the empty canvas of nature. Then the train was in the sharp clear air of the Rockies, a spirit cleansed and released.

By now, they were running well behind schedule and the train crew was harried and sweating. The man paid to keep passengers happy, the service manager – who used to be called the conductor – was all out of soothing words. 'If you're wondering why we are stopped,' came one helpless announcement, 'we are waiting for orders to go on. The next station is just two miles away. There we will take on food and water. As soon as we've done that we'll proceed.' They jogged into Jasper twelve hours late.

From Jasper, reduced now to two engines, the train hurried out of the mountains and on to the prairies. There, the rangelands were dry and burnt, victim of the disordered seasons of an increasingly disordered globe. Going between the carriages on his way to dome car or dining car, Lew could smell the acrid smoke. He saw cattle – though he might have been imagining that's how they would be – looking lean and frazzled. No cowboys anywhere. But he noticed narrow wheeltracks along the fence lines, and even ascending almost vertical knolls, and then he saw the modern cowboy, a dude in a wide hat seated on a little Honda ATV – All-Terrain Vehicle – capable of going damn near everywhere, perhaps even to the moon.

Nothing could make the prairie look anything but beautiful to Lew, a vastness so long and so sad, a sadness intensified by dereliction. Farmhouses, barns, granaries were sinking back into the earth, roofs caved, casements smashed, sashes hanging loose, walls tumbling, blind windows broken. And the old grain elevators were also falling into disuse, pieces of redundant technology, though some now desperately preserved as 'heritage'. Somewhere in Saskatchewan he saw what might never have occurred to him, a graveyard for farm machinery, a Sargasso Sea of rusting hulks, as big as any dead town. All good for nothing. Too costly to redeem or recycle, these wrecks made way for the gigantic machines of the present. The farmer now sits in the hermetically sealed, air-conditioned cabin of a mammoth costing a king's fortune. He has music, CD player, two-way radio, video cameras to show on a screen the far extremities of his vehicle. It's a wonder, Lew thought, that the farmer knows where he is.

The prairies receded, like a fading beauty falling behind the times, and on the third morning Lew lifted the blind above his bunk to see thin snow flurries in Ontario. Little shrunken trees grew by the track, growing about as thick as the hair on a dog's back, and Lew knew from experience that he was entering bitter cold territory. It was hard living here, and the small stations were generally in disrepair. The effort of keeping life sane and safe left not much over for the upkeep of stations. Yet the chief reason for the existence of most of these isolated places was the economy to be gleaned along a railway line. Lean pickings nowadays. The telegraph poles were tumbling too; no one used the telegraph any more.

When the train reached Toronto, Lew transferred for the only unpleasant part of the journey, shooting from Toronto to Montreal in what was called a 'corridor' train, as bland, faceless and uncomfortable as any aeroplane. The seats, like those of a plane, were crammed together, and the food came on a cart down the aisle, vying with airline food on all points of poor quality and tastelessness. The woman sitting next to Lew, a matron with a pile of silver hair and startling blue eyeshadow, tasted it and shuddered.

'A case,' she said contemptuously, 'of competition driving down standards, as seems to be normal in our day and age.'

Nova Scotia

On the night train from Montreal to Halifax his spirits revived. For this last leg of the journey he had taken a roomette, considering that he might need a night for privacy and silent thought to compose himself for the arrival. And then he almost forgot to go to bed, sitting up in the dome car, staring into the night in the faint glow of stars, drinking rather too much, and at last teetering down to his bed at about two a.m. He closed his eyes, thinking it was one of the saddest things in the world, the last night of a long journey, a passage laid to rest like old leaves pressed in an album.

The early morning was clear with a promise of fine weather, and then Lew began to see in rural Quebec the brick houses in the villages and the small fields around them and the maples bursting out of hedgerows and tall spires of churches spearing upwards, and he knew he was in rare country, older, deeper, more reticent than the land of flaring optimism and energy he had grown used to on the West Coast. In New Brunswick the world looked so neat and ordered that he wanted to fold it into his pocket and carry it away with him. And when he had his first sight of a Cape Island boat, those friendly stumpy lines, he thought, though he was not a nautical man, that he never wanted to see again the aluminium box of a Pacific coast herring skiff or the rusting steel of a salmon boat.

All the way to Halifax he took with him this feeling of triumph and surprise, stepping lightfooted on to the platform at the end of the line on a sunny Sunday afternoon.

He rented a car and drove out of town. The city did not interest him. It had grown rich and brash, in the way of cities generally, and he did not recognize it. He had some duties to his relatives and visited those few left, often to their amazement, in modest houses in modest communities. He had been away too long; memories were fuddled, interests had wandered far apart, though on parting there was some subtle unspoken sense of loss on both sides. He knew he would not see them again.

In the rental car he meandered down the south shore, then crossed the province to the Annapolis Valley, to his home town. He stopped on the overpass that used to stride above the old railway line and the nearby station. No tracks any more, no station, everything buried in weeds and fallen masonry. Looking back in time he could see the day, the mild October day, when he had arrived at that station as a kid. He could recall, with no feeling of nostalgia, every moment of that occasion. He felt a kind of excitement that if he stood there long enough it would all happen again; his life nudged forward by changes in the initial conditions would have become another sort of adventure. He let the fantasy drop. It was not something he wished for anyway.

He took lodgings for a few nights in a bed-and-breakfast that had been the old Catholic rectory, a gaunt respectable house built about 1860. It had a look of austerity but the bed was most comfortable. Then he wandered the town, taking lanes and byways he half knew, remarking how large and substantial the houses were. They looked set for a few more centuries. He had an excellent dinner of seafood and later, in a bar as well behaved as a Sunday school, he saw a black Canadian who had been his schoolmate so many years ago. After some cordial slaps on the back Lew got the scoop on who was alive and who was dead, on the unexceptional leaps and plunges of an old colonial town.

'I guess to you we all seem to be lacking in jizz down here,' his friend appeared to be apologizing, 'seeing as how you've been all over the world and done so much, So help me, I blink here and ten years have passed. Not bad years, not memorable years, but years you can live with any time. You grow old, as I'm beginning to do, and looking back life seems to have been pretty good. I wouldn't move. No sir, I would not.'

Next day, Lew went to visit his father's old farm, where he himself had grown up, and where he learnt the work of a man. Nothing was left. Not one building was standing and he could hardly discern the foundations of what had been there. Everything was overgrown, as silent about his past as a torn chronicle with cancelled pages. It was a surpassingly beautiful morning, and as Lew blundered through the undergrowth, trying to find something he could recall, some landmark, he heard the cawing of crows, and that was the only sound.

'For God's sake,' he burst out aloud, 'this is like some bad film, made by an Italian director.'

He was bemused by the emptiness, the blank past. He had it in mind to walk around the lane and go up the fields, and perhaps come back through the woodlot, for surely the remains of the old wood road would still be there. And then maybe he'd walk up as far as the mountain. Sit awhile where the field ended at the foot of the mountain. There were no fields any more, no wood road, no woodlot, only a few gnarled and twisted orchard trees left to die amid rotting apples. Scrub and bush, like a warrior band, had descended from the hills and overrun the land.

Everything changed. Yet he knew the landscape had not changed any more than he had.

He drove back through the Annapolis Valley, most of the time keeping to the old roads. Traffic flicked by fast and efficiently on the highway, but he wanted to run the film of the past more slowly, to stop and start at will. On some stretch of the road everything seemed different, and then around the next bend land and sea and sky were unchanged. He reached no conclusion, content to have observed and noted and passed on. He had discovered, since his return from Europe, that memory settles nothing. At best, it was a sleeve to wipe away the tears of the present.

After ten days his wallet and his credit card were showing signs of fatigue, so he took up the offer of his nephew, flying home free on frequent-flyer points. Compared to the train, the flight was short and brutal, and it was raining when he arrived in Vancouver. Under low skies blotting out the mountains to the north he went downtown to see about the bus up the coast. There was nothing that evening and he had to take a hotel. The city was full and wet and angry, the taxis occupied, and the bars frightful. But this was the frontier after all, and he was braced for whatever might come.

He was lighter in spirit and steadier than when he had set out. A weight of doubt and perplexity had dropped from him. But though he had divested himself of much, there was one new thing he carried back. On his right forearm he now had a tattoo, a fine illustration of a big-eyed Greek owl. The owl of Athene. He could highly recommend it, if only for the pain.

THE CABIN

His mother used to claim that she had second sight – perhaps she had – and Lew at a few times in his life had seen portents in dreams that laid down the future exactly. Now, he needed no message from dreams, no push from another world; a man who plans his own demise is already a condemned man.

He knew it was cancer, of course, an insidious cancer that had crept into his jaw over many years, recognized at first as pain, then as constant pain, and now on its way to becoming unbearable pain. It was not inoperable – almost anything medical, in our time, can be made subject to the knife – but a few years before he had seen a woman roughly of his own age with her jaw cut away. It left her face no more than a pathetic fright, a hollowed shell for Halloween. Her eyes pleaded with him not to look, for she was nothing but human tatters left over from the surgeon's table. A species of medical monster. Lew would never let the doctors get hold of him like that. Pain could be endured up to any point you cared to choose; loss of human dignity was unconscionable. Some time ago he had made his decision in principle, and he judged this to be the moment to put it into practice.

He had prepared carefully, taught by the lessons of his blood, the inheritance passed on to him by the first Holle in North America, the German mercenary quartermaster who arranged his own future so expeditiously in and after the War of Independence. Lew found a virtue in giving attention to small mundane things, matters of no great importance but needing to be fixed if his friends were not to suffer from his inaction. He had a few trifles to dispose of, some books, some papers, his battered truck, some favoured objects. Not many dollars in his account. He would write out simple instructions, wafting it all away. The cabin, though he had built it, was the property of his landlady. He did not care what happened to it. What worried him most was the fate of his goats, and they received a small codicil to his instructions.

That morning, he washed carefully, folded his clothes away, cleared the dishes from the draining board. He fed the cat and put it out of doors with a saucer of milk. He knew it would soon make its own peace. Then he sat at the table to compose whatever he had to say. He was not sorry for himself, nor for his friends, for he considered that the shock of his death was easier for them than having to endure day after day the long contemplation of his suffering. They should not be worried by his failure. It was inevitable. Death was always and everywhere a failure of living, yet none could avoid it. In his own mind he was as justified as any other man.

His instructions were short, without sentiment or self-pity, almost serene. He left the piece of paper in full view in the middle of the table, held down securely by one of his own beer bottles.

In an envelope next to these instructions he placed his contract with the funeral director.

*

In a while he walked down the slope to Alicia's cabin to use the telephone. The man's voice on the other end was loud and fruity. Sounded like he'd had a good breakfast.

'I've got some trouble to report,' Lew said calmly, 'but first let me give you some details.'

He gave his name and his exact location, which was not easy to find, even for the RCMP.

'Go on,' said the comfortable voice.

'I've got a message for the Mounties.'

'Yeah? Well, shoot away.'

'Strange that you should say that, because it's what I'm just about to do.'

'What do you mean? Say that again.' The voice had lost its complacency and was taking notice.

'In about ten minutes I'm going to shoot myself. Commit suicide.'

'Hey, you're not kidding me, are you? You don't sound as if you're joking.'

'No, I'm quite serious. I'm going to commit suicide and I don't want any of my friends to find the body. It will not be pleasant. If you send a cruiser out now you'll find me dead. I'm sorry to impose this on you, but you'll know what to expect.'

'Sir, hold hard there.' The voice was urgent and agitated now. 'We can be with you in about half and hour, maybe twenty minutes. However you feel now, there isn't any reason to kill yourself. Life's worth more than that. Take a look round. There are good folk ready to help.'

'There are reasons,' Lew replied, his voice still quiet and steady. No hysteria.

'Private reasons that I can't measure against the pains and miseries of anyone else. The reasons are good enough for me.'

'Wait, sir, please wait,' the voice was almost yelping now. 'We're on our way, don't . . .'

'I'm putting the phone down now. I hope you got the message clear. Goodbye.'

Gently, he replaced the handset in its cradle.

The Road Taken

22 April 1999

There were two of them in the police cruiser, an experienced cop and a rookie who was driving. The young man took off at a furious pace, tense as a grand prix driver, full tilt into the flow of cars. In a couple of blocks his companion put his hand on the rookie's shoulder.

'Ease up there, Dale,' he cautioned. 'Not so fast. If this guy's serious he'll be gone by the time we get there. If not, he'll be waiting for us. In the meantime let's get there safely. It would be a pity to clip a couple of innocent citizens on the way. Not good for our reputation.'

Dale slowed the car but kept the roof light flashing. He did not want to be cheated of all excitement, and watched with approval as the light traffic pulled out of his way. Through the Indian reservation he went down almost to regulation speed and then nudged up towards the eighties, running free.

There was not much conversation. 'Do you think he means it?' Dale had asked at the beginning of the ride.

'Always hard to say in these cases,' the older cop replied. 'Most times they don't really mean it, just need someone to reach out a hand. But sometimes they do it anyway. Like riding a rapids and unable to break out of the current.'

'Damned if I'd do it. I can't imagine having that sort of desperation.' He paused, before adding, 'Or courage.'

They were quiet then, looking at the woods and listening to the insistent swish of the tyres.

Where the old sawmill had been Dale swung sharply off the highway, the rear tyres twitching on loose gravel before they gripped the blacktop of the minor road. They had to go cautiously now, searching for the dirt driveway, the right break in the trees. In a minute or so they saw the break and went to the left, bumped over the potholes for four hundred yards and pulled up in the rough clearing before the fence that Lew had put up to try to keep his goats corralled. Ahead, on a rise, was the cabin. A hundred feet to the right was a small blue Datsun truck, and behind that the battered wooden shed that might well be its garage. That was the place to look.

They got out of the car, leaving the doors open, and stood for a few moments bareheaded in the sunshine, assessing the lie of the land. Nothing stirred, no sound but the rural murmurings of the clearing. They knew what the next step must be, but were reluctant to take it. Then the older cop sighed. 'Wait here,' he said and walked slowly towards the shed.

He was gone several minutes, hidden from the gaze of the rookie by the bulk of the Datsun. The young cop propped his bottom against the bonnet of the police car and wiped his brow, more from anxiety than on account of the warmth. He glanced around the clearing in the woods and wondered if he could ever afford a place like this. He was a country boy from the Okanagan and was not yet happy in the town.

Then his partner returned looking pale and shocked.

'Gone,' he said laconically. 'Looks like he took one in the mouth. That will do it.' He turned aside, taking a couple of gulps of air, feeling a constriction in the throat.

'I've been a cop a long time,' he added, 'but I can never get used to this. You don't want to see it. You stay here, I've got to go check the cabin.'

He fetched his hat from the back seat of the car, adjusted it with care, and started up the slope. After a few steps he hesitated then stopped and faced the young cop.

'Get your hat, Dale,' he said in a tired voice, 'and then just call this in.'